Best of Bridge

Sunday Suppers

All-New Recipes for Family & Friends

Robert
ROSE

Best of Bridge Sunday Suppers
Text copyright © 2017 Elizabeth Chorney-Booth, Sue Duncan and Julie Van Rosendaal
Photographs copyright © 2017 Robert Rose Inc.
Cover and text design copyright © 2017 Robert Rose Inc.

For complete cataloguing information, see page 324.

Disclaimer

The recipes in this book have been carefully tested by our kitchen and our tasters. To the best of our knowledge, they are safe and nutritious for ordinary use and users. For those people with food or other allergies, or who have special food requirements or health issues, please read the suggested contents of each recipe carefully and determine whether or not they may create a problem for you. All recipes are used at the risk of the consumer.

We cannot be responsible for any hazards, loss or damage that may occur as a result of any recipe use.

For those with special needs, allergies, requirements or health problems, in the event of any doubt, please contact your medical adviser prior to the use of any recipe.

Design and production: PageWave Graphics Inc.
Editor: Sue Sumeraj
Recipe editor: Jennifer MacKenzie
Proofreader: Kelly Jones
Indexer: Gillian Watts
Photographer: Matt Johannsson, Reflector Inc.
Food stylist: Michael Elliott
Prop stylist: Charlene Erricson

The publisher gratefully acknowledges the financial support of our publishing program by the Government of Canada through the Canada Book Fund.

Canada

Published by Robert Rose Inc.
120 Eglinton Avenue East, Suite 800, Toronto, Ontario, Canada M4P 1E2
Tel: (416) 322-6552 Fax: (416) 322-6936
www.robertrose.ca

Printed and bound in China

1 2 3 4 5 6 7 8 9 PPLS 25 24 23 22 21 20 19 18 17

CONTENTS

INTRODUCTION

QUICK AND EASY MEALS WILL ALWAYS HAVE A PLACE IN OUR KITCHEN. LIKE YOU, OUR LIVES ARE BUSY, AND THE IDEA OF WHIPPING UP SOMETHING THAT CAN BE ON OUR PLATES IN 15 TO 30 MINUTES IS PRETTY APPEALING. BUT SOMETIMES WE LIKE TO TAKE OUR TIME, PUT A MEAL TOGETHER WITH A LITTLE EXTRA CARE AND LOVE, AND SIT AROUND THE TABLE WITH FAMILY AND FRIENDS TO SAVOR BOTH THE FOOD AND THE COMPANY. HENCE THE CONCEPT OF SUNDAY SUPPERS: DINNERS SPENT TALKING AND LAUGHING WITH THE PEOPLE WHO ARE MOST IMPORTANT TO US, CELL PHONES AND CURRENT EVENTS FORGOTTEN.

THE ORIGINAL BEST OF BRIDGE LADIES WERE ALL ABOUT HOME ENTERTAINING, INVITING PEOPLE IN AND FEEDING THEM WELL — SOCIALIZING AND CONNECTING AROUND A GOOD MEAL. IT DOESN'T HAVE TO BE EXTRAVAGANT: BATCHES OF DOUGH AND TOPPINGS FOR PIZZA NIGHT OR A POT OF BRAISED MEAT SET OUT ON THE TABLE WITH TORTILLAS AND ACCOMPANIMENTS FOR TACO NIGHT. SUMMER PROVIDES AN EXCUSE TO FIRE UP THE GRILL AND EAT IN YOUR FLIP-FLOPS. WHETHER YOU LOVE TO SPEND THE DAY IN THE KITCHEN PULLING OFF PRIME RIB AND YORKSHIRE PUDDINGS, HAVE A SPECIAL OCCASION THAT CALLS FOR SOMETHING DIFFERENT OR NEED SOME SIMPLE IDEAS THAT WILL BRING THE FAMILY BACK AROUND THE TABLE ANY DAY OF THE WEEK, THIS COLLECTION OF RECIPES CELEBRATES WHAT'S ON THE TABLE — AND WHO'S AROUND IT.

ENJOY!

— SUE, JULIE & ELIZABETH

SALADS

ALL-PURPOSE COLESLAW

THIS EASY COLESLAW IS PERFECT TO THROW ALONGSIDE ALMOST ANY MEAL THAT NEEDS AN EXTRA DASH OF VEG. IT GOES GREAT ON A PULLED PORK SANDWICH, WITH A FISH FILLET OR ON THE TABLE AT A SUMMER SUPPER BARBECUE.

1	BAG (12 OZ/340 G) SHREDDED COLESLAW MIX (OR ABOUT 4 CUPS/1 L CABBAGE, MATCHSTICK CARROTS AND OTHER SLAW-WORTHY VEGETABLES)	1
$1/4$ CUP	SUNFLOWER OIL (OR ANOTHER VEGETABLE OIL OF YOUR CHOICE)	60 ML
2 TBSP	WHITE WINE VINEGAR	30 ML
1 TSP	GRAINY MUSTARD	5 ML
$1/2$ TSP	FENNEL OR CELERY SEEDS, CRUSHED	2 ML
PINCH	PAPRIKA	PINCH
	SALT AND BLACK PEPPER TO TASTE	

PLACE COLESLAW IN A LARGE SALAD BOWL. IN A SMALL BOWL, WHISK TOGETHER OIL, VINEGAR, MUSTARD, FENNEL SEEDS, PAPRIKA, SALT AND PEPPER. TASTE THE DRESSING AND ADJUST THE SEASONING (A LITTLE MORE SALT OR PAPRIKA MAY BE IN ORDER). POUR THE DRESSING ON THE SLAW AND TOSS UNTIL EVENLY COATED. SERVE IMMEDIATELY OR LET IT LINGER IN THE FRIDGE WHILE YOU PREPARE THE REST OF YOUR MEAL. SERVES 6 TO 8.

MY MOM'S ICHIBAN SALAD

WE KEPT THIS A GENERAL REFERENCE TO "MOM," SINCE MOST OF OUR MOMS MAKE A MEAN ICHIBAN SALAD. THOSE PACKETS OF DRY NOODLES MAKE A CRUNCHY ADDITION, ESPECIALLY IF YOU TOAST THEM FIRST.

1	PACKAGE DRY ASIAN NOODLES WITH FLAVOR PACKET (SUCH AS ICHIBAN)	1
1/3 CUP	SLICED OR SLIVERED ALMONDS	75 ML
1/2	PACKAGE (12 OZ/340 G) SHREDDED COLESLAW MIX	1/2
1/4 CUP	VEGETABLE OIL	60 ML
3 TBSP	RICE VINEGAR	45 ML
2 TSP	SUGAR	10 ML

IF YOU LIKE, TOAST THE NOODLES AND ALMONDS: CRUSH THE NOODLES ONTO A RIMMED BAKING SHEET, ADD THE ALMONDS AND TOAST IN A 350°F (180°C) OVEN (OR TOASTER OVEN) FOR 5 TO 7 MINUTES OR UNTIL PALE GOLDEN AND FRAGRANT. SET ASIDE TO COOL.

PLACE COLESLAW IN A SHALLOW BOWL. IN A SMALL BOWL OR A JAR WITH A LID, STIR OR SHAKE TOGETHER OIL, VINEGAR, SUGAR AND ABOUT HALF THE CONTENTS OF THE FLAVOR PACKET, OR TO TASTE. DRIZZLE OVER COLESLAW AND TOSS UNTIL EVENLY COATED. ADD NOODLES AND ALMONDS; TOSS TO COAT AGAIN. SERVE IMMEDIATELY, SO THE NOODLES DON'T SOFTEN.

SERVES 4 TO 6.

UNCOMPLICATED ARUGULA SALAD

ARUGULA IS SUCH A LIGHT AND REFRESHING GREEN. THIS UNCOMPLICATED SALAD LETS IT SHINE, BUT FEEL FREE TO DRESS IT UP WITH APPLES, PECANS, DIFFERENT CHEESES OR WHATEVER OTHER GOODIES YOU HAVE IN YOUR FRIDGE OR PANTRY.

5 OZ	ARUGULA	150 G
1/4	RED ONION, THINLY SLICED	1/4
2 OZ	GOAT CHEESE, CRUMBLED	60 G
1/4 CUP	PINE NUTS	60 ML
1/4 CUP	OLIVE OIL	60 ML
	JUICE OF 1/2 LEMON	
	SALT AND BLACK PEPPER TO TASTE	

IN A LARGE SALAD BOWL, COMBINE ARUGULA, RED ONION, GOAT CHEESE AND PINE NUTS. IN A SMALL BOWL, WHISK TOGETHER OIL AND LEMON JUICE, THEN SEASON LIBERALLY WITH SALT AND PEPPER. (ARUGULA LOVES PEPPER, SO DON'T BE SHY WITH IT!) POUR THE DRESSING ON THE SALAD AND TOSS UNTIL EVENLY COATED. SERVE IMMEDIATELY SO THE GREENS DON'T WILT. SERVES 4 TO 6.

THE KEY TO EATING HEALTHY? NEVER EAT ANYTHING THAT HAS A TV COMMERCIAL.
— MIKE BIRBIGLIA

KALE CAESAR SALAD

HARDY KALE MAKES AN AMAZING CAESAR SALAD.
TO MAKE IT A MORE SUBSTANTIAL ONE-DISH MEAL,
TOP IT WITH GRILLED OR ROASTED CHICKEN.

SALAD

1	SMALL BUNCH CURLY KALE (ABOUT 6 CUPS/1.5 L PACKED)	1
6	BACON STRIPS, COOKED CRISP AND CRUMBLED	6
1 CUP	CROUTONS	250 ML
1/3 CUP	GRATED PARMESAN CHEESE	75 ML

DRESSING

1/4 CUP	MAYONNAISE	60 ML
2 TBSP	LEMON JUICE	30 ML
2 TBSP	WHITE WINE VINEGAR OR RICE VINEGAR	30 ML
1/4 CUP	GRATED PARMESAN CHEESE	60 ML
1	GARLIC CLOVE, MINCED	1
1 TSP	WORCESTERSHIRE SAUCE	5 ML
1/2 TSP	BLACK PEPPER	2 ML

SALAD: WASH KALE AND SHAKE THE LEAVES DRY. PULL THE LEAVES OFF THE STEMS AND TEAR OR SLICE THE LEAVES INTO A WIDE BOWL. (DISCARD THE STEMS AND TOUGH CENTER RIBS.)

DRESSING: IN A SMALL BOWL, WHISK TOGETHER MAYONNAISE, LEMON JUICE, VINEGAR, PARMESAN, GARLIC, WORCESTERSHIRE AND PEPPER.

POUR THE DRESSING ON THE KALE AND TOSS UNTIL EVENLY COATED. TOP WITH BACON, CROUTONS AND A SHOWER OF PARMESAN CHEESE. SERVES 6.

FRIENDSHIP SALAD

SHOW UP AT A DINNER PARTY WITH THIS PRETTY SALAD AND YOU'RE BOUND TO MAKE A LIFELONG FRIEND OR TWO.

1	LARGE AVOCADO	1
	JUICE OF 1 LIME	
4	GREEN ONIONS, SLICED	4
2 to 4	RADISHES, THINLY SLICED	2 to 4
1/2	CUCUMBER, SLICED	1/2
4 CUPS	BABY SPINACH	1 L
1/2 CUP	HALVED CHERRY TOMATOES	125 ML
1/2 CUP	SLICED MUSHROOMS	125 ML
4 OZ	SOFT SILKEN TOFU	125 G
3 TBSP	MILK	45 ML
2 TSP	MUSTARD	10 ML
1/2 TSP	WHITE WINE VINEGAR	2 ML
PINCH	CAYENNE PEPPER	PINCH
	SALT AND BLACK PEPPER TO TASTE	

CUT AVOCADO INTO 1/4-INCH (0.5 CM) CUBES AND DRIZZLE WITH LIME JUICE. IN A LARGE SALAD BOWL, TOSS TOGETHER AVOCADO, GREEN ONIONS, RADISHES, CUCUMBER, SPINACH, TOMATOES AND MUSHROOMS.

IN A MEDIUM BOWL OR SMALL BLENDER, COMBINE TOFU, MILK, MUSTARD, VINEGAR, CAYENNE, SALT AND BLACK PEPPER. BLEND (USING EITHER THE BLENDER OR AN IMMERSION BLENDER) UNTIL SMOOTH. TASTE AND ADJUST THE SEASONING IF NECESSARY. DRESS THE SALAD TO TASTE AND TOSS UNTIL EVENLY COATED. SERVES 6 TO 8.

FATTOUSH

THIS MIDDLE EASTERN SALAD IS MADE SPECIAL WITH THE ADDITION OF CRISPY BITS OF TOASTED PITA.

2	10- TO 12-INCH (25 TO 30 CM) PITAS	2
3 TBSP	OLIVE OIL, DIVIDED	45 ML
6	GREEN ONIONS, CHOPPED	6
1	ENGLISH CUCUMBER, HALVED AND SLICED	1
1	RED BELL PEPPER, CHOPPED	1
5 CUPS	CHOPPED ROMAINE HEARTS	1.25 L
2 CUPS	HALVED CHERRY TOMATOES	500 ML
1	BUNCH FRESH PARSLEY, CHOPPED	1
2 TBSP	CHOPPED FRESH MINT	30 ML
1	GARLIC CLOVE, MINCED	1
1/4 CUP	LEMON JUICE	60 ML
	SALT AND BLACK PEPPER TO TASTE	
1/4 CUP	CRUMBLED FETA CHEESE	60 ML

PREHEAT OVEN TO 400°F (200°C). OPEN EACH PITA AND SEPARATE THE TWO SIDES SO THAT YOU HAVE 4 SEPARATE ROUNDS. LAY THE ROUNDS OUT ON A BAKING SHEET AND BRUSH WITH OIL ON BOTH SIDES, USING ABOUT 1 TBSP (15 ML) OIL. BAKE FOR 8 MINUTES OR UNTIL CRISP AND GOLDEN, FLIPPING HALFWAY THROUGH. LET COOL, THEN BREAK INTO BITE-SIZE PIECES.

IN A LARGE BOWL, TOSS TOGETHER GREEN ONIONS, CUCUMBER, RED PEPPER, ROMAINE, TOMATOES, PARSLEY, MINT AND PITA PIECES. IN A SMALL BOWL, WHISK TOGETHER GARLIC, THE REMAINING OIL, LEMON JUICE, SALT AND PEPPER. POUR ON THE SALAD AND TOSS TO COAT. SPRINKLE WITH FETA. SERVES 8 TO 10.

MEG'S SPINACH, POTATO AND BLUEBERRY SALAD

THIS UNIQUE SALAD CONTAINS MORE GREENS THAN THE USUAL ALL-POTATO SALAD; IT POPS WITH FRESH BLUEBERRIES AND IS DELICIOUS ALONGSIDE ROASTED CHICKEN OR GRILLED SAUSAGES.

1 LB	SMALL WHITE OR RED POTATOES	500 G
	SALT TO TASTE	
6 CUPS	BABY SPINACH	1.5 L
2	LARGE EGGS, HARD-COOKED AND CHOPPED	2
2	GREEN ONIONS, CHOPPED	2
1 CUP	FRESH BLUEBERRIES	250 ML
1/4 CUP	MAYONNAISE (REGULAR OR LIGHT)	60 ML
2 TBSP	RICE VINEGAR	30 ML
1 TBSP	GRAINY MUSTARD	15 ML
1/2 TSP	SUGAR	2 ML
1/4 TSP	BLACK PEPPER	1 ML
1/4 CUP	SLICED ALMONDS, TOASTED (OPTIONAL)	60 ML

CUT ANY LARGER POTATOES INTO ONE OR TWO PIECES (SO THAT ALL ARE ABOUT THE SAME SIZE) AND PLACE IN A LARGE SAUCEPAN. ADD ENOUGH WATER TO COVER BY ABOUT 1 INCH (2.5 CM), ADD A BIG PINCH OF SALT AND BRING TO A BOIL. REDUCE THE HEAT SO THE WATER JUST MAINTAINS A BOIL AND COOK FOR 15 TO 20 MINUTES OR UNTIL FORK-TENDER. DRAIN AND LET COOL JUST UNTIL YOU CAN HANDLE THE POTATOES, THEN, IF YOU LIKE, CUT THEM INTO LARGE BITE-SIZE PIECES.

PLACE SPINACH IN A LARGE BOWL AND TOP WITH POTATOES, EGGS, GREEN ONIONS AND BLUEBERRIES. IN A SMALL BOWL, STIR TOGETHER MAYONNAISE, VINEGAR, MUSTARD, SUGAR AND PEPPER. POUR THE DRESSING ON THE SALAD AND GENTLY TOSS UNTIL EVENLY COATED. TOP WITH TOASTED ALMONDS, IF DESIRED. SERVES 6.

TIP: TO TOAST ALMONDS, SPREAD THEM IN A SINGLE LAYER IN A SMALL SKILLET AND TOAST OVER MEDIUM HEAT, SHAKING THE PAN OFTEN, UNTIL PALE GOLDEN AND FRAGRANT. REMOVE FROM THE SKILLET AND SET ASIDE TO COOL COMPLETELY.

HEARD OF MURPHY'S LAW? WHAT ABOUT COLE'S LAW? IT'S THINLY SLICED CABBAGE.

COUSCOUS SALAD

A TYPE OF PASTA MADE FROM TINY GRANULES OF DURUM WHEAT, COUSCOUS COOKS QUICKLY AND MAKES A TASTY BASE FOR A SALAD THAT LOOKS NICE SERVED ON A PLATTER FOR A CROWD. EXPERIMENT WITH VEGGIES THAT ARE IN SEASON OR THAT YOU HAVE ON HAND.

1 1/4 CUPS	BASIC CHICKEN STOCK (PAGE 28), READY-TO-USE CHICKEN OR VEGETABLE BROTH, OR WATER	300 ML
1 CUP	COUSCOUS	250 ML
1	SMALL ZUCCHINI	1
3	GREEN ONIONS, THINLY SLICED	3
2 CUPS	CHERRY OR GRAPE TOMATOES, HALVED	500 ML
1 CUP	DICED MOZZARELLA CHEESE OR BABY BOCCONCINI	250 ML
1/4 CUP	THINLY SLICED FRESH BASIL	60 ML
1	SMALL GARLIC CLOVE, MINCED	1
1/4 CUP	OLIVE OIL	60 ML
3 TBSP	BALSAMIC VINEGAR	45 ML
	SALT AND BLACK PEPPER TO TASTE	

IN A MEDIUM SAUCEPAN, BRING STOCK TO A BOIL. STIR IN COUSCOUS, REMOVE FROM HEAT, COVER AND LET STAND FOR 5 MINUTES. FLUFF WITH A FORK AND SET ASIDE TO COOL.

TRANSFER COOLED COUSCOUS TO A LARGE BOWL. USE A VEGETABLE PEELER TO SLICE RIBBONS OF ZUCCHINI INTO THE COUSCOUS. ADD GREEN ONIONS, TOMATOES, CHEESE AND BASIL. IN A SMALL BOWL, STIR TOGETHER GARLIC, OIL AND VINEGAR. POUR THE DRESSING ON THE SALAD, SEASON WITH SALT AND PEPPER AND TOSS GENTLY UNTIL EVENLY COATED. SERVES 6.

ANN'S BEAN AND COUSCOUS SALAD

AN EASY ASSEMBLY OF A FEW STORE-BOUGHT ITEMS MAKES THE MOST UNIQUE, ADDICTIVE AND REQUESTED SALAD JULIE'S COUSIN-IN-LAW ANN MAKES FOR ALL THEIR FAMILY GET-TOGETHERS. BECAUSE IT'S BUILT ON COUSCOUS AND MARINATED BEANS, IT TRAVELS WELL TOO.

I CUP	COUSCOUS	250 ML
1¼ CUPS	BOILING WATER	300 ML
I	JAR (14 OZ/398 ML) PREPARED BEAN SALAD, WELL DRAINED	I
½ CUP	CRUMBLED FETA CHEESE	125 ML
¼ CUP	BOTTLED GREEK OR ITALIAN DRESSING (OR TO TASTE)	60 ML

PLACE COUSCOUS IN A GLASS OR STAINLESS STEEL BOWL AND POUR IN BOILING WATER. COVER WITH A PLATE OR PLASTIC WRAP AND LET STAND FOR 5 MINUTES. FLUFF WITH A FORK AND SET ASIDE, UNCOVERED, TO COOL.

ADD BEAN SALAD AND FETA TO THE COOLED COUSCOUS. ADD DRESSING AND TOSS UNTIL EVENLY COATED.

SERVES 8.

QUINOA SLAW WITH PANCETTA AND TOASTED SEEDS

THIS SLAW IS A GREAT MIX OF SWEET AND SAVORY, HEALTHY AND INDULGENT.

QUINOA

1/2 CUP	QUINOA, RINSED	125 ML
1 CUP	WATER	250 ML
	SALT TO TASTE	

DRESSING

1	GARLIC CLOVE, MINCED	1
1/2 CUP	OLIVE OR VEGETABLE OIL	125 ML
1/4 CUP	WHITE WINE VINEGAR	60 ML
	GRATED ZEST OF 1 ORANGE	
1/4 CUP	ORANGE JUICE	60 ML
1/2 TSP	LIQUID HONEY	2 ML
	SALT AND BLACK PEPPER TO TASTE	

SALAD

5 OZ	PANCETTA, CHOPPED	150 G
1/3 CUP	SUNFLOWER SEEDS	75 ML
1/3 CUP	GREEN PUMPKIN SEEDS (PEPITAS)	75 ML
PINCH	SALT	PINCH
1	LARGE CARROT, GRATED	1
1	CELERY STALK, CHOPPED	1
1	LARGE SWEET, CRISP APPLE (SUCH AS AMBROSIA), CHOPPED	1
6 CUPS	THINLY SLICED RED CABBAGE (SEE TIP)	1.5 L
1/2 CUP	PACKED FRESH PARSLEY LEAVES, CHOPPED	125 ML
1/4 CUP	RAISINS, CHOPPED (OPTIONAL)	60 ML

QUINOA: IN A MEDIUM SAUCEPAN, COMBINE QUINOA, WATER AND A PINCH OF SALT. BRING TO A BOIL OVER MEDIUM-HIGH

HEAT, THEN REDUCE HEAT AND SIMMER, PARTIALLY COVERED, UNTIL WATER IS ABSORBED AND QUINOA IS TENDER BUT NOT MUSHY, ABOUT 15 MINUTES. REMOVE PAN FROM HEAT. PLACE A FOLDED CLEAN TEA TOWEL UNDER LID AND LET STEAM FOR 10 MINUTES. REMOVE LID AND LET COOL COMPLETELY.

DRESSING: MEANWHILE, IN A SMALL BOWL OR A JAR WITH A LID, STIR OR SHAKE TOGETHER GARLIC, OIL, VINEGAR, ORANGE ZEST, ORANGE JUICE, HONEY, SALT AND PEPPER.

SALAD: HEAT A MEDIUM SKILLET OVER MEDIUM-LOW HEAT. ADD PANCETTA AND SAUTÉ FOR 5 TO 10 MINUTES OR UNTIL CRISP AND BROWNED. USING A SLOTTED SPOON, TRANSFER PANCETTA TO A SMALL BOWL LINED WITH A PAPER TOWEL. DISCARD FAT FROM PAN AND GIVE PAN A QUICK WIPE WITH A PAPER TOWEL. ADD SUNFLOWER SEEDS, PUMPKIN SEEDS AND SALT TO PAN AND TOAST, STIRRING, OVER MEDIUM-LOW HEAT UNTIL SEEDS ARE JUST STARTING TO BROWN, ABOUT 5 MINUTES. DISCARD PAPER TOWEL UNDER PANCETTA. ADD SEEDS AND LET COOL.

IN A LARGE BOWL, TOSS TOGETHER COOLED QUINOA, CARROT, CELERY, APPLE, CABBAGE, PARSLEY AND RAISINS (IF USING). ADD DRESSING AND TOSS UNTIL EVENLY COATED. LET STAND FOR 10 MINUTES, THEN TOSS AGAIN. TOP WITH PANCETTA AND SEEDS JUST BEFORE SERVING. SERVES 8.

TIP: RED CABBAGE IS PRETTY IN THIS DISH, BUT GREEN CABBAGE WORKS JUST AS WELL. YOU CAN ALSO USE A 14-OZ (400 G) BAG OF SHREDDED COLESLAW MIX.

VARIATION: SUBSTITUTE 1/2 CUP (125 ML) DRY COUSCOUS, COOKED, FOR THE COOKED QUINOA.

QUINOA SALAD WITH MINT AND BLUEBERRIES

*THE FRESH FLAVORS OF THIS SALAD ARE
A CONSISTENT HIT.*

1 CUP	QUINOA, RINSED	250 ML
2 CUPS	WATER	500 ML
	SALT TO TASTE	
2 CUPS	FRESH BLUEBERRIES	500 ML
6	GREEN ONIONS, SLICED	6
1	BUNCH FRESH PARSLEY, FINELY CHOPPED	1
1 CUP	FINELY CHOPPED MINT	250 ML
1/2 CUP	CRUMBLED FETA CHEESE	125 ML
1/4 CUP	LEMON JUICE	60 ML
2 TBSP	OLIVE OIL	30 ML
1 TBSP	DIJON MUSTARD	15 ML

IN A MEDIUM SAUCEPAN, COMBINE QUINOA, WATER AND A PINCH OF SALT. BRING TO A BOIL OVER MEDIUM-HIGH HEAT, THEN REDUCE HEAT AND SIMMER, PARTIALLY COVERED, UNTIL WATER IS ABSORBED AND QUINOA IS TENDER BUT NOT MUSHY, ABOUT 15 MINUTES. REMOVE PAN FROM HEAT. PLACE A FOLDED CLEAN TEA TOWEL UNDER LID AND LET STEAM FOR 10 MINUTES. REMOVE LID AND LET COOL COMPLETELY.

TRANSFER QUINOA TO A LARGE BOWL AND ADD BLUEBERRIES, GREEN ONIONS, PARSLEY, MINT AND FETA, TOSSING LIGHTLY. IN A SMALL BOWL, WHISK TOGETHER LEMON JUICE, OIL AND MUSTARD. POUR OVER SALAD AND TOSS TO COAT. SERVES 6 TO 8.

HERBED POTATO SALAD

A COMPLETELY FRESH TAKE ON AN OLD FAVORITE.

2 LBS	SMALL WHITE OR RED POTATOES	1 KG
	SALT TO TASTE	
1	GARLIC CLOVE, MINCED	1
3 TBSP	WHITE WINE VINEGAR	45 ML
	BLACK PEPPER TO TASTE	
1/3 CUP	PACKED FINELY CHOPPED FRESH MINT	75 ML
1/3 CUP	PACKED FINELY CHOPPED FRESH PARSLEY	75 ML
1/3 CUP	PACKED FINELY CHOPPED FRESH DILL	75 ML
1/4 CUP	PACKED FINELY CHOPPED FRESH BASIL	60 ML
1/2 CUP	MAYONNAISE	125 ML
4	LARGE EGGS, HARD-COOKED AND CUT INTO QUARTERS	4

CUT ANY LARGER POTATOES INTO ONE OR TWO PIECES (SO THAT ALL ARE ABOUT THE SAME SIZE) AND PLACE IN A LARGE SAUCEPAN. ADD ENOUGH WATER TO COVER BY ABOUT 1 INCH (2.5 CM), ADD A BIG PINCH OF SALT AND BRING TO A BOIL. REDUCE THE HEAT SO THE WATER JUST MAINTAINS A BOIL AND COOK FOR 15 TO 20 MINUTES OR UNTIL FORK-TENDER. DRAIN AND LET COOL JUST UNTIL YOU CAN HANDLE THE POTATOES, THEN, IF YOU LIKE, CUT THEM INTO LARGE BITE-SIZE PIECES.

MEANWHILE, IN A LARGE BOWL, COMBINE GARLIC, VINEGAR, SALT AND PEPPER. TOSS POTATOES WITH DRESSING WHILE STILL VERY WARM, THEN LET COOL, TOSSING ONCE OR TWICE. ADD MINT, PARSLEY, DILL AND BASIL, TOSSING TO COMBINE. STIR IN MAYONNAISE. GENTLY FOLD IN EGGS. SERVES 6.

ASIAN NOODLE SALAD

THIS MAKES A GREAT SUMMER SUPPER. IF IT'S TOO HOT TO USE THE STOVE, WE USE A CAST-IRON PAN ON THE GRILL TO COOK THE ONION AND CHICKEN.

CHICKEN

2	GARLIC CLOVES, MINCED	2
2 TBSP	FINELY CHOPPED FRESH CILANTRO	30 ML
	VEGETABLE OIL	
	SALT AND BLACK PEPPER TO TASTE	
I LB	BONELESS SKINLESS CHICKEN BREASTS, CUT INTO BITE-SIZE PIECES	500 G

DRESSING

2	GARLIC CLOVES, MINCED	2
I TBSP	PACKED BROWN SUGAR (OR TO TASTE)	15 ML
1/4 CUP	VEGETABLE OIL	60 ML
3 TBSP	LIME JUICE (OR TO TASTE)	45 ML
3 TBSP	RICE VINEGAR	45 ML
3 TBSP	FISH SAUCE	45 ML
1/2 TSP	SRIRACHA (OR TO TASTE)	2 ML

SALAD

8 OZ	DRY RICE NOODLES (MEDIUM WIDTH)	250 G
I	RED ONION, CUT INTO QUARTERS, THEN SLICED	I
I	RED BELL PEPPER, CUT INTO THIN STRIPS	I
3/4 CUP	MIXED FRESH HERBS (SUCH AS CILANTRO, BASIL AND MINT), LEAVES AND SMALL TENDER STEMS ROUGHLY CHOPPED	175 ML

CHICKEN: IN A MEDIUM BOWL, COMBINE GARLIC, CILANTRO, 2 TBSP (30 ML) OIL, SALT AND PEPPER. ADD CHICKEN

AND TOSS TO COAT. SET ASIDE TO MARINATE FOR 15 TO 30 MINUTES.

DRESSING: MEANWHILE, IN A SMALL BOWL OR A JAR WITH A LID, COMBINE GARLIC, BROWN SUGAR, OIL, LIME JUICE, VINEGAR, FISH SAUCE AND SRIRACHA. LET STAND FOR 10 MINUTES, THEN TASTE AND ADD MORE SUGAR, LIME JUICE OR SRIRACHA IF YOU WISH. SET ASIDE.

SALAD: COOK RICE NOODLES ACCORDING TO PACKAGE DIRECTIONS (MAKING SURE THEY'RE STILL AL DENTE). DRAIN AND RINSE, THEN USE A PAPER TOWEL TO BLOT EXCESS MOISTURE. SET ASIDE.

IN A LARGE SKILLET, HEAT A SKIFF OF OIL OVER MEDIUM-HIGH HEAT. SAUTÉ ONION UNTIL IT HAS A LITTLE COLOR BUT HASN'T SOFTENED, ABOUT 2 MINUTES. TRANSFER TO A PLATE. IN THE SAME PAN, SAUTÉ CHICKEN, WITH ITS MARINADE, IN BATCHES UNTIL WELL BROWNED AND NO LONGER PINK INSIDE, 4 TO 6 MINUTES PER BATCH, ADDING MORE OIL AS NEEDED. TRANSFER CHICKEN TO A PLATE AND LET COOL.

TRANSFER COOLED CHICKEN TO A LARGE BOWL AND ADD ONION, NOODLES, RED PEPPER AND DRESSING. TOSS UNTIL EVENLY COATED, THEN LET STAND FOR 10 MINUTES, TOSSING AGAIN SEVERAL TIMES. MIX IN FRESH HERBS RIGHT BEFORE SERVING. SERVES 4 TO 6 AS A MAIN, OR MORE AS A SIDE.

CURRIED CHICKEN SALAD WITH PEACHES

THIS IS A WONDERFUL SALAD TO MAKE IN THE HEIGHT OF SUMMER WHEN PEACHES ARE AT THEIR BEST. A MANGO OR 1 CUP (250 ML) OF HALVED GRAPES CAN BE SUBSTITUTED DURING THE REST OF THE YEAR.

1 LB	BONELESS SKINLESS CHICKEN BREASTS	500 G
3	GARLIC CLOVES (LEFT WHOLE)	3
1/2 TSP	SALT	2 ML
	COLD WATER	
1 TBSP	VEGETABLE OIL	15 ML
1	SMALL ONION, FINELY CHOPPED	1
3 TBSP	MILD CURRY PASTE	45 ML
1/2 CUP	MAYONNAISE	125 ML
1/2 CUP	PLAIN GREEK YOGURT	125 ML
1/4 CUP	PEACH OR MANGO CHUTNEY, LARGE PIECES MASHED	60 ML
1 CUP	TRIMMED SUGAR SNAP PEAS, CUT INTO 1/2-INCH (1 CM) PIECES	250 ML
1	CELERY STALK, SLICED	1
1	SWEET, CRISP APPLE (SUCH AS AMBROSIA), CHOPPED	1
1	LARGE RIPE BUT FIRM PEACH	1
1/2 CUP	PACKED FRESH CILANTRO LEAVES, ROUGHLY CHOPPED	125 ML
1/4 CUP	ROASTED CASHEWS, CHOPPED (SALTED OR UNSALTED)	60 ML

PLACE CHICKEN IN A SINGLE LAYER IN A LARGE SAUCEPAN. ADD GARLIC, SALT AND ENOUGH COLD WATER TO COVER BY 1 INCH (2.5 CM). BRING TO A SIMMER OVER HIGH HEAT,

THEN REDUCE HEAT TO VERY LOW, PARTIALLY COVER AND COOK CHICKEN AT A BARE SIMMER UNTIL NO LONGER PINK INSIDE, ABOUT 15 MINUTES. TRANSFER CHICKEN TO A PLATE AND LET COOL, THEN SHRED INTO LARGE BITE-SIZE PIECES. (THE POACHING LIQUID CAN BE STRAINED AND USED AS STOCK IN ANOTHER RECIPE.)

MEANWHILE, IN A MEDIUM SAUCEPAN, HEAT OIL OVER MEDIUM HEAT. SAUTÉ ONION UNTIL VERY BROWNED AND SOFT, ABOUT 10 MINUTES. STIR IN CURRY PASTE AND COOK FOR 1 MINUTE, THEN TRANSFER TO A LARGE BOWL AND LET COOL.

STIR MAYONNAISE, YOGURT AND CHUTNEY INTO COOLED ONION MIXTURE. ADD CHICKEN, PEAS, CELERY AND APPLE, TOSSING TO COMBINE. JUST BEFORE SERVING, CHOP THE PEACH (NO NEED TO PEEL) AND ADD TO THE SALAD. TOSS GENTLY AND TOP WITH CILANTRO AND CASHEWS. SERVES 4 TO 6.

TIP: YOU CAN SUBSTITUTE 2 TO 3 CUPS (500 TO 750 ML) LEFTOVER ROAST CHICKEN FOR THE POACHED CHICKEN IN THIS RECIPE, IF YOU WISH.

I MADE A CHICKEN SALAD EARLIER. THAT UNGRATEFUL BIRD DIDN'T EVEN SAY THANK YOU.

BACON AND AVOCADO SALAD WITH ROASTED TOMATOES

ALMOST LIKE A BLT, WITH AVOCADOS AS WELL, THIS IS A SURE WAY TO GET RELUCTANT SALAD EATERS TO FINISH THEIR GREENS!

CROUTONS

2 CUPS	LARGE BREAD CUBES, SLIGHTLY STALE (ABOUT 3 SLICES BREAD)	500 ML
3 TBSP	OLIVE OIL	45 ML
I	GARLIC CLOVE, MINCED	I
	BLACK PEPPER TO TASTE	
$1/4$ CUP	GRATED PARMESAN CHEESE	60 ML

SALAD

I CUP	GRAPE OR CHERRY TOMATOES, HALVED	250 ML
	OLIVE OIL	
	SALT AND BLACK PEPPER TO TASTE	
6	BACON SLICES	6
I	PACKAGE (5 OZ/142 G) MIXED BABY GREENS	I
6 TBSP	HONEY MUSTARD VINAIGRETTE (PAGE 254), DIVIDED	90 ML
I	AVOCADO, SLICED	I

CROUTONS: PREHEAT OVEN TO 400°F (200°C). PLACE BREAD CUBES ON A RIMMED BAKING SHEET LINED WITH PARCHMENT PAPER AND DRIZZLE WITH OIL. ADD GARLIC AND BLACK PEPPER; TOSS TO COMBINE, THEN SPREAD OUT IN A SINGLE LAYER. BAKE UNTIL NEARLY CRISP, ABOUT 4 MINUTES. SPRINKLE WITH PARMESAN AND BAKE UNTIL GOLDEN AND CRISP, ABOUT 3 MINUTES. REMOVE FROM

OVEN, LEAVING OVEN ON, TRANSFER CROUTONS TO A PLATE AND LET COOL COMPLETELY.

SALAD: PLACE TOMATOES ON PARCHMENT-LINED SHEET (YOU CAN REUSE THE PARCHMENT FROM THE CROUTONS) AND DRIZZLE WITH OIL. ADD SALT AND PEPPER; TOSS TO COMBINE, THEN SPREAD OUT IN A SINGLE LAYER. BAKE FOR 25 TO 30 MINUTES, STIRRING ONCE OR TWICE, UNTIL THEY START TO SHRIVEL AND ALMOST BLACKEN ON THE UNDERSIDES. LET COOL.

IN A LARGE SKILLET OVER MEDIUM HEAT, COOK BACON UNTIL VERY CRISP BUT NOT BLACKENED. DRAIN ON A PLATE LINED WITH A PAPER TOWEL AND LET COOL. BREAK EACH SLICE INTO 4 OR 5 PIECES.

IN A LARGE SALAD BOWL, TOSS GREENS WITH 4 TBSP (60 ML) DRESSING. ADD CROUTONS AND TOSS AGAIN. SCATTER AVOCADO, TOMATOES AND BACON PIECES OVER THE TOP AND DRIZZLE WITH THE REMAINING DRESSING. SERVES 4 TO 6.

"TRUST ME, YOU CAN DANCE."
— VODKA

ORZO SALAD WITH CHERRIES AND LIME DRESSING

A COOL SUMMER SALAD FOR WARM DAYS WHEN FRESH CHERRIES ARE IN SEASON.

1 CUP	ORZO PASTA	250 ML
1	AVOCADO, CHOPPED	1
1 CUP	CHERRIES, HALVED AND PITTED	250 ML
1/2 CUP	CHOPPED RED BELL PEPPER	125 ML
2 TBSP	CHOPPED FRESH CILANTRO	30 ML
2 TBSP	SLIVERED ALMONDS	30 ML
1	GARLIC CLOVE, MINCED	1
1/4 CUP	OLIVE OIL	60 ML
	GRATED ZEST AND JUICE OF 1 LIME	
1/2 TSP	SUGAR	2 ML
	SALT AND BLACK PEPPER TO TASTE	

COOK THE ORZO ACCORDING TO PACKAGE DIRECTIONS, DRAIN (IN A STRAINER WITH SMALL HOLES — WATCH OUT; THOSE LITTLE PASTA PIECES ARE SMALL AND SLIPPERY!), RINSE IN COLD WATER AND LET COOL. TRANSFER TO A LARGE SALAD BOWL AND ADD AVOCADO, CHERRIES, RED PEPPER, CILANTRO AND ALMONDS. IN A SMALL BOWL, WHISK TOGETHER GARLIC, OIL, LIME ZEST, LIME JUICE, SUGAR, SALT AND PEPPER. TASTE THE DRESSING AND ADJUST THE SEASONING AS NEEDED. POUR THE DRESSING ON THE SALAD AND TOSS UNTIL EVENLY COATED. REFRIGERATE FOR AN HOUR OR UNTIL READY TO SERVE. SERVES 6 TO 8.

TIP: THIS IS A PRETTY HARDY SALAD WITH MINIMAL DRESSING, SO IT STANDS WELL IN THE FRIDGE. ANY LEFTOVERS WILL MAKE FOR A TASTY LUNCH THE NEXT DAY.

SOUPS

BASIC CHICKEN STOCK

HOMEMADE CHICKEN STOCK IS EASY AND INEXPENSIVE TO MAKE, FREEZES WELL AND IS MUCH BETTER THAN ANYTHING YOU CAN BUY IN A STORE.

4 LBS	CHICKEN BACKS	2 KG
2	CELERY STALKS, CUT IN HALF	2
I	LARGE ONION, CUT INTO 8 PIECES	I
I	CARROT, CUT IN HALF	I
	SALT TO TASTE	
I4 CUPS	WATER	3.5 L

PREHEAT OVEN TO 425°F (220°C). PLACE CHICKEN, CELERY, ONION AND CARROT IN A LARGE ROASTING PAN AND SPRINKLE WITH A FEW PINCHES OF SALT. ROAST UNTIL BROWNED, ABOUT 45 MINUTES. TRANSFER EVERYTHING (INCLUDING ANY LIQUID IN PAN) TO A LARGE STOCKPOT SET OVER HIGH HEAT. ADD WATER AND BRING TO A SIMMER; ADJUST HEAT TO MAINTAIN A SIMMER. COOK FOR 2 HOURS (OR MORE), UNTIL THE BROTH IS RICH AND FLAVORFUL. DISCARD SOLIDS, THEN POUR LIQUID THROUGH A DOUBLE LAYER OF CHEESECLOTH OR A CLEAN TEA TOWEL. CHILL, THEN REMOVE THE FAT FROM THE SURFACE ONCE IT SOLIDIFIES. MAKES ABOUT I2 CUPS (3 L).

BEN'S FAVORITE BROCCOLI CHEESE SOUP

BROCCOLI AND CHEESE ARE A CLASSIC KID-FRIENDLY COMBO, ALWAYS ENTHUSIASTICALLY WELCOMED AT OUR DINNER TABLES.

	VEGETABLE OIL	
2 TBSP	BUTTER	30 ML
2	CELERY STALKS, CHOPPED	2
1	SMALL ONION, CHOPPED	1
1	CARROT, CHOPPED	1
3 TBSP	ALL-PURPOSE FLOUR	45 ML
	SALT AND BLACK PEPPER TO TASTE	
4 CUPS	BROCCOLI FLORETS	1 L
4 CUPS	BASIC CHICKEN STOCK (OPPOSITE) OR READY-TO-USE CHICKEN BROTH	1 L
1 CUP	HALF-AND-HALF (10%) CREAM	250 ML
1 CUP	SHREDDED SHARP (OLD) CHEDDAR CHEESE	250 ML

IN A MEDIUM POT, HEAT A DRIZZLE OF OIL ALONG WITH THE BUTTER OVER MEDIUM-HIGH HEAT. SAUTÉ CELERY, ONION AND CARROT FOR 4 TO 5 MINUTES OR UNTIL SOFT. ADD FLOUR AND SEASON WITH SALT AND PEPPER, STIRRING TO COAT THE VEGETABLES; COOK FOR A MINUTE OR TWO. STIR IN BROCCOLI AND STOCK; BRING TO A SIMMER. REDUCE HEAT AND SIMMER FOR 20 MINUTES OR UNTIL BROCCOLI IS VERY TENDER. ADD CREAM AND CHEESE; COOK, STIRRING, FOR A MINUTE OR TWO, THEN REMOVE FROM HEAT AND PURÉE WITH AN IMMERSION BLENDER RIGHT IN THE POT (OR LET COOL SLIGHTLY AND PURÉE SOUP IN BATCHES IN A BLENDER, THEN RETURN TO THE POT AND REHEAT UNTIL STEAMING). SEASON WITH SALT AND PEPPER, IF IT NEEDS IT. SERVES 6.

ROASTED RED PEPPER
AND TOMATO SOUP

SMOKY ROASTED RED PEPPERS AND RIPE TOMATOES
GO SO WELL TOGETHER. WE LIKE TO MAKE THIS SOUP
IN LATE SUMMER AND FALL, WHEN BOTH ARE AT THEIR
PEAK AND INEXPENSIVE AT FARMERS' MARKETS. THE
SOUP FREEZES WELL, SO YOU CAN PULL IT OUT FOR
A TASTE OF SUMMER IN THE BLEAK MIDWINTER.

4	RED BELL PEPPERS	4
	VEGETABLE OIL	
1	ONION, CHOPPED	1
2	GARLIC CLOVES, MINCED	2
1 TSP	CHOPPED FRESH THYME	5 ML
1	CAN (14 OZ/398 ML) DICED OR WHOLE TOMATOES, WITH JUICE	1
4 CUPS	BASIC CHICKEN STOCK (PAGE 28) OR READY-TO-USE CHICKEN BROTH	1 L
1/2 CUP	HALF-AND-HALF (10%) CREAM	125 ML
	SALT AND BLACK PEPPER TO TASTE	

PREHEAT OVEN TO 450°F (230°C). CUT RED PEPPERS
IN HALF LENGTHWISE, PULL OUT THE SEEDS AND
MEMBRANES AND PLACE PEPPERS, CUT SIDE DOWN, ON
A BAKING SHEET LINED WITH PARCHMENT PAPER OR FOIL.
ROAST FOR ABOUT 30 MINUTES OR UNTIL BLACKENED AND
BLISTERED, ROTATING THE SHEET IF NECESSARY FOR THE
PEPPERS TO COOK EVENLY. TRANSFER PEPPERS TO A
BOWL, COVER WITH FOIL OR A PLATE AND LET COOL. WHEN
COOL ENOUGH TO HANDLE, PEEL OFF AND DISCARD SKINS,
DROPPING THE PEPPERS BACK INTO THE BOWL.

IN A MEDIUM POT OR DUTCH OVEN, HEAT A DRIZZLE OF OIL OVER MEDIUM-HIGH HEAT. SAUTÉ ONION FOR 4 TO 5 MINUTES OR UNTIL SOFT. ADD GARLIC AND SAUTÉ FOR 1 MINUTE. ADD THYME, TOMATOES AND STOCK; BRING TO A SIMMER. ADD ROASTED PEPPERS AND ANY JUICES THAT HAVE ACCUMULATED IN THE BOWL; REDUCE HEAT AND SIMMER FOR ABOUT 20 MINUTES OR UNTIL VEGETABLES ARE VERY SOFT. REDUCE HEAT TO LOW AND ADD CREAM, SALT AND PEPPER. REMOVE FROM HEAT AND PURÉE WITH AN IMMERSION BLENDER RIGHT IN THE POT UNTIL SMOOTH (OR LET COOL SLIGHTLY AND PURÉE SOUP IN BATCHES IN A BLENDER, THEN RETURN TO THE POT AND REHEAT UNTIL STEAMING). SERVES 6.

THE MORE I LEARN ABOUT PEOPLE,
THE MORE I LIKE MY DOG.
— MARK TWAIN

FRENCH ONION SOUP FOR A CROWD

THE KEYS TO A GREAT ONION SOUP ARE GREAT INGREDIENTS AND LONG, SLOW COOKING.

SOUP

1/4 CUP	BUTTER	60 ML
3 1/2 LBS	ONIONS, THINLY SLICED	1.75 KG
3	SHALLOTS, THINLY SLICED	3
	SALT TO TASTE	
1/2 CUP	DRY WHITE WINE	125 ML
12 CUPS	BASIC CHICKEN STOCK (PAGE 28)	3 L
2	BAY LEAVES	2
1/2 TSP	DRIED ROSEMARY, CRUSHED	2 ML
12 OZ	GRUYÈRE CHEESE, SHREDDED	375 G
3/4 CUP	GRATED PARMESAN CHEESE	175 ML

CROUTONS

2	GARLIC CLOVES, MINCED	2
1/2 CUP	BUTTER, SOFTENED	125 ML
2	BAGUETTES, CUT INTO 1/2-INCH (1 CM) SLICES	2

SOUP: SET 2 LARGE SKILLETS OVER MEDIUM HEAT. DIVIDE BUTTER BETWEEN THEM, THEN ADD HALF THE ONIONS AND SHALLOTS TO EACH PAN. ADD A COUPLE PINCHES OF SALT TO EACH PAN. COVER AND COOK, STIRRING OCCASIONALLY, FOR 20 TO 30 MINUTES OR UNTIL ONIONS HAVE WILTED. UNCOVER AND COOK, STIRRING AS NEEDED, UNTIL ONIONS ARE CARAMELIZED. IF THE RESIDUE IN THE PANS IS IN DANGER OF GETTING TOO DARK, ADD A FEW SPOONFULS OF WATER AND SCRAPE UP ALL THE BITS.

AS ONIONS GET CLOSER TO BEING DONE, TURN HEAT DOWN GRADUALLY TO ENSURE THEY DON'T BURN. THIS WILL TAKE ABOUT 1½ HOURS FROM RAW TO CARAMELIZED.

POUR HALF THE WINE INTO EACH PAN. ADD ¼ CUP (60 ML) STOCK TO EACH. SCRAPE UP ALL THE BROWNED BITS. TRANSFER THE CONTENTS OF BOTH PANS TO A LARGE SOUP POT AND ADD THE REMAINING STOCK, BAY LEAVES AND ROSEMARY; BRING TO A SIMMER OVER MEDIUM-HIGH HEAT. REDUCE HEAT AND SIMMER FOR 45 MINUTES. DISCARD BAY LEAVES AND ADD SALT TO TASTE.

CROUTONS: PREHEAT OVEN TO 400°F (200°C). IN A SMALL BOWL, STIR TOGETHER GARLIC AND BUTTER. BUTTER ONE SIDE OF EACH BAGUETTE SLICE WITH THIS MIXTURE AND ARRANGE BREAD, BUTTER SIDE UP, ON 2 RIMMED BAKING SHEETS (OR COOK IN TWO BATCHES). BAKE FOR 5 TO 7 MINUTES OR UNTIL CRUNCHY AROUND THE OUTSIDE AND VERY PALE GOLDEN. THE CROUTONS WILL GET CRUNCHIER AS THEY COOL.

PREHEAT THE BROILER AND SET A RACK 6 INCHES (15 CM) BELOW THE HEAT. IN A MEDIUM BOWL, COMBINE GRUYÈRE AND PARMESAN. LADLE 1 CUP (250 ML) OF SOUP INTO EACH OF 6 OVENPROOF BOWLS; SET BOWLS ON A RIMMED BAKING SHEET. STIR 1½ TBSP (22 ML) CHEESE INTO EACH BOWL. FLOAT 2 OR 3 CROUTONS ON TOP, THEN SPRINKLE MORE CHEESE ON THE CROUTONS. BROIL UNTIL CHEESE IS MELTED AND BUBBLY, 1 TO 2 MINUTES. REPEAT WITH ANOTHER 6 BOWLS. LET COOL FOR A FEW MINUTES BEFORE SERVING. SERVES 12.

BEET BORSCHT

A HEARTY BORSCHT IS PRAIRIE COMFORT FOOD. MAKE IT
MORE SUBSTANTIAL BY ADDING CHOPPED OR CRUMBLED
SAUSAGE ALONG WITH THE CARROTS AND ONION,
OR BRAISE SOME STEWING BEEF AND STIR IT INTO
THE SOUP ALONG WITH THE WATER.

2	MEDIUM BEETS, TRIMMED	2
	VEGETABLE OIL	
2	LARGE CARROTS, COARSELY GRATED	2
1	MEDIUM ONION, CHOPPED	1
1/4 CUP	KETCHUP	60 ML
2	MEDIUM THIN-SKINNED POTATOES, SLICED OR DICED	2
1/2	SMALL HEAD CABBAGE, THINLY SLICED	1/2
1	CAN (19 OZ/540 ML) RED KIDNEY BEANS, RINSED AND DRAINED (2 CUPS/500 ML)	1
4 CUPS	BASIC CHICKEN STOCK (PAGE 28) OR READY-TO-USE CHICKEN, BEEF OR VEGETABLE BROTH	1 L
2 TBSP	LEMON JUICE	30 ML
2	BAY LEAVES	2
	SALT AND BLACK PEPPER TO TASTE	
1/2 CUP	CHOPPED FRESH DILL, DIVIDED	125 ML
	SOUR CREAM	

COOK THE BEETS: EITHER WRAP THEM IN FOIL AND ROAST
DIRECTLY ON THE OVEN RACK AT 350°F (180°C) FOR
1 HOUR, UNTIL TENDER, OR PLACE THEM IN A SAUCEPAN,
COVER WITH WATER, BRING TO A SIMMER, THEN REDUCE
HEAT AND SIMMER FOR 45 MINUTES OR UNTIL TENDER.
(IF YOU SIMMER THEM, RESERVE THE COOKING WATER
FOR THE SOUP.) SET BEETS ASIDE UNTIL THEY'RE COOL

ENOUGH TO HANDLE, THEN PEEL THEM WITH YOUR FINGERS AND COARSELY SHRED OR JULIENNE THEM.

IN A LARGE POT OR DUTCH OVEN, HEAT A DRIZZLE OF OIL OVER MEDIUM-HIGH HEAT. SAUTÉ CARROTS AND ONION FOR A FEW MINUTES, UNTIL SOFT. ADD KETCHUP AND COOK, STIRRING, FOR 1 MINUTE. STIR IN BEETS, POTATOES, CABBAGE, BEANS, STOCK, LEMON JUICE AND BAY LEAVES. ADD ENOUGH WATER TO COVER ALL THE VEGGIES (IF YOU HAVE BEET COOKING WATER, USE IT HERE). SEASON WITH SALT AND PEPPER. BRING TO A SIMMER, THEN REDUCE HEAT AND SIMMER FOR 20 MINUTES OR UNTIL VEGGIES ARE TENDER. STIR IN ABOUT HALF THE DILL AND ADJUST THE SALT IF IT NEEDS IT. SERVE WITH A DOLLOP OF SOUR CREAM, SCATTERED WITH MORE FRESH DILL. SERVES 8.

TIP: THE BEETS CAN BE ROASTED AHEAD OF TIME. TUCK THEM IN THE OVEN WHILE YOU'RE BAKING SOMETHING ELSE, THEN STORE IN THEIR FOIL IN A BOWL IN THE FRIDGE FOR UP TO 5 DAYS. THEY'RE EASY TO PEEL WITH YOUR FINGERS.

CAULIFLOWER AND STILTON SOUP

THIS IS AN ELEGANT, CREAMY SOUP THAT MAKES FOR A RICH STARTER OR A DELICIOUS MAIN EVENT.

2 TBSP	BUTTER	30 ML
2	LEEKS (WHITE AND PALE GREEN PARTS ONLY), THINLY SLICED	2
1	CELERY STALK, CHOPPED	1
	SALT AND WHITE OR BLACK PEPPER TO TASTE	
3	GARLIC CLOVES, MINCED	3
2 TBSP	ALL-PURPOSE FLOUR	30 ML
1	HEAD CAULIFLOWER (ABOUT 2 LBS/1 KG BEFORE TRIMMING), CUT INTO MEDIUM FLORETS	1
5 CUPS	BASIC CHICKEN STOCK (SEE PAGE 28) OR READY-TO-USE CHICKEN BROTH	1.25 L
2 CUPS	MILK	500 ML
7 OZ	CRUMBLED STILTON CHEESE	210 G

IN A LARGE SAUCEPAN, MELT BUTTER OVER MEDIUM-LOW HEAT. ADD LEEK, CELERY, SALT AND PEPPER; COVER AND SWEAT FOR 4 MINUTES OR UNTIL VEGETABLES ARE SOFTENED. ADD GARLIC AND FLOUR; COOK, STIRRING, FOR 2 MINUTES. ADD CAULIFLOWER AND STOCK; INCREASE HEAT AND BRING TO A SIMMER. REDUCE HEAT AND SIMMER, PARTIALLY COVERED, UNTIL VEGETABLES ARE VERY TENDER, ABOUT 45 MINUTES. ADD MILK, REMOVE FROM HEAT AND PURÉE WITH AN IMMERSION BLENDER UNTIL AS SMOOTH AS POSSIBLE. REHEAT SOUP SO IT'S NEARLY AT A SIMMER AGAIN (DON'T BOIL). STIR IN STILTON UNTIL MELTED. SERVES 6 TO 8.

Friendship Salad (page 10)

French Onion Soup
for a Crowd (page 32)

Roasted Carrot and Sweet Potato Soup
with Apple and Sage (page 40)

Chicken Soup with Tortellini (page 52)

WINTER ROOT VEGETABLE SOUP

THIS FENNEL-SPICED, HALF-PURÉED SOUP WILL GET KIDS
OF ALL AGES HAPPILY EATING RUTABAGA AND PARSNIPS.

	VEGETABLE OIL	
1	LARGE ONION, CHOPPED	1
2	CLOVES GARLIC, MINCED	2
1 TSP	FENNEL SEEDS, LIGHTLY CRUSHED	5 ML
2	LARGE CARROTS, CHOPPED	2
2	PARSNIPS, CHOPPED	2
2	MEDIUM POTATOES, PEELED AND CHOPPED	2
1 CUP	DICED PEELED RUTABAGA	250 ML
4 CUPS	BASIC CHICKEN STOCK (PAGE 28) OR READY-TO-USE CHICKEN OR VEGETABLE BROTH	1 L
PINCH	HOT PEPPER FLAKES	PINCH
	SALT AND BLACK PEPPER TO TASTE	
2 TSP	LEMON JUICE (APPROX.)	10 ML

IN A SOUP POT, HEAT A DRIZZLE OF OIL OVER MEDIUM
HEAT. SAUTÉ ONION UNTIL IT BEGINS TO SOFTEN. ADD
GARLIC AND FENNEL SEEDS; SAUTÉ FOR 1 MINUTE. ADD
CARROTS, PARSNIPS, POTATOES, RUTABAGA, STOCK, HOT
PEPPER FLAKES, SALT AND BLACK PEPPER; INCREASE HEAT
AND BRING TO A BOIL. REDUCE HEAT AND SIMMER FOR
30 TO 40 MINUTES OR UNTIL VEGETABLES ARE SOFT.
USING AN IMMERSION BLENDER, PURÉE THE SOUP RIGHT
IN THE POT SO ABOUT HALF THE VEGETABLES REMAIN
CHUNKY BUT THE BROTH IS THICKENED. IF THE SOUP IS
TOO THICK, THIN WITH HOT WATER. STIR IN LEMON JUICE.
ADJUST SEASONING WITH SALT, PEPPER AND LEMON
JUICE, IF NECESSARY. SERVES 4 TO 6.

GINGER CARROT SOUP

A HEALTHY DOSE OF FRESH GINGER MAKES THIS
CREAMY ORANGE SOUP A WINNER FOR SICK DAYS
OR A SPICY STARTER FOR A WINTER MEAL.

	VEGETABLE OIL	
1	LARGE ONION, CHOPPED	1
2	GARLIC CLOVES, MINCED	2
5 CUPS	SLICED CARROTS (SEE TIP)	1.25 L
1 1/2 TBSP	GRATED FRESH GINGER	22 ML
1 TSP	GROUND CORIANDER	5 ML
	SALT AND BLACK PEPPER TO TASTE	
4 CUPS	BASIC CHICKEN STOCK (PAGE 28) OR READY-TO-USE CHICKEN OR VEGETABLE BROTH	1 L
1	CAN (14 OZ/400 ML) COCONUT MILK	1
	CHOPPED GREEN ONIONS	

IN A LARGE POT OR DUTCH OVEN, HEAT A DRIZZLE OF
OIL OVER MEDIUM-HIGH HEAT. SAUTÉ ONIONS FOR 4 TO
5 MINUTES OR UNTIL SOFT. ADD GARLIC, CARROTS AND
GINGER; SAUTÉ FOR 1 MINUTE. STIR IN CORIANDER, SALT,
PEPPER, STOCK AND COCONUT MILK; INCREASE HEAT AND
BRING TO A BOIL. REDUCE HEAT AND SIMMER FOR 20 TO
25 MINUTES OR UNTIL CARROTS ARE SOFT. REMOVE FROM
HEAT AND PURÉE WITH AN IMMERSION BLENDER RIGHT IN
THE POT UNTIL SMOOTH (OR LET COOL SLIGHTLY AND
PURÉE SOUP IN BATCHES IN A BLENDER, THEN RETURN
TO THE POT AND REHEAT UNTIL STEAMING). SERVE
GARNISHED WITH GREEN ONIONS. SERVES 4 TO 6.

TIP: WHEN SHOPPING, BUY ABOUT 2 LBS (1 KG) OF CARROTS
TO YIELD 5 CUPS (1.25 L) SLICED.

COCONUT SWEET POTATO SOUP

WE'VE ALWAYS LOVED ADDING COCONUT MILK TO
BUTTERNUT SQUASH SOUP, BUT ONE THANKSGIVING,
WHEN THE STORE WAS SOLD OUT OF SQUASH,
WE SUBBED IN SWEET POTATOES, AND IT PROVED
TO BE JUST AS GOOD.

	VEGETABLE OIL	
1	LARGE ONION, CHOPPED	1
1	GARLIC CLOVE, MINCED	1
8 CUPS	CHOPPED PEELED SWEET POTATOES (ABOUT 4 MEDIUM)	2 L
2 TSP	CURRY POWDER	10 ML
4 CUPS	BASIC CHICKEN STOCK (PAGE 28) OR READY-TO-USE CHICKEN OR VEGETABLE BROTH	1 L
1	CAN (14 OZ/400 ML) COCONUT MILK	1
PINCH	CAYENNE PEPPER	PINCH
	SALT AND BLACK PEPPER TO TASTE	
1 TBSP	LIME JUICE	15 ML

IN A SOUP POT, HEAT A DRIZZLE OF OIL OVER MEDIUM-
HIGH HEAT. SAUTÉ ONION UNTIL IT BEGINS TO SOFTEN.
ADD GARLIC AND SAUTÉ FOR 1 MINUTE. ADD SWEET
POTATOES AND CURRY POWDER; SAUTÉ FOR 2 MINUTES.
STIR IN STOCK, COCONUT MILK, CAYENNE, SALT AND BLACK
PEPPER; BRING TO A BOIL. REDUCE HEAT AND SIMMER
FOR 20 MINUTES OR UNTIL SWEET POTATOES ARE SOFT.
REMOVE FROM HEAT AND PURÉE WITH AN IMMERSION
BLENDER UNTIL SMOOTH (OR LET COOL SLIGHTLY AND
PURÉE IN BATCHES IN A BLENDER, THEN RETURN TO THE
POT AND REHEAT UNTIL STEAMING). STIR IN LIME JUICE. IF
SOUP IS TOO THICK, THIN WITH WATER. SERVES 6 TO 8.

ROASTED CARROT AND SWEET POTATO SOUP WITH APPLE AND SAGE

THE SWEETNESS OF CARROTS, SWEET POTATO AND APPLE MAKE THIS A DELICIOUSLY SIMPLE FALL SOUP. IT ALSO FREEZES WELL — A GREAT WAY TO PRESERVE THE BEST OF THE SEASON.

2	LARGE CARROTS, CHOPPED	2
1	MEDIUM SWEET POTATO, PEELED AND DICED	1
	VEGETABLE OIL	
1 TBSP	BUTTER	15 ML
1	ONION, CHOPPED	1
1	TART APPLE, PEELED AND CHOPPED	1
1 TSP	DRIED SAGE	5 ML
4 CUPS	BASIC CHICKEN STOCK (PAGE 28) OR READY-TO-USE CHICKEN BROTH	1 L
1 CUP	APPLE JUICE OR CIDER	250 ML
	SALT AND BLACK PEPPER TO TASTE	
1/2 CUP	HALF-AND-HALF (10%) OR HEAVY OR WHIPPING (35%) CREAM (OPTIONAL)	125 ML

PREHEAT OVEN TO 450°F (230°C). PLACE CARROTS AND SWEET POTATO ON A RIMMED BAKING SHEET LINED WITH PARCHMENT PAPER. DRIZZLE WITH OIL, TOSS TO COAT WELL, THEN SPREAD OUT IN A SINGLE LAYER. ROAST FOR 20 MINUTES, UNTIL STARTING TO TURN GOLDEN ON THE EDGES.

IN A MEDIUM POT OR DUTCH OVEN, HEAT A DRIZZLE OF OIL ALONG WITH THE BUTTER OVER MEDIUM-HIGH HEAT. WHEN THE FOAM SUBSIDES, ADD ONION AND SAUTÉ FOR

5 MINUTES, UNTIL SOFT. ADD ROASTED CARROTS AND SWEET POTATO, SCRAPING ANY FLAVORFUL BROWNED BITS FROM THE PAN. ADD APPLE, SAGE, STOCK AND APPLE JUICE; BRING TO A SIMMER. REDUCE HEAT AND SIMMER FOR 15 TO 20 MINUTES OR UNTIL EVERYTHING IS SOFT. SEASON WITH SALT AND PEPPER. REMOVE FROM HEAT AND PURÉE WITH AN IMMERSION BLENDER RIGHT IN THE POT UNTIL SMOOTH (OR LET COOL SLIGHTLY AND PURÉE SOUP IN BATCHES IN A BLENDER, THEN RETURN TO THE POT AND REHEAT UNTIL STEAMING). STIR IN CREAM, IF YOU'RE USING IT. SERVE HOT. SERVES 6.

I HATE WHEN I THINK I'M BUYING ORGANIC VEGETABLES AND WHEN I GET HOME I DISCOVER THEY'RE JUST REGULAR DONUTS.

MANGO BUTTERNUT SOUP

WE ADORE A MANGO BUTTERNUT SOUP OUR FRIEND
MARGARET MAKES, SO WE CREATED OUR OWN VERSION.

	VEGETABLE OIL	
1	ONION, CHOPPED	1
2	MEDIUM POTATOES, PEELED AND CHOPPED	2
1	MEDIUM BUTTERNUT SQUASH, PEELED AND CHOPPED	1
1	SMALL MANGO, PEELED AND CHOPPED	1
4 CUPS	BASIC CHICKEN STOCK (PAGE 28) OR READY-TO-USE CHICKEN OR VEGETABLE BROTH	1 L
1 TSP	BROWN SUGAR	5 ML
1/2 TSP	GROUND CINNAMON	2 ML
1/4 TSP	GROUND GINGER	1 ML
1/4 TSP	GROUND NUTMEG	1 ML
PINCH	GROUND CLOVES	PINCH
	SALT AND BLACK PEPPER TO TASTE	
1/4 CUP	HEAVY OR WHIPPING (35%) CREAM	60 ML

IN A SOUP POT, HEAT A DRIZZLE OF OIL OVER MEDIUM
HEAT. SAUTÉ ONION UNTIL IT BEGINS TO SOFTEN. ADD
POTATOES, SQUASH AND MANGO; SAUTÉ FOR A FEW
MINUTES. STIR IN STOCK, BROWN SUGAR, CINNAMON,
GINGER, NUTMEG, CLOVES, SALT AND PEPPER; BRING TO A
BOIL. REDUCE HEAT, COVER AND SIMMER FOR 40 MINUTES
OR UNTIL VEGGIES ARE SOFT. REMOVE FROM HEAT AND
PURÉE WITH AN IMMERSION BLENDER UNTIL SMOOTH
(OR LET COOL SLIGHTLY AND PURÉE IN BATCHES IN A
BLENDER, THEN RETURN TO THE POT AND REHEAT UNTIL
STEAMING). STIR IN CREAM. SERVES 4 TO 6.

DAVE'S MEXICAN POTATO SOUP

ELIZABETH HAS ALWAYS REMEMBERED A SPICY LIME-DRENCHED POTATO SOUP HER DAD MADE. THE ORIGINAL RECIPE IS LONG GONE, BUT THIS IS A CLOSE APPROXIMATION.

	VEGETABLE OIL	
6	GARLIC CLOVES, THINLY SLICED	6
3	JALAPEÑO PEPPERS, SEEDED, RINSED AND FINELY CHOPPED	3
1	ONION, THINLY SLICED	1
2 CUPS	QUARTERED BABY POTATOES	500 ML
4 CUPS	BASIC CHICKEN STOCK (PAGE 28) OR READY-TO-USE CHICKEN BROTH	1 L
1 CUP	WATER	250 ML
1½ CUPS	SHREDDED COOKED CHICKEN (SEE TIP, PAGE 55)	375 ML
¼ CUP	CHOPPED FRESH CILANTRO	60 ML
¼ CUP	LIME JUICE (PREFERABLY FRESH)	60 ML
	SALT TO TASTE	

IN A LARGE SAUCEPAN OR DUTCH OVEN, HEAT A DRIZZLE OF OIL OVER MEDIUM HEAT. SAUTÉ GARLIC, JALAPEÑOS AND ONION FOR 5 TO 10 MINUTES OR UNTIL ONION IS SOFT AND EVERYTHING IS FRAGRANT. KEEP AN EYE ON THE HEAT TO MAKE SURE THE GARLIC DOESN'T BURN AND NOTHING STARTS TO BROWN. STIR IN POTATOES AND COOK FOR 1 TO 2 MINUTES TO BLEND THE FLAVORS. STIR IN STOCK AND WATER; BRING TO A BOIL. REDUCE HEAT AND SIMMER FOR ABOUT 20 MINUTES OR UNTIL POTATOES ARE TENDER. STIR IN CHICKEN, CILANTRO AND LIME JUICE AND COOK UNTIL HEATED THROUGH. SEASON WITH SALT. SERVES 4 TO 6.

GUIDO'S LEEK AND POTATO SOUP (VICHYSSOISE)

THIS IS JULIE'S DAD'S FAVORITE SOUP: IT'S EASY TO MAKE AND DELICIOUS WARM OR COLD. SERVED CHILLED, IT'S CALLED VICHYSSOISE — PERFECT FOR SUMMER DAYS ON THE PATIO.

2	MEDIUM LEEKS	2
1 TBSP	VEGETABLE OIL	15 ML
1 TBSP	BUTTER	15 ML
1	SMALL ONION, CHOPPED	1
2	GARLIC CLOVES, MINCED	2
1 LB	RUSSET OR YELLOW POTATOES, PEELED AND CHOPPED	500 G
4 CUPS	BASIC CHICKEN STOCK (PAGE 28) OR READY-TO-USE CHICKEN OR VEGETABLE BROTH	1 L
	SALT AND BLACK PEPPER TO TASTE	
1/2 CUP	HALF-AND-HALF (10%) OR HEAVY OR WHIPPING (35%) CREAM (OPTIONAL)	125 ML
	CHOPPED FRESH CHIVES (OPTIONAL)	

CUT LEEKS IN HALF LENGTHWISE AND WASH THEM THOROUGHLY UNDER RUNNING WATER (SAND AND GRIT TEND TO WORK THEIR WAY IN BETWEEN THE LAYERS). THINLY SLICE THE WHITE AND PALE GREEN PARTS CROSSWISE. DISCARD THE DARK GREEN TOPS.

IN A MEDIUM POT OR DUTCH OVEN, HEAT OIL AND BUTTER OVER MEDIUM-HIGH HEAT. WHEN THE FOAM SUBSIDES, ADD LEEKS AND ONION; SAUTÉ FOR 5 TO 7 MINUTES OR UNTIL SOFT AND TRANSLUCENT. ADD GARLIC AND SAUTÉ FOR 1 MINUTE. STIR IN POTATOES AND STOCK; BRING TO A BOIL. REDUCE HEAT AND SIMMER

FOR ABOUT 20 MINUTES OR UNTIL POTATOES ARE VERY TENDER. SEASON WITH SALT AND PEPPER. REMOVE FROM HEAT AND PURÉE WITH AN IMMERSION BLENDER RIGHT IN THE POT UNTIL SMOOTH (OR LET COOL SLIGHTLY AND PURÉE SOUP IN BATCHES IN A BLENDER, THEN RETURN TO THE POT). RETURN TO MEDIUM HEAT AND STIR IN CREAM (IF USING); HEAT THROUGH WITHOUT BRINGING TO A BOIL. SERVE HOT OR AT ROOM TEMPERATURE, OR LET COOL, REFRIGERATE AND SERVE CHILLED. IF DESIRED, SPRINKLE WITH CHIVES JUST BEFORE SERVING. SERVES 6.

RED AND WHITE BEAN SOUP WITH PICO DE GALLO

THIS IS A FLAVORFUL SOUP THAT'S EASY ON THE POCKETBOOK. SERVE WITH BUTTERMILK CORNBREAD (PAGE 252) OR CRUSTY ROLLS.

5	BACON SLICES, CHOPPED	5
I	CARROT, CHOPPED	I
I	CELERY STALK, CHOPPED	I
I	ONION, CHOPPED	I
	SALT AND BLACK PEPPER TO TASTE	
3	GARLIC CLOVES, MINCED	3
2 TBSP	ALL-PURPOSE FLOUR	30 ML
I TBSP	TOMATO PASTE	15 ML
4 CUPS	BASIC CHICKEN STOCK (PAGE 28) OR READY-TO-USE CHICKEN BROTH	I L
I	CAN (19 OZ/540 ML) WHITE KIDNEY BEANS, RINSED AND DRAINED (2 CUPS/500 ML)	I
I	CAN (19 OZ/540 ML) RED KIDNEY BEANS, RINSED AND DRAINED (2 CUPS/500 ML)	I
	GRATED CHEDDAR CHEESE	
	PICO DE GALLO (PAGE 262)	

IN A LARGE SAUCEPAN SET OVER MEDIUM HEAT, COOK BACON UNTIL CRISP. ADD CARROT, CELERY, ONION, SALT AND PEPPER; COVER AND SWEAT FOR 3 MINUTES. UNCOVER AND SAUTÉ UNTIL VEGETABLES ARE STARTING TO BROWN, ABOUT 3 MINUTES. ADD GARLIC, FLOUR AND TOMATO PASTE; COOK, STIRRING, FOR I MINUTE. STIR IN STOCK AND BEANS; BRING TO A SIMMER. REDUCE HEAT AND SIMMER FOR 30 TO 40 MINUTES OR UNTIL FLAVORS HAVE COMBINED. SERVE TOPPED WITH CHEESE AND A GENEROUS SCOOP OF PICO DE GALLO. SERVES 4.

SPLIT PEA SOUP WITH HAM

HAM HOCKS FLAVOR THIS CLASSIC SOUP.

	VEGETABLE OIL	
2	CELERY STALKS, CHOPPED	2
1	ONION, CHOPPED	1
1	CARROT, CHOPPED	1
PINCH	SALT	PINCH
	BLACK PEPPER TO TASTE	
1 LB	DRIED SPLIT PEAS (YELLOW OR GREEN)	500 G
1½ TBSP	CHOPPED CHIPOTLE PEPPERS IN ADOBO SAUCE	22 ML
4 CUPS	BASIC CHICKEN STOCK (PAGE 28) OR READY-TO-USE CHICKEN BROTH	1 L
2 CUPS	WATER (APPROX.)	500 ML
2	HAM HOCKS (EACH ABOUT 1 LB/500 G), SCRUBBED	2

IN A LARGE, HEAVY SOUP POT, HEAT A DRIZZLE OF OIL OVER MEDIUM HEAT. ADD CELERY, ONION, CARROT, SALT AND PEPPER; COVER AND SWEAT FOR 5 MINUTES. STIR IN PEAS, CHIPOTLES, STOCK AND WATER. ADD HAM HOCKS AND BRING TO A SIMMER. REDUCE HEAT AND SIMMER, STIRRING AS NEEDED TO KEEP PEAS FROM STICKING, FOR 1 TO 2 HOURS OR UNTIL PEAS ARE SOFT BUT STILL HAVE SOME SHAPE. ADD MORE WATER IF THE SOUP BECOMES TOO THICK. TRANSFER HAM HOCKS TO A PLATE AND LET COOL UNTIL THEY CAN BE HANDLED. MEANWHILE, REMOVE SOUP FROM HEAT AND PARTIALLY PURÉE IT WITH AN IMMERSION BLENDER (OR USE A POTATO MASHER). REMOVE AND DISCARD SKIN AND LARGE CHUNKS OF FAT FROM HAM HOCKS. SHRED MEAT OFF THE BONES AND RETURN MEAT TO SOUP, DISCARDING BONES. SERVES 6 TO 8.

SMOKED FISH CHOWDER
WITH SCALLOPS

YOU CAN SUBSTITUTE OTHER FISH OR SHELLFISH FOR THE SCALLOPS IN THIS RECIPE — USE WHATEVER IS AVAILABLE AND LOOKS GOOD!

1 LB	RED OR YELLOW POTATOES (UNPEELED), CUT INTO LARGE BITE-SIZE PIECES	500 G
	SALT TO TASTE	
5	BACON SLICES, CHOPPED	5
2	CELERY STALKS, CHOPPED	2
1	LARGE ONION, CHOPPED	1
1/4 CUP	ALL-PURPOSE FLOUR	60 ML
2	BOTTLES (EACH 8 OZ/225 ML) CLAM JUICE	2
2 CUPS	MILK (PREFERABLY WHOLE OR 2%)	500 ML
4	FRESH THYME SPRIGS	4
2	BAY LEAVES	2
1/8 TSP	CAYENNE PEPPER (OR TO TASTE)	0.5 ML
	BLACK PEPPER TO TASTE	
1 1/4 LBS	SMOKED WHITE FISH (SUCH AS COD OR HADDOCK), CUT INTO LARGE BITE-SIZE PIECES	625 G
1 1/4 LBS	SKINLESS WHITE FISH (SUCH AS ROCKFISH, TILAPIA OR COD), CUT INTO LARGE BITE-SIZE PIECES	625 G
10 OZ	BAY SCALLOPS, TRIMMED OF HARD SIDE MUSCLES	300 G
1 TBSP	LEMON JUICE	15 ML

PLACE POTATOES IN A MEDIUM SAUCEPAN AND ADD ENOUGH WATER TO COVER BY 1 INCH (2.5 CM). SALT LIGHTLY (THE SMOKED FISH WILL ADD A LOT OF SALT TO THE CHOWDER) AND BRING TO A BOIL OVER HIGH HEAT.

BOIL FOR 15 TO 20 MINUTES OR UNTIL FORK-TENDER. DRAIN AND SET ASIDE.

IN A LARGE SAUCEPAN SET OVER MEDIUM HEAT, COOK BACON UNTIL NEARLY CRISP. ADD CELERY AND ONION; COVER AND SWEAT FOR 3 MINUTES. UNCOVER AND SAUTÉ UNTIL STARTING TO BROWN, ABOUT 3 MINUTES. ADD FLOUR AND COOK, STIRRING, FOR 2 MINUTES. STIR IN CLAM JUICE, MILK, THYME, BAY LEAVES, CAYENNE AND BLACK PEPPER; BRING TO A SIMMER. REDUCE HEAT AND SIMMER FOR 10 MINUTES TO LET FLAVORS DEVELOP. STIR IN SMOKED FISH AND FRESH FISH; SIMMER FOR 5 MINUTES. STIR IN SCALLOPS AND POTATOES; SIMMER FOR 3 TO 5 MINUTES OR UNTIL FRESH FISH AND SCALLOPS ARE OPAQUE AND FISH FLAKES EASILY WHEN TESTED WITH A FORK. DISCARD BAY LEAVES AND THYME. STIR IN LEMON JUICE. SERVES 6.

CHILDREN'S SCIENCE EXAM QUESTION:
NAME THE FOUR SEASONS.
ANSWER: SALT, PEPPER, MUSTARD AND KETCHUP.

MEG'S THAI SHRIMP BISQUE

THIS IS ONE OF JULIE'S MOM'S STAND-BY DINNER PARTY RECIPES — IT'S SIMPLE AND CALLS FOR EASY-TO-FIND INGREDIENTS, YET CREATES A DELICIOUSLY COMPLEX BROTH THAT TASTES LIKE SOMETHING YOU'D GET AT A RESTAURANT.

SHRIMP

1½ LBS	MEDIUM SHRIMP	750 G
2	GARLIC CLOVES, MINCED	2
1 TBSP	FINELY CHOPPED FRESH CILANTRO	15 ML
1 TBSP	GRATED FRESH GINGER	15 ML
1½ TSP	SUGAR	7 ML
1½ TSP	CURRY POWDER	7 ML
¼ TSP	HOT PEPPER FLAKES	1 ML
	GRATED ZEST OF 1 LIME	
⅓ CUP	LIME JUICE	75 ML

SHRIMP STOCK

2 CUPS	WATER	500 ML
¼ CUP	DRY WHITE WINE	60 ML
1 TBSP	TOMATO PASTE	15 L

SOUP

1 TBSP	OLIVE OIL	15 ML
2	CELERY STALKS, CHOPPED	2
1	SMALL ONION, CHOPPED	1
¼ CUP	ALL-PURPOSE FLOUR	60 ML
1	CAN (14 OZ/400 ML) REGULAR OR LIGHT COCONUT MILK (OPTIONAL)	1
2 CUPS	WATER	500 ML
1½ CUPS	TOMATO SAUCE	375 ML
	JUICE OF 1 LIME	
¼ CUP	CHOPPED FRESH CILANTRO, DIVIDED	60 ML
	SALT TO TASTE (OPTIONAL)	

SHRIMP: PEEL AND DEVEIN SHRIMP, RESERVING THE SHELLS. IN A LARGE BOWL OR SEALABLE PLASTIC BAG, COMBINE GARLIC, CILANTRO, GINGER, SUGAR, CURRY POWDER, HOT PEPPER FLAKES, LIME ZEST AND LIME JUICE. ADD SHRIMP AND TOSS TO COAT. COVER OR SEAL AND MARINATE IN THE REFRIGERATOR FOR 30 MINUTES.

SHRIMP STOCK: MEANWHILE, IN A LARGE POT OR DUTCH OVEN, COMBINE THE RESERVED SHRIMP SHELLS, WATER, WINE AND TOMATO PASTE. BRING TO A BOIL OVER MEDIUM-HIGH HEAT. REDUCE HEAT AND SIMMER FOR ABOUT 10 MINUTES OR UNTIL LIQUID IS REDUCED BY ABOUT HALF. STRAIN THROUGH A SIEVE SET OVER A BOWL, DISCARDING SOLIDS.

SOUP: IN THE SAME POT, HEAT OIL OVER MEDIUM-HIGH HEAT. SAUTÉ CELERY AND ONION FOR 5 TO 6 MINUTES OR UNTIL SOFT AND TURNING GOLDEN. ADD FLOUR, STIRRING TO COAT THE VEGETABLES, AND COOK, STIRRING, FOR 1 MINUTE. ADD SHRIMP STOCK, COCONUT MILK (IF USING), WATER AND TOMATO SAUCE, SCRAPING THE BOTTOM OF THE PAN TO LOOSEN ANY BROWNED BITS; BRING TO A SIMMER. STIR IN LIME JUICE AND HALF THE CILANTRO. REMOVE FROM HEAT AND PURÉE WITH AN IMMERSION BLENDER RIGHT IN THE POT UNTIL SMOOTH (OR LET COOL SLIGHTLY AND PURÉE IN BATCHES IN A BLENDER, THEN RETURN TO THE POT). BRING TO A SIMMER OVER MEDIUM HEAT, THEN REDUCE HEAT AND SIMMER UNTIL THICKENED. ADD SHRIMP AND ITS MARINADE; SIMMER UNTIL SHRIMP ARE PINK, FIRM AND OPAQUE — THIS SHOULD TAKE JUST A FEW MINUTES. TASTE AND SEASON WITH SALT IF IT NEEDS IT. SERVE IMMEDIATELY, TOPPED WITH THE REMAINING CILANTRO. SERVES 4 TO 6.

CHICKEN SOUP WITH TORTELLINI

THIS IS A COMFORTING SOUP WITH A LITTLE MORE
SUBSTANCE THAN A BARE-BONES CHICKEN NOODLE SOUP.

8 CUPS	BASIC CHICKEN STOCK (PAGE 28) OR READY-TO-USE CHICKEN BROTH, DIVIDED	2 L
1 1/2 LBS	BONELESS SKINLESS CHICKEN BREASTS OR THIGHS	750 G
2 TBSP	BUTTER	30 ML
1	LARGE ONION, FINELY CHOPPED	1
	SALT AND BLACK PEPPER TO TASTE	
4	GARLIC CLOVES, MINCED	4
3 TBSP	ALL-PURPOSE FLOUR	45 ML
1/2 TSP	DRIED SAGE	2 ML
1/2 TSP	DRIED ROSEMARY	2 ML
1/4 TSP	DRIED THYME	1 ML
1 TSP	SRIRACHA (OPTIONAL)	5 ML
8 OZ	FRESH TORTELLINI OR RAVIOLI (SAUSAGE- OR CHEESE-FILLED)	250 G
2 CUPS	SLIVERED SWISS CHARD LEAVES	500 ML
	GRATED PARMESAN CHEESE	
	SLIVERED FRESH BASIL	

POUR 2 CUPS (500 ML) STOCK INTO A MEDIUM SAUCEPAN
SET OVER MEDIUM-HIGH HEAT. ADD CHICKEN AND BRING
TO A SIMMER. REDUCE HEAT TO VERY LOW, PARTIALLY
COVER AND COOK AT A BARE SIMMER FOR ABOUT
12 MINUTES OR UNTIL BREASTS ARE NO LONGER PINK
INSIDE OR JUICES RUN CLEAR WHEN THIGHS ARE PIERCED.
TRANSFER CHICKEN TO A PLATE AND SET COOKING LIQUID
ASIDE. LET CHICKEN COOL, THEN CUT IN HALF ACROSS THE
GRAIN AND PULL INTO LARGE BITE-SIZE PIECES.

IN A LARGE SAUCEPAN, HEAT BUTTER OVER MEDIUM
HEAT. ADD ONION, SALT AND PEPPER; SAUTÉ FOR 5 TO
10 MINUTES OR UNTIL ONION IS SOFTENED AND BROWN. ADD
GARLIC AND FLOUR; COOK, STIRRING, FOR 2 MINUTES. STRAIN
POACHING LIQUID THROUGH A SIEVE INTO THE SAUCEPAN.
STIR IN THE REMAINING STOCK, SAGE, ROSEMARY,
THYME AND SRIRACHA (IF USING); BRING TO A SIMMER.
REDUCE HEAT AND SIMMER, STIRRING OCCASIONALLY, FOR
30 MINUTES TO COMBINE THE FLAVORS. INCREASE HEAT
AND BRING TO A BOIL. ADD TORTELLINI, REDUCE HEAT AND
SIMMER FOR 3 MINUTES. ADD CHICKEN AND CHARD; COOK
FOR 2 MINUTES OR UNTIL HEATED THROUGH. ADJUST
SEASONING WITH SALT AND PEPPER, IF NEEDED. SERVE
TOPPED WITH PARMESAN AND BASIL. SERVES 6 TO 8.

HOT-AND-SOUR CHICKEN SOUP

TRADITIONAL CHINESE HOT-AND-SOUR SOUP IS FULL OF TOFU AND PORK, BUT THIS EASY (AND VERY UNTRADITIONAL) VERSION USES CHICKEN. SERVE IT AT THE BEGINNING OF AN ASIAN-INSPIRED DINNER.

4 CUPS	BASIC CHICKEN STOCK (PAGE 28) OR READY-TO-USE CHICKEN BROTH	1 L
2¼ CUPS	WATER, DIVIDED	550 ML
1 TBSP	SOY SAUCE	15 ML
2 CUPS	SHREDDED COOKED CHICKEN (SEE TIP)	500 ML
1 CUP	CHOPPED SHIITAKE MUSHROOM CAPS	250 ML
½ CUP	DRAINED CANNED BAMBOO SHOOTS, SLICED	125 ML
½ TSP	WHITE OR BLACK PEPPER	2 ML
PINCH	HOT PEPPER FLAKES	PINCH
¼ CUP	WHITE WINE VINEGAR	60 ML
1 TSP	LIQUID HONEY	5 ML
3 TBSP	CORNSTARCH	45 ML
2 CUPS	BABY SPINACH	500 ML
1	LARGE EGG, LIGHTLY BEATEN	1
1	GREEN ONION, CHOPPED	1
1 TBSP	FINELY CHOPPED FRESH CILANTRO	15 ML
	SESAME OIL	

IN A LARGE POT, COMBINE STOCK, 2 CUPS (500 ML) WATER AND SOY SAUCE. BRING TO A GENTLE SIMMER OVER MEDIUM-HIGH HEAT. ADD CHICKEN, MUSHROOMS, BAMBOO SHOOTS, WHITE PEPPER, HOT PEPPER FLAKES, VINEGAR AND HONEY; REDUCE HEAT AND CONTINUE TO SIMMER. IN A SMALL BOWL, COMBINE CORNSTARCH AND

THE REMAINING WATER, STIRRING UNTIL CORNSTARCH
IS DISSOLVED. STIR INTO SOUP AND SIMMER, STIRRING,
FOR 3 TO 4 MINUTES OR UNTIL THE BROTH THICKENS.
ADD SPINACH AND SIMMER UNTIL WILTED. REMOVE FROM
HEAT AND SLOWLY POUR IN EGG, STIRRING CONSTANTLY.
STIR IN GREEN ONION AND CILANTRO. LADLE INTO BOWLS
AND TOP EACH SERVING WITH A DRIZZLE OF SESAME OIL.
SERVES 4 TO 6.

TIP: SAVE LEFTOVER CHICKEN FROM ANOTHER MEAL
FOR THIS SOUP, OR GRAB A ROTISSERIE CHICKEN FROM
THE GROCERY STORE IF YOU DON'T HAVE TIME TO
STICK A CHICKEN BREAST OR TWO IN THE OVEN BEFORE
MAKING SOUP.

TIDY PEOPLE NEVER MAKE THE EXCITING
DISCOVERIES I DO.

SAUSAGE, CORN, POTATO AND CHEDDAR CHOWDER

THIS HEARTY CHOWDER MAKES A COMFORTING CASUAL SUPPER FOR A SMALL FAMILY AND CAN BE DOUBLED TO FEED MORE (OR FOR HEARTIER APPETITES). JUST ADD CRUSTY BREAD OR BISCUITS AND A GREEN SALAD.

	VEGETABLE OIL	
1	MILD OR HOT ITALIAN SAUSAGE	1
1	LARGE ONION, FINELY CHOPPED	1
1	CELERY STALK, CHOPPED	1
1	CARROT, DICED	1
2 TBSP	ALL-PURPOSE FLOUR	30 ML
1 TSP	GROUND CUMIN	5 ML
2	SMALL THIN-SKINNED POTATOES, DICED	2
3 CUPS	BASIC CHICKEN STOCK (PAGE 28) OR READY-TO-USE CHICKEN BROTH	750 ML
1 CUP	CORN KERNELS	250 ML
1/2 CUP	HALF-AND-HALF (10%) CREAM (OPTIONAL)	125 ML
1 CUP	SHREDDED SHARP (OLD) CHEDDAR CHEESE	250 ML
	SALT AND BLACK PEPPER TO TASTE	

IN A MEDIUM POT, HEAT A DRIZZLE OF OIL OVER MEDIUM-HIGH HEAT. SQUEEZE SAUSAGE OUT OF ITS CASING INTO THE POT AND COOK, BREAKING IT UP WITH A SPOON, FOR 4 TO 5 MINUTES OR UNTIL NO LONGER PINK. ADD ONION, CELERY AND CARROT; SAUTÉ FOR 4 TO 5 MINUTES OR UNTIL SOFT. ADD FLOUR AND CUMIN; COOK, STIRRING, FOR 1 MINUTE. STIR IN POTATOES AND STOCK; BRING TO A SIMMER. REDUCE HEAT AND SIMMER FOR 10 TO 15 MINUTES OR UNTIL POTATOES ARE TENDER. STIR IN CORN AND CREAM, IF USING. ADD CHEESE, SEASON WITH SALT AND PEPPER AND STIR UNTIL THE CHEESE MELTS. SERVES 4.

BIG ROASTS

CLASSIC ROAST CHICKEN

ROAST CHICKEN IS ONE OF THE EASIEST, YET MOST
IMPRESSIVE THINGS YOU CAN COOK YOURSELF. IT
CAN BE AS SIMPLE AS THIS RECIPE, OR YOU CAN
SPRUCE IT UP BY ADDING A LITTLE CHOPPED THYME
OR ROSEMARY WITH THE SALT AND PEPPER, PLUS
A SPRIG FOR THE CAVITY.

3½ LB	WHOLE CHICKEN	1.75 KG
	SALT AND BLACK PEPPER TO TASTE	
1½ TBSP	VEGETABLE OIL OR MELTED BUTTER (PLUS SOME FOR OILING THE PAN)	22 ML
½	LEMON	½

PAT CHICKEN DRY WITH PAPER TOWELS, THEN SEASON
WELL WITH SALT AND PEPPER, INCLUDING RUBBING THE
SEASONING AS FAR UNDERNEATH THE SKIN ON THE
BREAST AND THIGH AS YOU CAN GO WITHOUT TEARING
THE SKIN. COVER AND REFRIGERATE FOR AS LONG AS
YOU HAVE OR UP TO 24 HOURS.

PREHEAT OVEN TO 425°F (220°C). PLACE CHICKEN
IN AN OILED ROASTING PAN (SEE TIP) AND BRUSH THE
SKIN WITH OIL. PLACE LEMON HALF INSIDE THE BIRD'S
CAVITY AND ROAST FOR 20 MINUTES. REDUCE OVEN
TEMPERATURE TO 375°F (190°C) AND ROAST, SPOONING
PAN JUICES OVER CHICKEN ONCE OR TWICE, UNTIL SKIN
IS BROWNED AND LEG JOINTS MOVE FREELY IN THEIR
SOCKETS, ABOUT 45 MINUTES (IF YOU WISH TO USE A
MEAT THERMOMETER, THE TEMPERATURE AT THE INNER
THIGH SHOULD BE 165°F/74°C). TRANSFER BIRD TO A
RIMMED PLATE OR BAKING SHEET, TENT WITH FOIL AND
LET REST FOR 10 MINUTES BEFORE CARVING. SERVES 4.

TIP: IF YOU WANT TO MAKE A JUS, SEE INSTRUCTIONS IN THE LAST PARAGRAPH ON PAGE 61. ADD A SQUEEZE OF LEMON JUICE OR A SPLASH OF WHITE WINE TO THE JUS, IF YOU WISH.

TIP: YOU CAN ROAST A BIRD EITHER BREAST UP OR BREAST DOWN — WHICH IS VERY HANDY IF YOU'RE NOT SURE WHICH IS WHICH! IF YOU ROAST BREAST DOWN (WHICH USUALLY RESULTS IN THE WHITE MEAT BEING MORE MOIST), USE A ROASTING RACK TO KEEP THE BREAST MEAT FROM BOILING IN THE PAN JUICES.

THE DINNER I WAS COOKING FOR MY FAMILY WAS GOING TO BE A SURPRISE, BUT THE FIRE TRUCKS RUINED IT.

ROAST CHICKEN WITH LIME AND CILANTRO

THIS ROAST CHICKEN IS BURSTING WITH FLAVOR. USE THE LEFTOVERS IN TACOS OR ON A MEXICAN-THEMED SALAD.

4	GARLIC CLOVES, MINCED	4
2/3 CUP	PACKED FINELY CHOPPED FRESH CILANTRO (LEAVES AND SMALL STEMS FROM 1 LARGE BUNCH)	150 ML
2 TSP	SALT (OR TO TASTE)	10 ML
	BLACK PEPPER TO TASTE	
1 TBSP	OLIVE OR VEGETABLE OIL	15 ML
1	LIME	1
4 to 5 LB	WHOLE CHICKEN	2 to 2.5 KG
1 CUP	WATER (APPROX.)	250 ML

IN A SMALL BOWL, COMBINE GARLIC, CILANTRO, SALT, PEPPER, OIL AND ZEST AND JUICE FROM HALF THE LIME (RESERVE OTHER HALF). PAT CHICKEN DRY WITH PAPER TOWELS, THEN SPREAD CILANTRO MIXTURE ALL OVER THE BIRD, INSIDE AND OUT, INCLUDING AS FAR UNDERNEATH THE SKIN ON THE BREAST AND THIGH AS YOU CAN GO WITHOUT TEARING THE SKIN. COVER AND REFRIGERATE FOR 8 TO 24 HOURS.

PREHEAT OVEN TO 425°F (220°C). PLACE CHICKEN IN AN OILED ROASTING PAN (SEE TIP, PAGE 59), PLACE RESERVED LIME HALF INSIDE THE CHICKEN CAVITY AND ROAST FOR 20 MINUTES. REDUCE OVEN TEMPERATURE TO 375°F (190°C) AND ROAST, SPOONING PAN JUICES OVER CHICKEN ONCE OR TWICE, UNTIL SKIN IS BROWNED AND LEG JOINTS MOVE FREELY IN THEIR SOCKETS, ABOUT

1 HOUR (IF YOU WISH TO USE A MEAT THERMOMETER, THE TEMPERATURE AT THE INNER THIGH SHOULD BE 165°F/74°C). TRANSFER BIRD TO A RIMMED PLATE OR BAKING SHEET, TENT WITH FOIL AND LET REST FOR 10 MINUTES BEFORE CARVING.

MEANWHILE, PLACE ROASTING PAN ON THE STOVE OVER MEDIUM HEAT. SPOON OUT AS MUCH FAT AS POSSIBLE, THEN ADD WATER TO THE PAN. SCRAPE UP BROWNED BITS UNTIL DISSOLVED (USE A LITTLE MORE WATER IF YOU NEED TO). ADD THE JUICES FROM THE RESTING CHICKEN AND SIMMER UNTIL THE JUS REACHES THE CONSISTENCY YOU WANT. DRIZZLE OVER CARVED CHICKEN. SERVES 4 TO 6.

EASY UNSTUFFED TURKEY

ROASTING A TURKEY IS EASY WITH A LITTLE PLANNING. START THAWING A FROZEN BIRD IN THE FRIDGE 2 TO 3 DAYS BEFORE YOU PLAN TO COOK IT (THAW FOR 5 HOURS PER LB/10 HOURS PER KG). PREP THE TURKEY FOR ROASTING THE NIGHT BEFORE IF POSSIBLE (FOR THE BEST FLAVOR), BUT DON"T WORRY IF YOU CAN"T.

1 TBSP	DRIED ROSEMARY	15 ML
1 1/2 TSP	DRIED SAGE	7 ML
1 1/2 TSP	DRIED THYME	7 ML
	SALT AND BLACK PEPPER TO TASTE	
	GRATED ZEST OF 1/2 LEMON	
	JUICE OF 1 LEMON	
1	WHOLE TURKEY (SEE TIP)	1
	VEGETABLE OIL OR MELTED BUTTER	
1	ONION, CUT IN HALF	1
1	CELERY STALK, CUT IN HALF	1
2	FRESH SAGE SPRIGS (OPTIONAL)	2

IN A SMALL BOWL, COMBINE ROSEMARY, DRIED SAGE, THYME, SALT, PEPPER, LEMON ZEST AND LEMON JUICE. REMOVE AND RESERVE THE NECK AND GIBLETS, THEN PAT TURKEY DRY WITH PAPER TOWELS. RUB SEASONING MIX ALL OVER BIRD, INCLUDING AS FAR UNDERNEATH THE SKIN ON THE BREAST AND THIGH AS YOU CAN GO WITHOUT TEARING THE SKIN. PLACE THE TURKEY IN A ROASTING PAN, COVER AND REFRIGERATE, ALONG WITH NECK AND GIBLETS, FOR UP TO 24 HOURS.

PREHEAT OVEN TO 325°F (160°C). RUB THE BIRD WITH A LITTLE OIL AND PLACE, BREAST SIDE UP, ON A ROASTING

RACK (IF YOU HAVE ONE) SET IN THE PAN. PLACE ONION, CELERY AND SAGE SPRIGS (IF USING) IN THE CAVITY. PLACE NECK AND GIBLETS IN THE BOTTOM OF THE PAN. LOOSELY COVER THE BREAST AREA WITH FOIL (DISCARD FOIL ABOUT HALFWAY THROUGH COOKING). ROAST (SEE TIP), BASTING TWO OR THREE TIMES WITH PAN JUICES, UNTIL LEG JOINTS MOVE FREELY IN THEIR SOCKETS AND JUICES RUN CLEAR WHEN MEAT IS PIERCED WITH A SKEWER (IF YOU WISH TO USE A MEAT THERMOMETER, THE TEMPERATURE AT THE THICKEST PART OF THE INNER THIGH SHOULD BE 165°F/74°C). LIFT THE BIRD AND ROASTING RACK (IF USING) OUT OF THE PAN AND PLACE ON A LARGE RIMMED BAKING SHEET. COVER WITH FOIL AND LET REST FOR 30 MINUTES BEFORE CARVING. SEE BASIC GRAVY, PAGE 266, IF YOU WANT TO MAKE GRAVY. SEE TIP FOR SERVING SIZES.

TIP: YOU CAN USE THIS RECIPE FOR A TURKEY OF ANY SIZE. WE FIND BIRDS IN THE 10- TO 18-LB (5 TO 9 KG) RANGE BOTH EASIEST AND TASTIEST. PLAN ON ABOUT 15 MINUTES PER LB (30 MINUTES PER KG) TO ROAST, BUT SEE ABOVE TO ENSURE THAT THE TURKEY IS DONE.

TIP: PLAN ON ABOUT 1 TO 1½ LBS (500 TO 750 G) TURKEY WEIGHT PER PERSON. FOR EXAMPLE, A 12-LB (6 KG) TURKEY WILL FEED 8 PEOPLE (WITH LEFTOVERS).

ROAST DUCK WITH APPLE CRANBERRY GLAZE

WHOLE DUCK IS BECOMING MORE AND MORE MAINSTREAM, AND IT'S NOW EASY TO FIND IN THE MEAT DEPARTMENT OR AT THE BUTCHER SHOP. ADDING THE ORANGE AND HERBS PARTWAY THROUGH GIVES YOU A CHANCE TO POUR OFF SOME OF THE FAT, UNFLAVORED, TO REFRIGERATE AND USE TO MAKE ROASTED POTATOES.

3 LB	WHOLE DUCK	1.5 KG
	VEGETABLE OIL	
	SALT AND BLACK PEPPER TO TASTE	
2	FRESH ROSEMARY SPRIGS	2
2	FRESH THYME SPRIGS	2
1	ORANGE, QUARTERED	1
10	WHOLE CRABAPPLES (OPTIONAL)	10

APPLE CRANBERRY GLAZE

1 CUP	ROUGHLY CHOPPED TART APPLES (OR CRABAPPLES)	250 ML
1 CUP	FRESH OR FROZEN CRANBERRIES	250 ML
1 CUP	WATER	250 ML
1/2 CUP	SUGAR (APPROX.)	125 ML

PREHEAT OVEN TO 450°F (230°C). PAT DUCK DRY WITH PAPER TOWELS AND PLACE IT IN A ROASTING PAN. POKE THROUGH THE SKIN (WITHOUT PIERCING THE MEAT) IN SEVERAL PLACES USING A BAMBOO SKEWER OR THE TIP OF A KNIFE, PULLING UP THE SKIN AND POKING THROUGH IT AS IF YOU WERE THREADING CLOTH. (THE HOLES WILL ALLOW THE EXCESS FAT, STORED UNDER THE DUCK'S SKIN, TO RENDER AWAY.) RUB THE DUCK WITH OIL AND SPRINKLE WITH SALT AND PEPPER. ROAST FOR 30 MINUTES.

GLAZE: MEANWHILE, IN A SMALL POT, COMBINE APPLES, CRANBERRIES AND WATER; BRING TO A SIMMER OVER MEDIUM-HIGH HEAT. REDUCE HEAT AND SIMMER FOR 20 MINUTES OR UNTIL FRUIT IS VERY SOFT. STRAIN THE FRUIT IN A SIEVE SET OVER A BOWL, PRESSING DOWN ON THE SOLIDS TO GET AS MUCH JUICE OUT AS POSSIBLE. DISCARD SOLIDS. TRANSFER JUICE TO A SAUCEPAN, ADD SUGAR (YOU SHOULD HAVE ABOUT HALF AS MUCH SUGAR AS JUICE) AND BRING TO A BOIL OVER MEDIUM-HIGH HEAT. REDUCE HEAT AND SIMMER FOR ABOUT 20 MINUTES OR UNTIL THICKENED. SET ASIDE. (YOU'LL LIKELY HAVE MORE GLAZE THAN YOU NEED; REFRIGERATE ABOUT HALF OF IT FOR UP TO A MONTH AND USE AS A SWEET-TART JELLY.)

REMOVE DUCK FROM THE OVEN AND POUR MOST OF THE FAT FROM THE PAN INTO A JAR (LET COOL, STORE IN THE FRIDGE FOR UP TO A MONTH AND USE TO MAKE THE VERY BEST ROASTED POTATOES EVER). BRUSH DUCK WITH GLAZE AND TUCK ROSEMARY, THYME AND ORANGE INTO THE CAVITY. IF USING CRABAPPLES, SCORE THEM AROUND THE MIDDLE AND SCATTER THEM AROUND THE DUCK IN THE PAN. REDUCE OVEN TEMPERATURE TO 350°F (180°C) AND ROAST FOR $1\frac{1}{2}$ TO 2 HOURS, UNTIL LEG JOINTS MOVE FREELY IN THEIR SOCKETS (IF YOU WISH TO USE A MEAT THERMOMETER, THE TEMPERATURE AT THE INNER THIGH SHOULD BE 165°F/74°C). TRANSFER BIRD TO A RIMMED PLATE OR BAKING SHEET, TENT WITH FOIL AND LET REST FOR 15 MINUTES BEFORE CARVING. SERVE THE ROASTED CRABAPPLES WITH THE DUCK. SERVES 4 TO 6.

ANNE'S BAKED HAM WITH PEARS

JULIE'S SISTER MAKES THIS SPECTACULAR-LOOKING BAKED HAM FOR SPECIAL OCCASIONS. IT WAS ORIGINALLY A MARTHA STEWART RECIPE, BUT THIS STREAMLINED VERSION HAS BECOME A FAMILY TRADITION. THE PEARS ARE QUARTERED LENGTHWISE AND ROASTED ALONGSIDE THE HAM, MAKING FOR A DRAMATIC PRESENTATION (AND A DELICIOUS SIDE DISH).

6 to 8 LB	FULLY COOKED HAM, WITH OR WITHOUT BONE	3 to 4 KG
2 CUPS	APPLE CIDER	500 ML
1 CUP	LIQUID HONEY, DIVIDED	250 ML
3	BOSC PEARS, QUARTERED LENGTHWISE AND CORED (LEAVE THE SKIN AND STEMS)	3
1	CINNAMON STICK	1
2 CUPS	FRESH OR FROZEN CRANBERRIES	500 ML
1/2 CUP	PACKED BROWN SUGAR	125 ML
1 TSP	GROUND GINGER	5 ML
	BLACK PEPPER TO TASTE	

PREHEAT OVEN TO 350°F (180°C). PLACE HAM IN A LARGE ROASTING PAN AND POUR CIDER AND HALF THE HONEY OVER TOP. BAKE FOR 1 HOUR, BASTING WITH PAN JUICES ONCE OR TWICE. SCATTER PEARS AND CINNAMON AROUND THE HAM. BAKE FOR 45 MINUTES, BASTING ONCE OR TWICE. SPRINKLE CRANBERRIES OVER PEARS AND BAKE FOR 30 TO 40 MINUTES OR UNTIL PEARS ARE TENDER AND CRANBERRIES BEGIN TO BURST. REMOVE FROM OVEN AND, USING A SLOTTED SPOON, TRANSFER FRUIT TO A SHALLOW BOWL; COVER WITH FOIL AND SET ASIDE. RETURN THE HAM TO THE OVEN.

LADLE PAN JUICES INTO A MEDIUM SAUCEPAN. STIR IN BROWN SUGAR, GINGER AND THE REMAINING HONEY; BRING TO A SIMMER OVER MEDIUM-LOW HEAT. SIMMER FOR ABOUT 20 MINUTES OR UNTIL GLAZE IS SYRUPY AND HAS REDUCED BY HALF. POUR GLAZE OVER HAM AND BAKE UNTIL A MEAT THERMOMETER INSERTED IN THE THICKEST PART OF THE HAM REGISTERS 165°F (74°C). REMOVE FROM OVEN AND BRUSH HAM WITH GLAZE FROM THE PAN. TRANSFER TO A CUTTING BOARD AND LET REST FOR 15 MINUTES BEFORE CARVING. POUR PAN JUICES OVER PEARS AND CRANBERRIES AND SERVE WITH THE HAM. SERVES 10 TO 12, WITH LEFTOVERS.

PORK CARNITAS

A POT OF FLAVORFUL BRAISED PORK SHOULDER IS A GREAT WAY TO FEED A SMALL CROWD — SET OUT TORTILLAS OR TACO SHELLS AND ACCOMPANIMENTS LIKE SALSA VERDE, AVOCADO, CILANTRO, LIME WEDGES AND SOUR CREAM, AND LET EVERYONE BUILD THEIR OWN. IF YOU LIKE, SWAP BEEF BRISKET FOR THE PORK SHOULDER, FOR BEEF CARNITAS — "LITTLE MEATS."

4 to 5 LB	BONELESS PORK SHOULDER BLADE ROAST, TRIMMED AND CUT INTO 3- TO 4-INCH (7.5 TO 10 CM) PIECES	2 to 2.5 KG
2 TBSP	CHILI POWDER	30 ML
	SALT TO TASTE	
	VEGETABLE OIL	
1 to 2 CUPS	BASIC CHICKEN STOCK (PAGE 28), READY-TO-USE CHICKEN BROTH OR WATER	250 to 500 ML
1 TSP	GROUND CUMIN	5 ML
1	BAY LEAF	1
	SOFT FLOUR TORTILLAS, WARMED	

ACCOMPANIMENTS

SALSA VERDE (PAGE 263)

SLICED AVOCADO

FRESH CILANTRO

LIME WEDGES

SOUR CREAM

PREHEAT OVEN TO 325°F (160°C). PLACE PORK ON A CUTTING BOARD AND PAT DRY WITH PAPER TOWELS. SPRINKLE WITH CHILI POWDER AND SALT, ROLLING THE PIECES AROUND WITH YOUR HANDS TO COAT. SET A

HEAVY, OVENPROOF BRAISING PAN OVER MEDIUM-HIGH
HEAT AND ADD A GENEROUS DRIZZLE OF OIL. BROWN THE
MEAT IN BATCHES, TRANSFERRING IT TO A PLATE AS YOU
GO. POUR OFF ANY EXCESS FAT AND ADD A SPLASH OF
WATER TO THE PAN, SCRAPING UP ANY BROWNED BITS
FROM THE BOTTOM. RETURN ALL THE MEAT TO THE PAN
AND ADD ENOUGH STOCK TO COME ABOUT HALFWAY UP
THE MEAT. ADD CUMIN AND BAY LEAF.

COVER THE PAN, PUT IT IN THE OVEN AND BAKE FOR
$2\frac{1}{2}$ TO 3 HOURS OR UNTIL MEAT IS VERY TENDER AND
CAN BE PULLED APART WITH A FORK. IF IT SEEMS TOO
LIQUIDY, PLACE THE PAN BACK ON THE STOVETOP AND
SIMMER, UNCOVERED, UNTIL ANY EXCESS LIQUID HAS
REDUCED. SET THE POT OUT ON THE TABLE WITH WARMED
TORTILLAS AND YOUR CHOICE OF ACCOMPANIMENTS
AND LET EVERYONE ASSEMBLE THEIR OWN CARNITAS.
SERVES 8 TO 10.

POT ROAST WITH MUSHROOM GRAVY

THIS CLASSIC POT ROAST IS COOKED LOW AND SLOW TO MAKE FOR DELICIOUSLY FALL-APART MEAT. THE MUSHROOM GRAVY COOKS RIGHT WITH IT AND IS FINISHED WITH THE WHIZZ OF A HANDHELD BLENDER. SERVE WITH POTATOES AND YOUR FAVORITE VEGGIES.

	VEGETABLE OIL	
3 to 4 LB	BONELESS BEEF CHUCK OR BLADE ROAST	1.5 to 2 KG
	SALT AND BLACK PEPPER TO TASTE	
2 CUPS	SLICED MUSHROOMS	500 ML
2	GARLIC CLOVES, MINCED	2
1	LARGE ONION, SLICED	1
4 CUPS	READY-TO-USE BEEF BROTH	1 L
2	FRESH ROSEMARY SPRIGS	2

PREHEAT OVEN TO 275°F (140°C). IN AN OVENPROOF DUTCH OVEN, HEAT A DRIZZLE OF OIL OVER MEDIUM-HIGH HEAT. SEASON ROAST WITH SALT AND PEPPER, PLACE IN THE POT AND BROWN ON ALL SIDES. TRANSFER ROAST TO A PLATE, REDUCE HEAT TO MEDIUM AND ADD MUSHROOMS TO THE POT, ADDING ANOTHER DRIZZLE OF OIL IF NECESSARY. COOK, STIRRING REGULARLY, FOR 5 TO 10 MINUTES OR UNTIL MUSHROOMS HAVE SOFTENED AND ARE STARTING TO RELEASE THEIR LIQUID. SCRAPE SOME OF THE BROWN BITS OFF THE BOTTOM OF THE POT (THE LIQUID FROM THE MUSHROOMS WILL HELP YOU DO THIS), THEN ADD GARLIC AND ONION; COOK, STIRRING, FOR ANOTHER MINUTE OR TWO, JUST SO THE ONION STARTS

TO SOFTEN. RETURN THE ROAST TO THE POT, POUR IN BROTH AND ADD ROSEMARY; BRING TO A SIMMER.

COVER THE POT, PUT IT IN THE OVEN AND BAKE FOR $2\frac{1}{2}$ HOURS. UNCOVER, FLIP THE ROAST OVER AND BAKE FOR 30 TO 60 MINUTES OR UNTIL MEAT IS VERY TENDER. TRANSFER ROAST TO A CUTTING BOARD, TENT WITH FOIL AND LET REST FOR 10 TO 15 MINUTES BEFORE SLICING.

MEANWHILE, USING A LARGE SPOON, SKIM ANY EXCESS FAT OFF THE COOKING LIQUID. DISCARD ROSEMARY. USING AN IMMERSION BLENDER, GIVE THE REMAINING COOKING LIQUID A COUPLE OF WHIZZES TO CHOP UP SOME OF THE MUSHROOMS AND CREATE A LITTLE BIT OF CREAMINESS WITHOUT COMPLETELY PURÉEING THE MUSHROOMS. TASTE THE SAUCE AND ADJUST THE SEASONING WITH SALT AND PEPPER. SERVE WITH SLICED ROAST. SERVES 6 TO 8.

MISSISSIPPI(ISH) POT ROAST

OUR VERSION OF THIS POPULAR DISH IS DONE IN THE OVEN, AND WE'VE SEASONED IT FROM SCRATCH TO CUT DOWN ON THE ORIGINAL'S SALTINESS.

3 TBSP	VEGETABLE OIL	45 ML
3 to 4 LB	BONELESS BEEF CHUCK OR BLADE ROAST	1.5 to 2 KG
	SALT AND BLACK PEPPER TO TASTE	
1 TSP	DRIED DILL	5 ML
1/2 TSP	PAPRIKA	2 ML
PINCH	CAYENNE PEPPER	PINCH
1/2 CUP	BUTTER, MELTED	125 ML
2 TBSP	MAYONNAISE	30 ML
1 TBSP	WORCESTERSHIRE SAUCE	15 ML
2 TSP	WHITE VINEGAR	10 ML
1 CUP	DRAINED PICKLED BANANA PEPPER RINGS, RINSED AND PATTED DRY	250 ML

PREHEAT OVEN TO 275°F (140°C). IN AN OVENPROOF DUTCH OVEN BIG ENOUGH TO HOUSE THE ROAST, HEAT OIL OVER HIGH HEAT. SEASON ROAST GENEROUSLY WITH SALT AND PEPPER AND BROWN ON ALL SIDES. REMOVE FROM HEAT. IN A MEDIUM BOWL, COMBINE DILL, PAPRIKA, CAYENNE, BUTTER, MAYONNAISE, WORCESTERSHIRE AND VINEGAR UNTIL SMOOTH. STIR IN BANANA PEPPERS. POUR OVER ROAST. COVER AND ROAST IN THE OVEN FOR 2 1/2 HOURS. UNCOVER, FLIP THE ROAST OVER AND ROAST FOR 30 TO 60 MINUTES OR UNTIL VERY TENDER. TRANSFER ROAST TO A CUTTING BOARD, TENT WITH FOIL AND LET REST FOR 10 TO 15 MINUTES BEFORE SLICING. SERVE WITH SAUCE FROM THE POT SPOONED OVER THE MEAT. SERVES 6 TO 8.

Classic Roast Chicken (page 58)

Anne's Baked Ham with Pears (page 66)

Pork Carnitas (page 68) with
Salsa Verde (page 263)

Foolproof Prime Rib (page 74)

JACKI'S BRISKET

ALTHOUGH JACKI'S BRISKET NEEDS TO BE STARTED A COUPLE OF DAYS AHEAD, IT DOESN'T REQUIRE A WHOLE LOT OF ACTUAL WORK.

4	WHITE ONIONS, THINLY SLICED	4
4	GARLIC CLOVES, PEELED	4
4 to 5 LB	BEEF BRISKET	2 to 2.5 KG
1/4 CUP	SOY SAUCE	60 ML
1	PACKAGE (1 OZ/28 G) DRY ONION SOUP MIX	1

STARTING ABOUT 48 HOURS IN ADVANCE, LINE A LARGE ROASTING PAN WITH ONIONS AND GARLIC. LAY BRISKET ON TOP. POUR SOY SAUCE OVER BRISKET, SPRINKLE WITH ONION SOUP MIX AND RUB ALL OVER THE MEAT. COVER WITH PLASTIC WRAP AND REFRIGERATE OVERNIGHT.

PREHEAT OVEN TO 325°F (160°C). COVER PAN TIGHTLY WITH A LID OR FOIL AND ROAST FOR 2 1/2 HOURS OR UNTIL THE END OF A WOODEN SPOON GOES EASILY THROUGH THE MEAT. REMOVE BRISKET AND SET IT ASIDE TO COOL FOR 30 MINUTES. STRAIN THE PAN JUICES, RESERVING BOTH THE JUICES AND THE ONIONS AND GARLIC IN SEPARATE AIRTIGHT CONTAINERS. REMOVE AS MUCH FAT AS YOU CAN FROM THE SURFACE OF THE LIQUID. COVER AND REFRIGERATE EVERYTHING OVERNIGHT.

TO PREPARE DINNER, PREHEAT OVEN TO 325°F (160°C), SLICE COLD BRISKET ACROSS THE GRAIN AND SPREAD SLICES OUT IN A BAKING DISH WITH THE RESERVED ONIONS, GARLIC AND LIQUID. BAKE FOR 20 TO 30 MINUTES OR UNTIL HEATED THROUGH. SERVES 6.

FOOLPROOF PRIME RIB

PRIME RIB CAN BE A SCARY CUT TO COOK: WHEN YOU SPEND SO MUCH ON A PIECE OF BEEF, YOU WANT TO MAKE SURE IT'S PROPERLY COOKED. THERE ARE PLENTY OF SIMPLE METHODS THAT GUARANTEE A PERFECT MEDIUM-RARE ROAST, AND THIS IS ONE OF THEM. ROASTING IT IN A CAST-IRON OR OTHER OVENPROOF SKILLET KICK-STARTS THE PROCESS AND ALLOWS YOU TO QUICKLY MAKE GRAVY RIGHT IN THE PAN.

3 to 6 LB	BONE-IN BEEF PRIME RIB ROAST	1.5 to 3 KG
2 to 4 TBSP	BUTTER, SOFTENED	30 to 60 ML
2 TSP	DRIED THYME	10 ML
	SALT AND BLACK PEPPER TO TASTE	

GRAVY

ALL-PURPOSE FLOUR

READY-TO-USE BEEF BROTH

DRY RED WINE

SALT AND BLACK PEPPER TO TASTE

PREHEAT OVEN TO 500°F (260°C) AND MAKE SURE IT'S UP TO TEMPERATURE (WE LIKE TO TURN IT ON A HALF-HOUR BEFORE WE PLAN TO START THE ROAST). RUB ROAST ALL OVER WITH BUTTER, THEN SPRINKLE WITH THYME, SALT AND PEPPER. SET A LARGE OVENPROOF SKILLET OVER MEDIUM-HIGH HEAT FOR A MINUTE OR TWO TO WARM IT UP. PUT THE ROAST, BONES DOWN, IN THE PAN AND SLIDE IT INTO THE OVEN. MULTIPLY THE WEIGHT OF THE ROAST IN POUNDS BY 6 (OR IN KILOGRAMS BY 12) AND ROAST IT FOR THAT MANY MINUTES — FOR EXAMPLE, A 4-LB ROAST X 6 (A 2 KG ROAST X 12) = 24 MINUTES. AFTER THAT

TIME, TURN THE OVEN DOWN TO 250°F (120°C) AND COOK FOR ABOUT 2 HOURS OR UNTIL A MEAT THERMOMETER INSERTED IN THE THICKEST PART OF THE ROAST REGISTERS 145°F (63°C) FOR MEDIUM-RARE.

GRAVY: WHEN YOU TAKE THE ROAST OUT OF THE OVEN, TRANSFER IT TO A CUTTING BOARD AND PUT THE SKILLET ON THE STOVETOP. DISCARD ALL BUT 1 TO 2 TBSP (15 TO 30 ML) OF THE FAT FROM THE SKILLET. ADD ABOUT 1 TBSP (15 ML) FLOUR AND WHISK OVER MEDIUM-HIGH HEAT UNTIL IT BUBBLES AND THICKENS. WHISK IN ABOUT 1 CUP (250 ML) BROTH AND A SPLASH OF WINE, BRING TO A SIMMER AND STIR UNTIL GRAVY HAS THE CONSISTENCY YOU WANT, ADDING A LITTLE MORE BROTH IF IT'S TOO THICK. IF IT'S TOO THIN, SIMMER UNTIL IT REDUCES. SEASON WITH SALT AND PEPPER.

SLICE AND SERVE PRIME RIB WITH THE GRAVY. SERVES ABOUT 3 PEOPLE PER LB (500 G) OF BEEF (BEFORE COOKING).

RACK OF LAMB

RACK OF LAMB IS A REAL TREAT, SOMETHING WE SAVE FOR SPECIAL OCCASIONS. WE PARTICULARLY LIKE THE SLIGHTLY SMALLER NEW ZEALAND RACKS FOR THE BEST FLAVOR. IF YOU PREFER TO USE LARGER RACKS, THEY CAN BE MORE LIKE 1½ LBS (750 G) EACH AND WILL NEED MORE TIME IN THE OVEN.

4	GARLIC CLOVES, MINCED	4
1 TBSP	FINELY CHOPPED FRESH ROSEMARY	15 ML
	SALT AND BLACK PEPPER TO TASTE	
2 TBSP	OLIVE OIL	30 ML
2	RACKS OF LAMB, FRENCHED (EACH ABOUT 1 LB/500 G)	2
2 TBSP	DIJON MUSTARD	30 ML

IN A SMALL BOWL, COMBINE GARLIC, ROSEMARY, SALT, PEPPER AND OIL. IF THE LAMB HAS MORE THAN ¼ INCH (0.5 CM) FAT ON THE BACK, TRIM IT DOWN A LITTLE; OTHERWISE, LEAVE IT BE. RUB THE GARLIC MIXTURE ALL OVER MEATY PARTS OF LAMB. PLACE IN A SEALABLE PLASTIC BAG OR A COVERED BOWL AND REFRIGERATE FOR 2 TO 24 HOURS.

PREHEAT OVEN TO 350°F (180°C). SCRAPE HERB MIXTURE OFF LAMB AND INTO A SMALL BOWL (IT DOESN'T NEED TO BE PERFECT, JUST REMOVE THE BULK OF IT). STIR MUSTARD INTO THE HERB MIXTURE AND SET ASIDE. IN A VERY LARGE OVENPROOF SKILLET SET OVER HIGH HEAT, SEAR FATTY SIDES OF LAMB UNTIL VERY BROWNED AND CRISP, THEN SEAR THE MEATY BOTTOMS. USING A BUTTER KNIFE, SMEAR MUSTARD MIXTURE OVER FATTY AND MEATY AREAS OF LAMB (DON'T WORRY TOO MUCH

ABOUT THE UNDERSIDE, WHERE THE RIBS ARE VISIBLE).
PLACE RACKS EITHER INTERLOCKING WITH ONE ANOTHER
(STANDING UP IN PAN) OR LYING FLAT, WITH FATTY
SIDE UP. ROAST (SEE TIP) UNTIL A MEAT THERMOMETER
INSERTED IN THE THICKEST PART REGISTERS 140°F (63°C)
FOR MEDIUM-RARE (THE TEMPERATURE WILL CONTINUE
TO RISE ABOUT ANOTHER 5°F/3°C WHILE THE LAMB
RESTS). TRANSFER LAMB TO A RIMMED BAKING SHEET,
COVER WITH FOIL AND LET REST FOR 10 MINUTES BEFORE
SLICING INTO INDIVIDUAL RIBS TO SERVE. SERVES 4.

TIP: IF THE EXPOSED RIB ENDS START TO BURN, FOLD
A SMALL PIECE OF FOIL OVER THE ENDS (ONE PIECE OF
FOIL PER RACK).

I WAS A VEGETARIAN UNTIL I STARTED
LEANING TOWARD THE SUNLIGHT.
— RITA RUDNER

SLOW-COOKED LEG OF LAMB WITH GARLICKY POTATOES

LEG OF LAMB MAKES A WONDERFULLY CELEBRATORY FAMILY MEAL BUT CAN BE INTIMIDATING TO COOK. IF YOU PICK UP A LEG WITH THE SHANK END TRIMMED, IT FITS NICELY IN A 6-QUART SLOW COOKER. THE RESULT IS ULTRA-TENDER LAMB WITH SOME BONUS STOCK IN THE BOTTOM TO EITHER MAKE GRAVY OR TURN INTO LENTIL SOUP OR SCOTCH BROTH THE NEXT DAY.

3 to 5 LB	LEG OF LAMB, WITH OR WITHOUT BONE, SHANK END TRIMMED	1.5 to 2.5 KG
	VEGETABLE OIL	
4	MEDIUM YELLOW POTATOES, CUT INTO 1-INCH (2.5 CM) PIECES	4
1	GARLIC BULB, CLOVES SEPARATED	1
	SALT TO TASTE	
2	FRESH ROSEMARY SPRIGS	2
1 CUP	DRY RED WINE OR READY-TO-USE BEEF BROTH	250 ML

PAT LAMB DRY WITH A PAPER TOWEL AND RUB IT ALL OVER WITH OIL. SET A LARGE, HEAVY SKILLET OVER MEDIUM-HIGH HEAT AND BROWN MEAT ON ALL SIDES (ALTERNATIVELY, YOU COULD DO THIS ON THE GRILL). MEANWHILE, TOSS POTATOES AND ABOUT HALF THE GARLIC CLOVES INTO YOUR SLOW COOKER. PLACE LAMB ON TOP OF POTATOES. SQUISH THE REMAINING CLOVES OF GARLIC AND RUB OVER THE SURFACE OF THE MEAT. SPRINKLE WITH SALT. TOSS IN ROSEMARY AND POUR WINE AROUND THE POTATOES. COVER AND COOK ON LOW FOR 6 TO 8 HOURS OR UNTIL LAMB IS VERY TENDER. DISCARD ROSEMARY SPRIGS. CARVE LAMB AND SERVE WITH POTATOES. SERVES 8.

SMALL MEATS

BAKED WHOLE SALMON

WE USUALLY LIKE TO KEEP IT SIMPLE WHEN WE COOK FISH. THIS PREPARATION HAS PLENTY OF SUBTLE FLAVOR AND REALLY ALLOWS THE SALMON TO SHINE.

2 LB	CLEANED WHOLE SALMON	1 KG
	SALT AND BLACK PEPPER TO TASTE	
3	LEMON SLICES, CUT IN HALF TO MAKE 6 HALF-CIRCLES	3
3	ORANGE SLICES, CUT IN HALF TO MAKE 6 HALF-CIRCLES	3
4	FRESH DILL SPRIGS, THICK STEMS DISCARDED	4
2	GREEN ONIONS, THINLY SLICED	2
1½ TBSP	BUTTER (SEE TIP)	22 ML

PREHEAT OVEN TO 425°F (220°C). RINSE SALMON AND PAT DRY, THEN PLACE ON A RIMMED BAKING SHEET LINED WITH PARCHMENT PAPER. USING A SHARP KNIFE, MAKE 4 SHALLOW SLICES, PERPENDICULAR TO THE SPINE, THROUGH THE SKIN ON TOP OF THE FISH. SEASON FISH INSIDE AND OUT WITH SALT AND PEPPER, THEN STUFF CAVITY WITH A THIRD OF THE LEMON AND ORANGE PIECES AND A THIRD OF THE DILL AND ONION (OR WHATEVER FITS). DOT A THIRD OF THE BUTTER INSIDE THE CAVITY. PLACE REMAINING LEMON AND ORANGE PIECES ON TOP OF FISH AND SCATTER THE REMAINING DILL AND ONION OVER TOP. DOT WITH THE REMAINING BUTTER.

BAKE FOR 20 TO 25 MINUTES OR UNTIL FLESH IS JUST OPAQUE AT THICKEST POINT. REMOVE CITRUS AND HERBS FROM OUTSIDE OF FISH AND CAVITY AND RESERVE. CUT OFF HEAD (IF SALMON WAS SOLD HEAD ON), THEN SCRAPE

SKIN FREE OF TOP FILLET. GENTLY REMOVE TOP FILLET BY SLICING DOWN TOWARD THE SPINE FROM THE TOP EDGE OF FISH, THEN PEELING FILLET OFF RIB BONES. TAKE CARE TO LEAVE BONES ATTACHED TO THE SPINE. STARTING FROM THE TAIL, CAREFULLY LIFT THE SPINE AND ALL ATTACHED BONES FROM THE LOWER FILLET. TURN LOWER FILLET OVER AND REMOVE SKIN. SERVE WITH RESERVED CITRUS AND HERBS ALONGSIDE. SERVES 4.

TIP: WHEN BAKING WILD FISH, IT'S A GOOD IDEA TO ADD A LITTLE BUTTER OR OIL, AS WILD FISH TENDS TO BE VERY LEAN. FARMED FISH (ALL ATLANTIC SALMON AND MOST STEELHEAD TROUT IS FARMED) ARE CONSIDERABLY MORE OILY; IF USING FARMED FISH, WE SUGGEST YOU OMIT THE BUTTER.

SALMON BURGERS

WE LOVE A GOOD SALMON BURGER! YOU CAN SERVE THESE WITH ALL THE USUAL BURGER TRIMMINGS OR BRANCH OUT AND ADD A BIG DOLLOP OF TZATZIKI (SEE PAGE 261). THE PATTIES WILL BE A LITTLE FRAGILE — WE SUGGEST EATING THEM OVER A PLATE.

	VEGETABLE OIL	
1	SHALLOT, FINELY CHOPPED	1
1 LB	SKINLESS SALMON FILLET	500 G
1/4 CUP	PANKO	60 ML
1 TBSP	FINELY CHOPPED FRESH DILL	15 ML
1 TBSP	RINSED CAPERS, PATTED DRY AND CHOPPED	15 ML
1	LARGE EGG YOLK	1
1 TSP	DIJON MUSTARD	5 ML
1 TSP	LEMON JUICE	5 ML
	SALT AND BLACK PEPPER TO TASTE	
	BUNS AND TYPICAL BURGER FIXINGS	

IN A SMALL SAUCEPAN, HEAT A DRIZZLE OF OIL OVER MEDIUM-LOW HEAT. SAUTÉ SHALLOT UNTIL SOFTENED AND BROWNED, ABOUT 5 MINUTES. LET COOL. CUT SALMON INTO VERY FINE PIECES (SEE TIP) AND PLACE IN A MEDIUM BOWL. STIR IN COOLED SHALLOTS, PANKO, DILL, CAPERS, EGG YOLK, MUSTARD, LEMON JUICE, SALT AND PEPPER. FORM INTO FOUR 3/4-INCH (2 CM) THICK PATTIES. LET PATTIES STAND FOR 5 MINUTES.

IN A LARGE NONSTICK OR CAST-IRON SKILLET, HEAT A SKIFF OF OIL OVER MEDIUM-LOW HEAT. USING A SPATULA, CAREFULLY SLIDE PATTIES INTO PAN. COOK UNTIL GOLDEN ON THE UNDERSIDE, ABOUT 4 MINUTES, THEN CAREFULLY

FLIP PATTIES OVER AND COOK UNTIL THE OTHER SIDE IS BROWNED AND THE PATTIES ARE COOKED THROUGH, ABOUT 4 MINUTES. MAKES 4 BURGERS.

TIP: TO CUT THE FISH INTO SMALL ENOUGH PIECES, FIRST SLICE THE FILLET INTO THIN RIBBONS (ABOUT $\frac{1}{8}$ INCH/3 MM), THEN SLICE A FEW RIBBONS AT A TIME INTO SMALLER PIECES. PIECES SHOULD BE SMALLER THAN $\frac{1}{4}$ INCH (0.5 CM) SQUARE IN ORDER FOR THE PATTIES TO HOLD TOGETHER WHEN COOKED.

ROOM AND BORED:
WHAT YOU GET AT A HOTEL WITH NO WI-FI.

JO-ANNA'S SMOTHERED CHICKEN DINNER

OUR FRIEND JO-ANNA MAKES THIS DISH FOR HER FAMILY OF FIVE. IT'S A CREAMY, COMFORTING DISH THAT THEY ALL LOVE. IF YOU LIKE, ADD 1/4 CUP (60 ML) WHITE WINE WITH THE CHICKEN BROTH AND WATER. THE FLAVOR THE WINE ADDS IS DELICIOUS, AND YOU CAN SERVE THE REST WITH DINNER!

1 TBSP	VEGETABLE OIL	15 ML
4	BONELESS SKINLESS CHICKEN BREASTS	4
	SALT AND BLACK PEPPER TO TASTE	
1 TBSP	BUTTER	15 ML
3	GARLIC CLOVES, MINCED	3
1	LARGE SWEET ONION, HALVED AND SLICED	1
2 CUPS	SLICED MUSHROOMS	500 ML
2 TBSP	ALL-PURPOSE FLOUR	30 ML
1 TSP	DRIED THYME	5 ML
1	CAN (10 OZ/284 ML) READY-TO-USE CHICKEN BROTH	1
1/4 CUP	WATER	60 ML
1/4 CUP	HEAVY OR WHIPPING (35%) CREAM	60 ML
1/4 CUP	SOUR CREAM	60 ML
2	GREEN ONIONS, CHOPPED	2
	HOT COOKED EGG NOODLES	

IN A HEAVY SKILLET, HEAT OIL OVER MEDIUM-HIGH HEAT. SEASON CHICKEN GENEROUSLY WITH SALT AND PEPPER. BROWN CHICKEN ON BOTH SIDES, ABOUT 3 MINUTES PER SIDE (IT DOESN'T NEED TO BE COOKED THROUGH YET). TRANSFER CHICKEN TO A PLATE. ADD BUTTER TO THE SKILLET AND SAUTÉ GARLIC, ONION AND MUSHROOMS

FOR 4 TO 5 MINUTES OR UNTIL SOFT AND THE MOISTURE FROM THE MUSHROOMS HAS COOKED OFF. ADD FLOUR AND THYME; COOK, STIRRING, FOR 1 MINUTE. STIR IN BROTH AND WATER; BRING TO A SIMMER. REDUCE HEAT AND COOK, SCRAPING UP ANY BROWNED BITS FROM THE BOTTOM OF THE PAN, UNTIL THE SAUCE THICKENS. STIR IN CREAM AND SOUR CREAM. RETURN CHICKEN AND ANY ACCUMULATED JUICES TO THE PAN; SIMMER FOR 15 TO 20 MINUTES OR UNTIL CHICKEN IS NO LONGER PINK INSIDE. SPRINKLE WITH GREEN ONIONS AND SERVE OVER EGG NOODLES. SERVES 4.

YELLOW CHICKEN

YELLOW CHICKEN — ISN'T THAT REDUNDANT?
THE YELLOW HERE IS THE COLOR OF THE SAUCE,
WHICH COMES FROM A BIT OF CURRY POWDER.
SERVE OVER STEAMED RICE.

6 to 8	BONELESS SKINLESS CHICKEN THIGHS	6 to 8
	SALT AND BLACK PEPPER TO TASTE	
3 TBSP	BUTTER	45 ML
3 TBSP	ALL-PURPOSE FLOUR	45 ML
1/2 CUP	BASIC CHICKEN STOCK (PAGE 28) OR READY-TO-USE CHICKEN BROTH	125 ML
1/2 CUP	MILK	125 ML
1/3 CUP	SHREDDED CHEDDAR CHEESE	75 ML
I TSP	CURRY POWDER	5 ML
1/2 CUP	MAYONNAISE	125 ML
1/2 TSP	LEMON JUICE	2 ML
1/4 CUP	DRY BREAD CRUMBS	60 ML
I TBSP	BUTTER, MELTED	15 ML

PLACE CHICKEN IN A LARGE, DEEP SKILLET OR SAUCEPAN AND COVER WITH ABOUT I INCH (2.5 CM) OF WATER. THROW IN A PINCH OF SALT AND A BIT OF PEPPER. BRING TO A SIMMER OVER MEDIUM-HIGH HEAT. REDUCE HEAT, COVER AND POACH FOR IO TO I5 MINUTES OR UNTIL JUICES RUN CLEAR WHEN CHICKEN IS PIERCED. REMOVE CHICKEN FROM WATER, PAT DRY AND PLACE IN AN 8-INCH (20 CM) SQUARE OR SIMILAR SIZE BAKING DISH.

PREHEAT OVEN TO 400°F (200°C). IN A SMALL SKILLET, MELT 3 TBSP (45 ML) BUTTER OVER MEDIUM HEAT. REDUCE HEAT TO MEDIUM-LOW AND WHISK IN FLOUR. COOK, WHISKING, FOR 2 TO 5 MINUTES OR UNTIL A

THICK PASTE FORMS. SLOWLY ADD STOCK, THEN MILK, WHISKING CONSTANTLY. COOK, WHISKING, UNTIL THE SAUCE THICKENS AND NO LUMPS REMAIN. REMOVE FROM HEAT AND STIR IN CHEESE, CURRY POWDER, MAYONNAISE, LEMON JUICE, SALT AND PEPPER UNTIL EVENLY COMBINED. POUR OVER CHICKEN AND TOSS SO THAT CHICKEN IS EVENLY COVERED. IN ANOTHER SMALL BOWL, COMBINE BREAD CRUMBS AND MELTED BUTTER; SPRINKLE OVER CHICKEN AND SAUCE. BAKE FOR 30 MINUTES OR UNTIL SAUCE IS BUBBLING. SERVES 4 TO 6.

TIP: IF YOU DON'T WANT TO POACH YOUR CHICKEN BREASTS, YOU CAN ROAST THEM IN THE OVEN BEFORE PUTTING THE REST OF THE DISH TOGETHER.

I WANT TO WRITE A MYSTERY NOVEL. OR DO I?

YVONNE'S POMEGRANATE CHICKEN

YVONNE LEARNED TO MAKE THIS STICKY SWEET-TANGY CHICKEN WHEN SHE LIVED IN IRAN. RICH WITH WALNUTS, ITS UNIQUE FLAVOR COMES FROM POMEGRANATE MOLASSES, WHICH IS BECOMING EASIER TO FIND IN THE INTERNATIONAL FOODS SECTION OF WELL-STOCKED GROCERY STORES. SERVE WITH RICE.

8	BONE-IN SKIN-ON CHICKEN THIGHS	8
$1/2$ TSP	POULTRY SEASONING OR DRIED SAGE	2 ML
	SALT AND BLACK PEPPER TO TASTE	
	VEGETABLE OIL	
3 TBSP	BUTTER	45 ML
I	LARGE ONION, FINELY CHOPPED	I
2 TBSP	TOMATO PASTE	30 ML
2 CUPS	WALNUT HALVES, CHOPPED	500 ML
3 CUPS	WATER	750 ML
3 TBSP	POMEGRANATE MOLASSES	45 ML
	JUICE OF I LEMON	
I TSP	SUGAR (APPROX.)	5 ML
$1/2$ TSP	GROUND CINNAMON	2 ML

PAT CHICKEN DRY WITH A PAPER TOWEL AND SPRINKLE WITH POULTRY SEASONING, SALT AND PEPPER. IN A LARGE, HEAVY SKILLET, HEAT A DRIZZLE OF OIL OVER MEDIUM-HIGH HEAT. WORKING IN BATCHES, BROWN CHICKEN THIGHS ON ALL SIDES, TRANSFERRING THEM TO A PLATE AS YOU GO AND ADDING MORE OIL TO THE PAN AS NEEDED BETWEEN BATCHES. ADD BUTTER TO THE PAN AND SAUTÉ ONION FOR 3 TO 4 MINUTES, UNTIL GOLDEN. ADD TOMATO PASTE AND COOK, STIRRING,

FOR A MINUTE OR TWO, UNTIL SLIGHTLY THICKENED. ADD WALNUTS AND COOK, STIRRING CONSTANTLY, FOR 5 MINUTES. ADD WATER, POMEGRANATE MOLASSES, LEMON JUICE, SUGAR AND CINNAMON. REDUCE HEAT TO LOW, COVER AND SIMMER FOR ABOUT 20 MINUTES OR UNTIL THICKENED. TASTE THE SAUCE; IF YOU FIND IT A LITTLE SOUR, ADD A BIT MORE SUGAR. ARRANGE CHICKEN IN SAUCE (SEE TIP), COVER AND SIMMER FOR 20 TO 25 MINUTES OR UNTIL JUICES RUN CLEAR WHEN CHICKEN IS PIERCED. SERVES 4 TO 6.

TIP: IF THE CHICKEN THIGHS DON'T ALL FIT IN THE PAN, ARRANGE THEM IN A BAKING DISH, POUR THE SAUCE OVER TOP, COVER AND BAKE AT 350°F (180°C) FOR 40 MINUTES OR UNTIL THE JUICES RUN CLEAR.

SHEET PAN CHICKEN WITH PISTACHIOS AND HONEY

THIS IS A VARIATION OF A SLIGHTLY MORE EXOTIC CHICKEN DISH CREATED BY YOTAM OTTOLENGHI. WE LOVED THE IDEA OF ROASTING CHICKEN PIECES WITH HONEY AND NUTS, BUT WANTED TO SIMPLIFY THE INGREDIENTS TO REFLECT WHAT'S USUALLY IN OUR OWN PANTRIES. THE RESULT IS JUST AS DELICIOUS. SERVE OVER RICE.

1	ONION, CHOPPED	1
1 TSP	GROUND GINGER	5 ML
1 TSP	GROUND CINNAMON	5 ML
PINCH	SAFFRON	PINCH
1/4 CUP	OLIVE OIL	60 ML
	JUICE OF 1 LEMON	
	SALT AND BLACK PEPPER TO TASTE	
2 LBS	ASSORTED BONE-IN SKIN-ON CHICKEN PIECES	1 KG
3 TBSP	LIQUID HONEY	45 ML
1/2 TSP	VANILLA	2 ML
1 TBSP	WARM WATER (APPROX.)	15 ML
3/4 CUP	SHELLED PISTACHIOS, ROUGHLY CHOPPED	175 ML

IN A SMALL BOWL, COMBINE ONION, GINGER, CINNAMON, SAFFRON, OIL, LEMON JUICE, SALT AND PEPPER. PLACE CHICKEN IN A SHALLOW DISH (OR SEALABLE PLASTIC BAG) AND COVER WITH MARINADE. COVER AND REFRIGERATE FOR A COUPLE OF HOURS OR OVERNIGHT.

PREHEAT OVEN TO 400°F (200°C). REMOVE CHICKEN FROM MARINADE AND ARRANGE ON A RIMMED BAKING SHEET, THEN POUR MARINADE OVER TOP. ROAST FOR 35 MINUTES.

MEANWHILE, IN ANOTHER SMALL BOWL, COMBINE HONEY AND VANILLA. STIR IN WARM WATER TO FORM A PASTE (START WITH A LITTLE WATER AND ADD MORE UNTIL YOU GET A WORKABLE CONSISTENCY). STIR IN PISTACHIOS. REMOVE CHICKEN FROM OVEN AND SPREAD PASTE EVENLY ON TOP OF CHICKEN. BAKE FOR 5 TO 10 MINUTES OR UNTIL JUICES RUN CLEAR WHEN CHICKEN IS PIERCED. SERVES 4 TO 6.

TIP: ANY COMBINATION OF BONE-IN SKIN-ON CHICKEN PIECES IS FINE IN THIS RECIPE, AND THE SAME AMOUNT OF MARINADE WILL WORK FOR A SLIGHTLY LARGER QUANTITY. IF YOU ARE COMFORTABLE WITH DISMANTLING A WHOLE CHICKEN (OR HAVE A BUTCHER WHO WILL DO IT FOR YOU), THAT WILL WORK. FOR EASE, WE ALSO LIKE BUYING A COUPLE OF PACKAGES OF CHICKEN THIGHS AND LEGS.

CHIMICHURRI CHICKEN LEGS

ARGENTINIAN CHIMICHURRI IS USED AS A MARINADE RATHER THAN A CONDIMENT IN THIS SIMPLE RECIPE.

4	BONE-IN SKIN-ON CHICKEN LEGS, WITH BACKS ATTACHED (ABOUT $2\frac{1}{2}$ LBS/1.25 KG TOTAL)	4
$\frac{1}{3}$ CUP	CHIMICHURRI (PAGE 264), PREFERABLY MADE WITH LEMON JUICE	75 ML
	SALT AND BLACK PEPPER TO TASTE	

PAT CHICKEN LEGS DRY WITH PAPER TOWELS AND SPREAD CHIMICHURRI ON MEAT UNDER THE SKIN OF EACH LEG. COVER SKIN WITH A LITTLE MORE CHIMICHURRI, USING A LITTLE MORE THAN 1 TBSP (15 ML) TOTAL PER LEG. SPRINKLE WITH SALT AND PEPPER, THEN COVER AND LET STAND FOR 30 MINUTES OR REFRIGERATE FOR UP TO 2 HOURS.

PREHEAT OVEN TO 425°F (220°C). PLACE CHICKEN ON A RIMMED BAKING SHEET LINED WITH PARCHMENT PAPER. BAKE FOR 40 TO 50 MINUTES (SEE TIP) OR UNTIL SKIN IS CRISPY AND JUICES RUN CLEAR WHEN CHICKEN IS PIERCED. SERVES 4.

TIP: IF A LOT OF JUICES ACCUMULATE IN THE PAN DURING COOKING, SPOON THEM OFF SO THAT THE CHICKEN ROASTS, RATHER THAN STEAMING.

AUNT BETTY'S SWEET-AND-SOUR CHICKEN WINGS

WHENEVER HER ADULT CHILDREN NEED SOME COMFORT FOOD, THIS IS WHAT ELIZABETH'S HUSBAND'S MUM MAKES FOR THEM. MAKE A BIG PLATTER FOR A POTLUCK OR SERVE THE WINGS OVER RICE WITH A DRIZZLE OF EXTRA SAUCE FOR DINNER.

2 LBS	CHICKEN WINGS, SPLIT, WITH TIPS REMOVED	1 KG
	ALL-PURPOSE FLOUR	
	VEGETABLE OIL	
1 1/3 CUPS	PACKED BROWN SUGAR	325 ML
2 TSP	GARLIC POWDER	10 ML
1/4 CUP	WHITE VINEGAR	60 ML
1/4 CUP	SOY SAUCE	60 ML

PREHEAT OVEN TO 325°F (160°C). PAT CHICKEN WINGS DRY AND FILL A SHALLOW BOWL WITH FLOUR. IN A SKILLET, HEAT A GENEROUS SPLASH OF OIL OVER HIGH HEAT. DREDGE EACH WING IN FLOUR, THEN BROWN IN HOT OIL FOR A COUPLE OF MINUTES ON EACH SIDE — YOU'LL LIKELY HAVE TO DO THIS IN BATCHES, REPLENISHING THE OIL IN THE PAN EACH TIME. (DISCARD ANY EXCESS FLOUR.) AS THEY ARE BROWNED, LAY THE WINGS IN A SINGLE LAYER IN A ROASTING PAN OR LARGE BAKING DISH.

IN A MEDIUM BOWL, STIR TOGETHER BROWN SUGAR, GARLIC POWDER, VINEGAR AND SOY SAUCE. POUR SAUCE EVENLY OVER CHICKEN WINGS, TURNING EACH WING OVER TO COAT FULLY. BAKE FOR 45 TO 60 MINUTES, TURNING THE WINGS EVERY 10 TO 15 MINUTES, UNTIL SAUCE IS THICK AND STICKS TO THE WINGS. SERVES 6 TO 8.

DUSTY'S BREADED CHICKEN

SUE'S GRANDMA DUSTY USED TO MAKE BAKED CHICKEN TO SERVE COLD AT PICNICS. THIS VERSION IS VERY LIKE HERS.

I CUP	PANKO	250 ML
2/3 CUP	GRATED PARMESAN CHEESE	150 ML
2 TBSP	FINELY CHOPPED FRESH PARSLEY	30 ML
I	GARLIC CLOVE, MINCED	I
3 TBSP	DIJON MUSTARD	45 ML
2 TBSP	BUTTER, MELTED	30 ML
1/2 TSP	SRIRACHA	2 ML
	SALT AND BLACK PEPPER TO TASTE	
2 LBS	BONELESS SKINLESS CHICKEN BREASTS	I KG

PREHEAT OVEN TO 375°F (190°C). IN A SHALLOW BOWL, COMBINE PANKO, PARMESAN AND PARSLEY. IN A SIMILAR BOWL, COMBINE GARLIC, DIJON, BUTTER, SRIRACHA, SALT AND PEPPER. PLACE A CHICKEN BREAST BETWEEN TWO SHEETS OF PLASTIC WRAP SET ON A WOODEN CUTTING BOARD. USING THE BOTTOM OF A SMALL SAUCEPAN, POUND THE CHICKEN SO THAT IT'S UNIFORMLY 1/2 INCH (I CM) THICK. REPEAT WITH THE REMAINING CHICKEN. CUT FLATTENED CHICKEN PIECES IN HALF. DREDGE EACH PIECE FIRST IN MUSTARD MIXTURE, THEN IN PANKO MIXTURE, PATTING CRUMBS TO ADHERE. PLACE ON A RIMMED BAKING SHEET LINED WITH PARCHMENT PAPER. DISCARD ANY EXCESS MUSTARD AND CRUMB MIXTURES. BAKE FOR 15 MINUTES, THEN TURN PIECES OVER AND BAKE FOR 10 TO 15 MINUTES OR UNTIL COATING IS BROWNED AND CHICKEN IS NO LONGER PINK INSIDE. SERVES 6.

CORN FLAKE-CRUSTED PORK CHOPS

CORN FLAKES CEREAL MAKES FOR A GREAT CRUNCHY CRUST THAT GIVES THESE OVEN-BAKED CHOPS A CHICKEN-FRIED STEAK FEEL.

2	LARGE EGGS	2
2	GARLIC CLOVES, MINCED	2
2 TBSP	MILK	30 ML
4 CUPS	CORN FLAKES CEREAL	1 L
2 TBSP	GRATED PARMESAN CHEESE	30 ML
	GRATED ZEST OF 1 LEMON	
6	BONELESS CENTER-CUT PORK LOIN CHOPS	6
	SALT AND BLACK PEPPER TO TASTE	

PREHEAT OVEN TO 350°F (180°C). IN A SHALLOW BOWL, LIGHTLY BEAT EGGS, THEN WHISK IN GARLIC AND MILK. IN A SEPARATE SHALLOW BOWL, LIGHTLY CRUSH CEREAL — YOU WANT TO BREAK THE FLAKES UP WELL SO THAT THEY FORM AN EVEN CRUST ON THE PORK, BUT YOU DON'T WANT TO PULVERIZE THEM INTO A POWDER — THEN STIR IN PARMESAN AND LEMON ZEST. PAT PORK DRY. DIP CHOPS, ONE BY ONE, IN EGG MIXTURE, TURNING TO COAT AND SHAKING OFF EXCESS, THEN DREDGE THEM IN CEREAL MIXTURE UNTIL EVENLY COVERED. DISCARD ANY EXCESS EGG MIXTURE AND CEREAL MIXTURE. PLACE BREADED CHOPS ON A BAKING SHEET. BAKE FOR 25 TO 30 MINUTES OR UNTIL JUST A HINT OF PINK REMAINS INSIDE PORK. IF THE CRUST ISN'T CRISP WHEN THE PORK CHOPS ARE COOKED, BROIL THEM FOR A MINUTE OR TWO TO CRISP THEM UP A BIT. SERVES 6.

BUTTERMILK PORK CHOPS WITH LEMON CAPER SAUCE

SOAKING PORK CHOPS IN BUTTERMILK BREAKS DOWN THE MEAT AND MAKES IT EXTRA-MOIST AND FLAVORFUL. THE CAPER PAN SAUCE MAKES THEM SUNDAY SUPPER-WORTHY. SERVE WITH YOUR CHOICE OF VEGETABLES.

4	1-INCH (2.5 CM) THICK CENTER-CUT BONE-IN PORK CHOPS (SEE TIP)	4
2 CUPS	BUTTERMILK	500 ML
	SALT AND BLACK PEPPER TO TASTE	
	VEGETABLE OIL	
2 TBSP	BUTTER	30 ML
1 TBSP	ALL-PURPOSE FLOUR	15 ML
1/2 TSP	DRIED THYME	2 ML
1 CUP	BASIC CHICKEN STOCK (PAGE 28) OR READY-TO-USE CHICKEN BROTH	250 ML
2 TBSP	LEMON JUICE	30 ML
2 TSP	DRY WHITE WINE	10 ML
2 TBSP	DRAINED CAPERS	30 ML

PUT THE PORK CHOPS IN A BAKING DISH OR A SEALABLE PLASTIC BAG. POUR IN BUTTERMILK SO THAT THE CHOPS ARE COMPLETELY COVERED. SEASON WITH SALT AND PEPPER. COVER OR SEAL AND REFRIGERATE FOR 4 HOURS OR OVERNIGHT.

PREHEAT OVEN TO 425°F (220°C). REMOVE CHOPS FROM BUTTERMILK AND PAT DRY. DISCARD BUTTERMILK. IN A LARGE SKILLET, HEAT A DRIZZLE OF OIL OVER HIGH HEAT. WORKING IN BATCHES AS NECESSARY, COOK PORK UNTIL GOLDEN ON BOTH SIDES, ADDING MORE OIL AS NEEDED

BETWEEN BATCHES. TRANSFER CHOPS TO A BAKING DISH AND BAKE FOR 15 TO 20 MINUTES OR UNTIL JUST A HINT OF PINK REMAINS INSIDE. LET REST FOR 5 MINUTES.

MEANWHILE, IN THE SAME SKILLET YOU USED TO COOK THE PORK (LEAVE ANY FAT OR BROWNED BITS IN THERE), MELT BUTTER OVER MEDIUM HEAT. WHISK IN FLOUR AND COOK, WHISKING, FOR 3 MINUTES. STIR IN THYME, STOCK, LEMON JUICE AND WINE; BRING TO A BOIL. ADD CAPERS, REDUCE HEAT AND SIMMER FOR 5 MINUTES. SERVE WITH PORK CHOPS. SERVES 4.

TIP: THE THICKNESS OF THE PORK CHOPS WILL GREATLY AFFECT THE COOKING TIME. IF YOUR CHOPS ARE THINNER THAN 1 INCH (2.5 CM), KEEP AN EYE ON THEM TO MAKE SURE THEY DON'T OVERCOOK AND DRY OUT; THICKER CHOPS MAY REQUIRE A LONGER COOKING TIME.

THE WORST THING ABOUT KITCHEN ACCIDENTS
IS THAT YOU USUALLY HAVE TO EAT THEM.

ALPHABET PORK CHOPS

THE ORIGINAL VERSION OF THIS RECIPE, HANDWRITTEN AND TUCKED INSIDE ELIZABETH'S GRANDMA VI'S OLD METAL RECIPE BOX, IS SIMPLY TITLED "TASTY DINNER," BUT IN THE FAMILY IT WAS ALWAYS KNOWN AS ALPHABET PORK CHOPS. THE ORIGINAL FEATURED A TIN OF VEGETABLE SOUP WITH ALPHABET PASTA, BUT HERE WE'VE COME UP WITH A FROM-SCRATCH ALPHABET TOMATO SAUCE THAT IS EVEN BETTER. SERVE WITH MASHED OR BAKED POTATOES AND, ACCORDING TO GRANDMA VI'S ORIGINAL INSTRUCTIONS, CABBAGE AND PICKLES.

1/2 CUP	ALPHABET PASTA (OR SIMILAR SMALL PASTA, SUCH AS ORZO)	125 ML
1 1/2 CUPS	BASIC CHICKEN STOCK (PAGE 28) OR READY-TO-USE CHICKEN BROTH	375 ML
1	LARGE CARROT, DICED	1
1/2 CUP	FROZEN PEAS	125 ML
1/2 TSP	DRIED THYME	2 ML
1/2 TSP	GARLIC POWDER	2 ML
1/4 TSP	DRIED OREGANO	1 ML
1/4 TSP	DRIED BASIL	1 ML
	SALT AND BLACK PEPPER TO TASTE	
2 TBSP	TOMATO PASTE	30 ML
1 TSP	WORCESTERSHIRE SAUCE	5 ML
1 TBSP	VEGETABLE OIL OR BACON FAT (APPROX.)	15 ML
6	BONELESS CENTER-CUT PORK LOIN CHOPS	6

PREHEAT OVEN TO 300°F (150°C). COOK PASTA ACCORDING TO PACKAGE DIRECTIONS UNTIL JUST AL DENTE, THEN DRAIN. BE CAREFUL NOT TO LET IT GET MUSHY. MEANWHILE, IN A MEDIUM SAUCEPAN, HEAT STOCK OVER MEDIUM-

HIGH HEAT. ADD CARROT, PEAS, THYME, GARLIC POWDER, OREGANO, BASIL, A LIBERAL AMOUNT OF SALT AND PEPPER, TOMATO PASTE AND WORCESTERSHIRE; BRING TO A SIMMER. REDUCE HEAT AND SIMMER, STIRRING OCCASIONALLY, FOR 15 MINUTES OR UNTIL LIQUID IS SLIGHTLY THICKENED. ADD PASTA TO PAN AND SIMMER FOR 5 MINUTES. ADJUST SEASONING IF NECESSARY (YOU'LL WANT TO USE A FAIR AMOUNT OF SALT TO SAVE IT FROM BEING BLAND) AND REMOVE FROM HEAT.

IN A LARGE SKILLET, HEAT OIL OVER MEDIUM-HIGH HEAT. WORKING IN BATCHES AS NECESSARY, BROWN PORK CHOPS ON BOTH SIDES, ADDING MORE OIL AS NEEDED BETWEEN BATCHES. TRANSFER TO A BAKING DISH AND POUR SAUCE OVER CHOPS, COVERING EVENLY. BAKE FOR 45 MINUTES OR UNTIL SAUCE IS BUBBLING AND JUST A HINT OF PINK REMAINS INSIDE PORK. SERVES 6.

TIP: THE THICKNESS OF YOUR PORK CHOPS WILL GREATLY AFFECT THE COOKING TIME. KEEP AN EYE ON THINNER CHOPS TO MAKE SURE THEY DON'T OVERCOOK AND DRY OUT; THICKER CHOPS MAY REQUIRE A LONGER COOKING TIME.

TIP: WHENEVER YOU FRY UP BACON FOR BREAKFAST, POUR THE EXCESS GREASE INTO A LITTLE JAR AND KEEP IT IN THE FRIDGE. KEEP ADDING TO THE JAR WHENEVER YOU MAKE BACON AND SCOOP OUT THE SOLID FAT WHEN YOU WANT SOME EXTRA FLAVOR WHEN BROWNING MEAT OR FRYING POTATOES.

PORK TENDERLOIN WITH A HONEY MUSTARD GLAZE

HONEY AND MUSTARD GO TOGETHER LIKE PEANUT BUTTER AND CHOCOLATE WHEN YOU TURN THEM INTO A GLAZE FOR PORK TENDERLOIN.

2	PORK TENDERLOINS (EACH ABOUT I LB/500 G)	2
	VEGETABLE OIL	
	SALT AND BLACK PEPPER TO TASTE	
1/2 CUP	LIQUID HONEY	125 ML
2 TBSP	BALSAMIC VINEGAR	30 ML
2 TBSP	GRAINY MUSTARD	30 ML
I TSP	DRIED ROSEMARY	5 ML
PINCH	CAYENNE PEPPER	PINCH

PREHEAT OVEN TO 375°F (190°C). CUT THE SILVERSKIN OFF THE TENDERLOINS. RUB PORK WITH OIL AND SEASON WITH SALT AND PEPPER. IN A LARGE SKILLET, HEAT A SPLASH OF OIL OVER MEDIUM-HIGH HEAT. BROWN PORK ON ALL SIDES, WORKING WITH ONE TENDERLOIN AT A TIME IF THEY DON'T FIT COMFORTABLY IN THE SAME PAN. TRANSFER PORK TO A ROASTING PAN.

IN A SMALL BOWL, USING A FORK, COMBINE HONEY, VINEGAR, MUSTARD, ROSEMARY AND CAYENNE. SPOON GLAZE OVER PORK. BAKE FOR 25 TO 30 MINUTES OR UNTIL A MEAT THERMOMETER INSERTED IN THE THICKEST PART OF A TENDERLOIN REGISTERS BETWEEN 145°F AND 160°F (63°C AND 71°C). COVER WITH FOIL AND LET REST FOR 10 MINUTES, THEN SLICE INTO MEDALLIONS. SERVES 6 TO 8.

MUFFULETTA

MUFFULETTA (A BIG, ROUND, DENSE ITALIAN SANDWICH OF CURED MEATS, CHEESES AND ROASTED PEPPERS, SERVED SLICED INTO WEDGES) MAKES FOR A PERFECT BACKYARD OR PICNIC DINNER. MEASUREMENTS HERE ARE APPROXIMATE — IT IS A SANDWICH, AFTER ALL.

I	ROUND LOAF RUSTIC ITALIAN BREAD, SUCH AS CIABATTA (OR TRY NO-KNEAD BREAD, PAGE 236)	I
1/4 CUP	BASIL OR SUN-DRIED TOMATO PESTO	60 ML
4	ROASTED RED BELL PEPPERS, SLICED	4
4 OZ	SOFT GOAT CHEESE, CRUMBLED	125 G
1/4 CUP	BALSAMIC VINAIGRETTE	60 ML
8 OZ	SLICED HAM OR PROSCIUTTO	250 G
4 OZ	THINLY SLICED SALAMI	125 G
I CUP	LOOSELY PACKED SMALL PEPPERY GREENS OR FRESH HERBS (SUCH AS ARUGULA, BASIL, CILANTRO OR FLAT-LEAF/ITALIAN PARSLEY)	250 ML

CUT THE LOAF OF BREAD IN HALF HORIZONTALLY AND PULL OUT THE INNARDS, LEAVING A SHELL WITH SOME OF THE SOFT CRUMB STILL INTACT (DON'T RAVAGE IT COMPLETELY). SPREAD PESTO ON THE BOTTOM HALF AND TOP WITH RED PEPPERS AND GOAT CHEESE. DRIZZLE WITH SOME OF THE VINAIGRETTE, THEN ARRANGE HAM AND SALAMI OVER TOP. DRIZZLE WITH THE REMAINING VINAIGRETTE. TOP WITH GREENS, THEN THE TOP HALF OF THE LOAF. WRAP TIGHTLY WITH PLASTIC WRAP, PLACE IN THE REFRIGERATOR AND SET A BIG, EVEN WEIGHT, SUCH AS A CAST-IRON SKILLET, ON TOP. CHILL FOR AT LEAST AN HOUR. WHEN READY TO SERVE, SLICE INTO WEDGES.

SERVES 8.

CHEESE-STUFFED MEATLOAF

*HOW TO RAISE MEATLOAF TO A WHOLE NEW LEVEL:
STUFF IT WITH CHEESE! TOTAL COMFORT FOOD
MAKES FOR A COZY FAMILY MEAL.*

1½ LBS	LEAN GROUND BEEF	750 G
8 OZ	GROUND PORK	250 G
½	SMALL ONION, GRATED	½
1 CUP	DRY BREAD CRUMBS, CRUSHED CRACKERS OR CRUSHED CROUTONS	250 ML
2 TBSP	GRATED PARMESAN CHEESE	30 ML
1	LARGE EGG	1
2 TBSP	KETCHUP	30 ML
1 TBSP	GRAINY OR YELLOW MUSTARD	15 ML
	SALT AND BLACK PEPPER TO TASTE	
1½ CUPS	SHREDDED SHARP (OLD) CHEDDAR OR GOUDA CHEESE	375 ML
1 TBSP	PACKED BROWN SUGAR	15 ML
¼ CUP	KETCHUP, TOMATO SAUCE OR CHILI SAUCE	60 ML
1 TBSP	GRAINY MUSTARD	15 ML

PREHEAT OVEN TO 350°F (180°C). IN A LARGE BOWL,
COMBINE BEEF, PORK, ONION, BREAD CRUMBS, PARMESAN,
EGG, KETCHUP, MUSTARD, SALT AND PEPPER. BLEND
GENTLY WITH YOUR HANDS, JUST UNTIL COMBINED.
LINE A RIMMED BAKING SHEET WITH FOIL OR PARCHMENT
PAPER. PAT THE MEAT MIXTURE INTO A 10- TO 12-INCH
(25 TO 30 CM) SQUARE AND SPRINKLE WITH CHEDDAR
CHEESE, LEAVING ONE EDGE BARE. ROLL UP LIKE A JELLY
ROLL, ENDING AT THE BARE EDGE, AND PLACE SEAM SIDE
DOWN ON THE BAKING SHEET. IN A SMALL BOWL, STIR

TOGETHER BROWN SUGAR, KETCHUP AND MUSTARD.
BRUSH HALF THE GLAZE OVER THE MEATLOAF. BAKE FOR
1 HOUR, BRUSHING AGAIN WITH GLAZE HALFWAY THROUGH,
UNTIL NO LONGER PINK INSIDE (IF YOU HAVE A MEAT
THERMOMETER, THE INTERNAL TEMPERATURE SHOULD BE
165°F/74°C). LET STAND FOR 10 MINUTES BEFORE SLICING.
SERVES 8.

WHY AREN'T JOKES ABOUT GERMAN SAUSAGES FUNNY?
BECAUSE THEY'RE THE WURST!

MAPLE-GLAZED MEATLOAF

NOTHING BEATS A GREAT MEATLOAF! THIS ONE
GETS ITS SWEET GLAZE FROM THE MORE ELEGANT
COMBINATION OF MAPLE SYRUP AND BALSAMIC VINEGAR,
RATHER THAN YOUR STANDARD BOTTLED KETCHUP.

	VEGETABLE OIL	
I	LARGE ONION, FINELY CHOPPED	I
3	GARLIC CLOVES, MINCED	3
$1\frac{1}{2}$ LBS	GROUND PORK	750 G
$1\frac{1}{2}$ LBS	LEAN GROUND BEEF	750 G
$\frac{1}{2}$ CUP	COARSE SALTINE CRACKER CRUMBS	125 ML
I TBSP	DRY MUSTARD	15 ML
$\frac{1}{2}$ TSP	DRIED THYME	2 ML
2	LARGE EGGS, LIGHTLY BEATEN	2
$\frac{1}{2}$ CUP	MILK	125 ML
I TSP	WORCESTERSHIRE SAUCE	5 ML
	SALT AND BLACK PEPPER TO TASTE	
$\frac{1}{4}$ CUP	PURE MAPLE SYRUP	60 ML
2 TBSP	GRAINY MUSTARD	30 ML
I TBSP	BALSAMIC VINEGAR	15 ML

PREHEAT OVEN TO 375°F (190°C). IN A SKILLET, HEAT A
SPLASH OF OIL OVER MEDIUM-LOW HEAT. SAUTÉ ONION
UNTIL VERY SOFT AND TRANSLUCENT, ABOUT 10 MINUTES.
ADD GARLIC AND SAUTÉ FOR I MINUTE. REMOVE FROM
HEAT. IN A LARGE BOWL, BREAK UP PORK AND BEEF WITH
A SPOON. ADD ONION MIXTURE AND CRACKER CRUMBS.
IN A SMALL BOWL, STIR TOGETHER DRY MUSTARD,
THYME, EGGS, MILK, WORCESTERSHIRE, SALT AND PEPPER.
POUR THE MILK MIXTURE INTO THE MEAT MIXTURE AND

GENTLY COMBINE WITH YOUR HANDS, BEING CAREFUL NOT TO OVERHANDLE.

PLACE MEAT MIXTURE ON A FOIL-LINED RIMMED BAKING SHEET AND SHAPE INTO A LOAF ABOUT 12 INCHES (30 CM) LONG. IN A SMALL BOWL, COMBINE MAPLE SYRUP, GRAINY MUSTARD AND VINEGAR; BRUSH GLAZE OVER MEATLOAF. BAKE FOR 1 TO $1\frac{1}{4}$ HOURS OR UNTIL NO LONGER PINK INSIDE (IF YOU HAVE A MEAT THERMOMETER, THE INTERNAL TEMPERATURE SHOULD BE 165°F/74°C). LET STAND FOR 10 MINUTES BEFORE SLICING. SERVES 8.

JAN'S SLOW-COOKED BEEF STROGANOFF

OUR FRIEND JAN SCOTT IS THE QUEEN OF HOME ENTERTAINING. WHILE THIS DISH ISN'T THE PRETTIEST YOU'LL EVER PUT ON THE TABLE, IT JUST MIGHT BE ONE OF THE TASTIEST. THE BEEF SIMMERS IN BROTH AND RED WINE, WITH SOUR CREAM STIRRED IN RIGHT AT THE END, YIELDING A RICH SAUCE THAT COULDN'T BE SIMPLER. THERE IS NO FUSSING WITH A ROUX, NO SPECIALTY INGREDIENTS TO SOURCE AND NO EXTRA HANDS-ON TIME REQUIRED TO TURN THIS SLOW-COOKED DINNER INTO ONE WORTHY OF SERVING TO GUESTS — AND IT'S A FAVORITE OF HER FAMILY OF FIVE, INCLUDING THREE GROWING BOYS.

2 LBS	STEWING BEEF, CUT INTO CUBES	1 KG
2 TBSP	ALL-PURPOSE FLOUR	30 ML
1 TSP	SALT	5 ML
$\frac{1}{2}$ TSP	BLACK PEPPER	2 ML
1 TBSP	VEGETABLE OIL (APPROX.)	15 ML
1 TBSP	BUTTER	15 ML
1	LARGE ONION, FINELY CHOPPED	1
1 LB	CREMINI MUSHROOMS, CUT INTO $\frac{1}{4}$-INCH (0.5 CM) SLICES	500 G
1 CUP	READY-TO-USE BEEF BROTH	250 ML
1 CUP	DRY RED WINE	250 ML
1 TBSP	DIJON MUSTARD	15 ML
1 CUP	SOUR CREAM	250 ML
	HOT BUTTERED EGG NOODLES	

PREHEAT OVEN TO 300°F (150°C). PLACE BEEF IN A LARGE BOWL AND SPRINKLE WITH FLOUR, SALT AND PEPPER, TOSSING TO COAT. IN A LARGE OVENPROOF DUTCH OVEN

OR SKILLET, HEAT OIL AND BUTTER OVER MEDIUM HEAT UNTIL BUTTER HAS MELTED. WORKING IN BATCHES SO AS NOT TO CROWD THE PAN, BROWN BEEF ON ALL SIDES, TRANSFERRING THE CUBES TO A PLATE AS THEY ARE DONE AND ADDING MORE OIL TO THE PAN AS NEEDED BETWEEN BATCHES. ADD ONION TO THE PAN AND SAUTÉ FOR 5 TO 7 MINUTES, STIRRING OFTEN TO SCRAPE UP ANY BROWNED BITS FROM THE BOTTOM OF THE PAN AND ADDING A LITTLE MORE OIL AS NEEDED TO KEEP THE ONIONS FROM STICKING AND BURNING.

RETURN BEEF TO THE PAN, ALONG WITH ANY ACCUMULATED JUICES, AND STIR IN MUSHROOMS, BROTH, WINE AND MUSTARD. COVER PAN, PUT IN THE OVEN AND BAKE FOR $2\frac{1}{2}$ TO 3 HOURS, UNTIL BEEF IS VERY TENDER. REMOVE FROM OVEN AND STIR IN SOUR CREAM JUST BEFORE SERVING OVER BUTTERED EGG NOODLES. SERVES 6 TO 8.

GIANT CHEESE-STUFFED MEATBALLS

WHO DOESN'T LOVE ENORMOUS MEATBALLS? THESE
MEATBALLS ARE STUFFED WITH CHEESE AND CAN BE
SERVED ON TOP OF SPAGHETTI, NESTLED INTO A SOFT
BUN WITH TOMATO SAUCE OR ON THEIR OWN WITH
A SIDE OF MASHED POTATOES AND PEAS.

I LB	MILD OR SPICY ITALIAN SAUSAGE (BULK OR REMOVED FROM CASING)	500 G
I LB	LEAN GROUND BEEF	500 G
I CUP	FRESH BREAD CRUMBS	250 ML
1/2 CUP	GRATED PARMESAN CHEESE	125 ML
I	LARGE EGG	I
	SALT AND BLACK PEPPER TO TASTE	
10	1/2-INCH (I CM) CUBES MOZZARELLA CHEESE	10
	VEGETABLE OIL	

PREHEAT OVEN TO 350°F (180°C). IN A LARGE BOWL, USING
YOUR HANDS, COMBINE SAUSAGE, BEEF, BREAD CRUMBS,
PARMESAN, EGG, SALT AND PEPPER, WITHOUT OVERWORKING
THE MEAT. SHAPE SMALL HANDFULS (ABOUT AS MUCH AS
YOU'D USE FOR A SMALL BURGER) AROUND EACH CHEESE
CUBE, PRESSING TO SEAL ANY GAPS AND MAKING SMOOTH
MEATBALLS ABOUT THE SIZE OF A SMALL ORANGE.

IN A LARGE OVENPROOF SKILLET (SEE TIP), HEAT A
DRIZZLE OF OIL OVER MEDIUM-HIGH HEAT. WORKING IN
BATCHES, BROWN MEATBALLS, ROLLING THEM AROUND
UNTIL THEY ARE GOLDEN AND CRISPY ON ALL SIDES.
TRANSFER THEM TO A PLATE AS THEY ARE BROWNED
AND ADD MORE OIL TO THE PAN IF YOU NEED TO BETWEEN
BATCHES. RETURN ALL MEATBALLS TO THE PAN, PUT PAN
IN THE OVEN AND BAKE FOR 20 TO 30 MINUTES OR UNTIL
NO LONGER PINK INSIDE. MAKES 10 GIANT MEATBALLS.

Salmon Burgers (page 82) with
Tzatziki (page 261)

Sheet Pan Chicken with Pistachios and Honey (page 90)

Buttermilk Pork Chops with Lemon Caper Sauce (page 96)

Vegetable Skewers (page 111)

ON THE GRILL

VEGETABLE PACKETS

EACH OF THE VARIATIONS WILL FILL A SINGLE PIE PLATE — MAKE AS MANY AS YOU NEED!

VARIATION 1

1 1/4 LBS	YELLOW OR RED POTATOES, THINLY SLICED	625 G
1	CARROT, THINLY SLICED	1
1/2	SMALL ONION, THINLY SLICED	1/2

VARIATION 2

12 OZ	SWEET POTATO, THINLY SLICED	375 G
12 OZ	PARSNIPS, THINLY SLICED	375 G
1 TSP	FINELY CHOPPED FRESH ROSEMARY	5 ML

VARIATION 3

1	CELERIAC (ABOUT 1 1/4 LBS/625 G), PEELED, CUT IN HALF AND THINLY SLICED	1
1	LARGE SHALLOT, THINLY SLICED	1
	SALT AND BLACK PEPPER TO TASTE	
	BUTTER OR VEGETABLE OIL	

PREHEAT BARBECUE GRILL TO MEDIUM-HIGH. LIGHTLY OIL A 9-INCH (23 CM) FOIL PIE PLATE FOR EACH PACKET. LAYER IN THE VEGETABLE COMBINATION OF YOUR CHOICE. SPRINKLE WITH SALT AND PEPPER AND DOT WITH BUTTER (OR TOSS VEGETABLES WITH SALT, PEPPER AND OIL TO TASTE IN A LARGE BOWL, THEN SPREAD IN PIE PLATE). COVER TIGHTLY WITH FOIL AND PLACE ON THE GRILL. CLOSE THE LID AND GRILL UNTIL VEGETABLES ARE TENDER THROUGHOUT AND BROWNED AND CRISP ON THE BOTTOM AND EDGES, ABOUT 35 TO 55 MINUTES (DEPENDING ON THE VEGETABLES USED). EACH PACKET SERVES 3 TO 4.

VEGETABLE SKEWERS

THE KEY TO COOKING VEGETABLES DIRECTLY ON THE GRILL IS KEEPING THE HEAT ON THE LOW SIDE. WE USE FLAT METAL SKEWERS HERE — THEY MAKE GRILLING VEGETABLES A BREEZE, ARE GENERALLY INEXPENSIVE AND LAST FOREVER.

4	GARLIC CLOVES, MINCED	4
2 TBSP	VEGETABLE OIL	30 ML
	SALT AND BLACK PEPPER TO TASTE	
6 CUPS	MIXED VEGETABLES, SUCH AS RED ONION, ZUCCHINI, EGGPLANT AND/OR SWEET PEPPERS	1.5 L
	BALSAMIC REDUCTION	

IN A LARGE BOWL, COMBINE GARLIC, OIL, SALT AND PEPPER. CUT VEGETABLES INTO $1\frac{1}{2}$-INCH (4 CM) PIECES. ADD ALL VEGGIES TO THE BOWL, TOSS WELL AND MARINATE FOR AT LEAST 45 MINUTES OR UP TO A FEW HOURS (COVER AND PUT IN THE FRIDGE IF MARINATING FOR MORE THAN 2 HOURS).

PREHEAT BARBECUE GRILL TO MEDIUM-LOW. THREAD VEGETABLES ONTO METAL SKEWERS, MAKING SURE THINGS LIKE EGGPLANT AND ZUCCHINI ARE PIERCED THROUGH THE SKIN RATHER THAN JUST THE INSIDE PORTION OF THE VEGETABLE (THIS WILL USUALLY ENSURE THAT THEY DON'T FALL OFF THE SKEWER AS THEY COOK). CLOSE THE LID AND GRILL, TURNING A FEW TIMES, FOR 10 TO 15 MINUTES OR UNTIL VEGETABLES ARE TENDER AND HAVE A FEW GRILL MARKS. TRANSFER SKEWERS TO A SERVING PLATTER AND DRIZZLE WITH BALSAMIC REDUCTION. SERVES 4 TO 6.

PLANKED SALMON

SUE'S UNCLE NORM AND AUNT VAL FIRST INTRODUCED HER TO COOKING SALMON THIS WAY. THE CEDAR IMPARTS A SPECIAL SMOKY FLAVOR TO THE FISH.

1½ to 2 LB	SKIN-ON SALMON FILLET	750 G to 1 KG
1½ TBSP	PACKED BROWN SUGAR	22 ML
1 TBSP	DIJON MUSTARD	15 ML
	COARSELY GROUND SALT AND BLACK PEPPER TO TASTE	

SOAK A CEDAR PLANK A LITTLE BIGGER THAN YOUR SALMON FILLET IN WATER FOR AT LEAST 2 HOURS OR AS LONG AS A DAY. WEIGH THE PLANK DOWN TO KEEP IT SUBMERGED. BE SURE TO HAVE A WATER-FILLED SPRAY BOTTLE HANDY TO COPE WITH FLARE-UPS ON THE GRILL, PARTICULARLY IF YOU ONLY HAVE 2 HOURS TO SOAK YOUR PLANK.

PREHEAT BARBECUE GRILL TO HIGH. RINSE SALMON AND PAT DRY. REMOVE PLANK FROM WATER AND SLUICE OFF EXCESS WATER. PLACE SALMON, SKIN SIDE DOWN, ON PLANK. IN A SMALL BOWL, COMBINE BROWN SUGAR AND MUSTARD. SPREAD OVER MEATY SIDE OF SALMON, THEN SPRINKLE WITH SALT AND PEPPER. PLACE PLANK ON GRILL, CLOSE THE LID AND GRILL FOR 10 TO 15 MINUTES, WITHOUT TURNING THE FISH OVER, UNTIL FISH IS OPAQUE AND FLAKES EASILY WHEN TESTED WITH A FORK.

USING TWO RIGID METAL FLIPPERS, LIFT THE PLANK ONTO A RIMMED BAKING SHEET. LET REST FOR 5 MINUTES. CUT FILLET INTO PORTIONS AND PLATE, LEAVING THE SKIN BEHIND WITH THE PLANK. DISCARD THE PLANK ONCE IT HAS COOLED COMPLETELY. SERVES 6 TO 8.

TROUT ON THE GRILL

TROUT IS A VERY MANAGEABLE FISH TO GRILL, PARTICULARLY IF YOU USE SMALLER TROUT.

2	CLEANED WHOLE FRESHWATER TROUT (EACH ABOUT 12 OZ/375 G)	2
1/4 CUP	SPINACH AND WALNUT PESTO (SEE PAGE 265), DIVIDED	60 ML
	VEGETABLE OIL	
	SALT TO TASTE	

PREHEAT BARBECUE GRILL TO HIGH. RINSE FISH INSIDE AND OUT AND PAT DRY. USE THE TIP OF A SHARP KNIFE TO CUT THROUGH THE MEMBRANE IN THE CAVITY (IN THE SAME DIRECTION AS THE BONES LIE) IN THREE OR FOUR PLACES AND ALSO UP THROUGH THE SPINE TOWARD THE MEATY BACK OF THE FISH. SPREAD 1 TBSP (15 ML) PESTO INSIDE EACH FISH, THEN COAT THE OUTSIDE WITH OIL AND SPRINKLE WITH SALT. PLACE FISH ON GRILL, CLOSE THE LID AND GRILL UNTIL THE SKIN IS BROWNED AND CRISP, ABOUT 3 MINUTES. TURN EACH FISH OVER, ROLLING THEM OVER THEIR SPINES. COOK FOR 3 TO 4 MINUTES OR UNTIL THE SECOND SIDE IS BROWNED AND CRISP AND THE FISH FLAKES EASILY WHEN TESTED WITH A FORK.

TRANSFER TROUT TO A PLATTER, THEN SCRAPE PESTO OUT OF THE CAVITIES AND RESERVE. CUT OFF HEADS, THEN GENTLY REMOVE THE TOP FILLET FROM EACH FISH (WE LEAVE THE SKIN ON), TAKING CARE TO LEAVE THE BONES ATTACHED TO THE SPINE. STARTING FROM THE TAIL, CAREFULLY REMOVE THE SPINE AND ALL ATTACHED BONES. SERVE THE FISH WITH THE RESERVED PESTO, PLUS THE REMAINING UNUSED PESTO. SERVES 4.

WHITE FISH WITH PARSLEY BEURRE BLANC

BEURRE BLANC ALSO GOES WELL WITH ROASTED BABY POTATOES AND VEGETABLES LIKE CAULIFLOWER OR SPROUTS. IF YOU WANT TO SAUCE MORE THAN JUST THE FISH, WE SUGGEST YOU DOUBLE THE QUANTITY OF BEURRE BLANC.

1¼ LBS	SKINLESS WHITE FISH FILLETS, SUCH AS TILAPIA OR ROCKFISH	625 G
8 TBSP	PARSLEY BEURRE BLANC (PAGE 258), DIVIDED	120 ML
6	THIN LEMON SLICES	6

PREHEAT BARBECUE GRILL TO MEDIUM. DIVIDE FISH INTO 2 PORTIONS. PLACE EACH ON A DOUBLED FOIL SHEET LARGE ENOUGH TO FULLY ENCLOSE FISH. ADD ABOUT 1 TBSP (15 ML) BEURRE BLANC TO EACH PACKET. TOP WITH LEMON SLICES, THEN FOLD FOIL OVER AND SEAL TIGHTLY. PLACE PACKETS ON THE GRILL, CLOSE THE LID AND GRILL UNTIL FISH IS OPAQUE AND FLAKES EASILY WHEN TESTED WITH A FORK (START CHECKING AT 10 MINUTES, BUT IT WILL LIKELY BE CLOSER TO 18 MINUTES). TRANSFER THE PACKETS TO A RIMMED BAKING SHEET AND CAREFULLY OPEN FOIL. LET COOL FOR A FEW MINUTES BEFORE PLATING (TO ENSURE THAT THE HOT FISH DOESN'T IMMEDIATELY MELT THE SAUCE).

ENSURE PLATES ARE SLIGHTLY WARMED (A LITTLE WARMER THAN ROOM TEMPERATURE). SPOON 1½ TBSP (22 ML) BEURRE BLANC ONTO EACH PLATE, THEN USE A THIN SPATULA TO SLIDE A FISH PORTION ON TOP. SERVES 4.

VARIATION: FISH PACKETS CAN ALSO BE COOKED IN THE OVEN AT 425°F (220°C) FOR A COMPARABLE LENGTH OF TIME.

GRILLED MUSSELS WITH LEMON

FRESH MUSSELS ARE THE ULTIMATE FAST FOOD WHEN COOKED ON THE GRILL. THIS MAKES A GREAT APPETIZER TO PUT OUT IN A WIDE, SHALLOW BOWL FOR EVERYONE TO NIBBLE ON WHILE YOU COOK DINNER, OR SERVE IT AS THE MAIN EVENT, WITH CRUSTY BREAD AND GRILLED VEGGIES.

2 LBS	FRESH MUSSELS	1 KG
2	LEMONS	2
	OLIVE OIL	
1/2 CUP	BUTTER	125 ML
1	GARLIC CLOVE, PEELED	1
	CHOPPED FRESH PARSLEY, FOR GARNISH	

PREHEAT BARBECUE GRILL TO MEDIUM-HIGH. MEANWHILE, RINSE MUSSELS, DISCARDING ANY THAT ARE OPEN AND DO NOT CLOSE WHEN TAPPED. CUT THE LEMONS INTO THICK WEDGES, OR IN HALF CROSSWISE, AND BRUSH THE CUT SIDES WITH OIL. SCATTER THE MUSSELS DIRECTLY ON THE GRILL ALONG WITH THE LEMONS, CUT SIDE DOWN. CLOSE THE LID AND GRILL FOR 5 MINUTES OR UNTIL MUSSELS OPEN.

MEANWHILE, IN A SMALL SAUCEPAN (OR IN A BOWL IN THE MICROWAVE), HEAT BUTTER AND GARLIC UNTIL BUTTER MELTS. DISCARD GARLIC.

REMOVE MUSSELS FROM THE GRILL AND DISCARD ANY THAT DID NOT OPEN. TRANSFER OPEN MUSSELS TO A BOWL, DRIZZLE WITH GARLICKY BUTTER AND TOSS TO COAT. TRANSFER TO ONE LARGE OR FOUR INDIVIDUAL SHALLOW BOWLS AND SCATTER WITH PARSLEY. SERVE WITH GRILLED LEMON. SERVES 4.

CHICKEN GRILLED UNDER A BRICK

OKAY — WE ACTUALLY USED TWO CAST-IRON SKILLETS, STACKED ONE UNDER THE OTHER, TO MAKE THIS. BUT ACTUAL FOIL-WRAPPED BRICKS WILL WORK EXACTLY THE SAME WAY. IN EITHER CASE, THE CHICKEN IS FLATTENED TO A UNIFORM THICKNESS AND SO COOKS VERY EVENLY.

1/4 CUP	OLIVE OR VEGETABLE OIL	60 ML
5	GARLIC CLOVES, MINCED	5
3 1/4 LB	WHOLE CHICKEN	1.625 KG
2 TBSP	CHOPPED FRESH PARSLEY	30 ML
I TSP	CHOPPED FRESH ROSEMARY	5 ML
I TSP	SALT (OR TO TASTE)	5 ML
	BLACK PEPPER TO TASTE	
I TSP	WHITE WINE VINEGAR	5 ML

IN A SMALL SAUCEPAN, HEAT OIL OVER MEDIUM-LOW HEAT. SAUTÉ GARLIC UNTIL SIZZLING AND VERY PALE GOLDEN. LET COOL. PAT CHICKEN DRY, THEN SPATCHCOCK (SEE TIP) AND PLACE IN A BOWL JUST LARGE ENOUGH TO HOLD IT.

POUR GARLIC AND OIL INTO A BLENDER OR MINI FOOD PROCESSOR. ADD PARSLEY, ROSEMARY, SALT, PEPPER AND VINEGAR; BLEND UNTIL COMBINED. RUB MARINADE ALL OVER BOTH SIDES OF CHICKEN, INCLUDING AS FAR UNDERNEATH THE SKIN ON THE BREAST AND THIGH AS YOU CAN GO WITHOUT TEARING THE SKIN. COVER AND REFRIGERATE FOR UP TO A DAY, OR AS LONG AS YOU HAVE.

PREHEAT BARBECUE GRILL SO IT IS VERY HOT, THEN TURN OFF THE BURNERS ON ONE SIDE (OR, IF USING

CHARCOAL, MOUND ALL OF THE COALS TO ONE SIDE). PLACE CHICKEN, SKIN SIDE DOWN, ON THE COOLER SIDE OF THE GRILL, THEN STACK TWO CAST-IRON SKILLETS ON TOP TO FLATTEN CHICKEN. CLOSE THE LID AND GRILL FOR 10 TO 15 MINUTES OR UNTIL THE SKIN IS WELL BROWNED AND CRISP. TURN CHICKEN OVER, REPLACE SKILLETS AND GRILL UNTIL LEG JOINTS MOVE FREELY IN THEIR SOCKETS (IF YOU WISH TO USE A MEAT THERMOMETER, THE TEMPERATURE AT THE INNER THIGH SHOULD BE 165°F/74°C). TRANSFER BIRD TO A PLATTER, TENT WITH FOIL AND LET REST FOR 10 MINUTES BEFORE CARVING. SERVES 4.

TIP: TO SPATCHCOCK A CHICKEN, USE STURDY POULTRY SHEARS TO CUT ALONG EITHER SIDE OF THE BACKBONE (BASICALLY YOU'RE JUST CUTTING THE BACKBONE OUT). PULL THE BIRD APART SO THAT THE CAVITY IS EXPOSED, THEN FLIP IT UPSIDE DOWN SO THE SKIN IS UP AND THE CAVITY IS OPEN AGAINST THE CUTTING BOARD. PRESS FIRMLY DOWN ON THE BREAST WITH BOTH HANDS SO THAT THE BIRD LIES NEARLY FLAT. SAVE THE SPINE FOR MAKING STOCK, IF YOU WISH.

BLACKENED PORK TENDERLOIN

WE LIKE TO MAKE THIS IN A LARGE CAST-IRON SKILLET SET ON AN OUTDOOR GAS GRILL (IT'S A SMOKY PROCESS).

IMPORTANT SAFETY TIP: ONCE THE CAST-IRON PAN IS ON THE GRILL, DON'T ATTEMPT TO REMOVE IT UNTIL THE ENTIRE GRILL HAS COOLED. IT WILL GET HOT ENOUGH TO CAUSE BURNS THROUGH SOME OVEN MITTS.

1 TBSP	PAPRIKA	15 ML
1 TSP	DRIED THYME	5 ML
1 TSP	GARLIC POWDER	5 ML
1 TSP	ONION POWDER	5 ML
1 TSP	SALT (OR TO TASTE)	5 ML
1 TSP	BLACK PEPPER	5 ML
1/4 TSP	CAYENNE PEPPER	1 ML
2	PORK TENDERLOINS (EACH ABOUT 1 LB/500 G)	2
	VEGETABLE OIL	
	LIME WEDGES (OPTIONAL)	

PREHEAT GAS BARBECUE GRILL TO HIGH, WITH A CAST-IRON SKILLET LARGE ENOUGH TO HOLD BOTH TENDERLOINS SET ON THE GRATE (OR USE TWO SMALLER SKILLETS). IN A SMALL BOWL, COMBINE PAPRIKA, THYME, GARLIC POWDER, ONION POWDER, SALT, BLACK PEPPER AND CAYENNE. CUT SILVERSKIN OFF TENDERLOINS AND COAT EACH TENDERLOIN WITH SPICE MIXTURE, USING IT ALL AND PATTING IT ONTO THE MEAT SO IT STICKS.

POUR A GENEROUS SKIFF OF OIL INTO THE SKILLET, THEN PLACE TENDERLOINS IN PAN, SPACING THEM APART.

CLOSE THE LID AND COOK FOR 3 MINUTES OR UNTIL MEAT IS VERY WELL SEARED (BLACKENED, IN FACT). TURN THE TENDERLOINS OVER AND BLACKEN THE OTHER SIDE. BLACKEN REMAINING SIDES IF THE SHAPE OF THE TENDERLOINS AND PAN ALLOW, ADDING MORE OIL AS NEEDED. REDUCE HEAT TO MEDIUM, CLOSE THE LID AND COOK UNTIL PORK IS BARELY PINK IN THE CENTER OR A MEAT THERMOMETER INSERTED IN THE THICKEST PART OF EACH TENDERLOIN REGISTERS 145°F TO 160°F (63°C TO 71°C). USING TONGS, TRANSFER TENDERLOINS TO A PLATTER, TENT WITH FOIL AND LET REST FOR 10 MINUTES BEFORE SLICING. SERVE WITH LIME WEDGES ALONGSIDE, IF YOU WISH. SERVES 4 TO 6.

GIVE A MAN A FISH AND HE'LL EAT FOR A DAY;
TEACH A MAN TO FISH AND HE'LL SIT IN A BOAT
AND DRINK BEER ALL DAY.

PORK SHOULDER CHOPS
WITH SALSA VERDE

SHOULDER CHOPS ARE SOMETIMES ALSO SOLD AS
SHOULDER STEAKS, AND CAN EITHER BE BONE-IN OR
BONELESS. THEY'RE GENERALLY WELL MARBLED,
WHICH MEANS THEY TEND TO STAY MOIST
AND FLAVORFUL ON THE GRILL.

1/2 TSP	DRIED SAGE	2 ML
1/2 TSP	DRIED ROSEMARY	2 ML
2	GARLIC CLOVES, MINCED	2
	SALT AND BLACK PEPPER TO TASTE	
1 1/2 TBSP	VEGETABLE OIL	22 ML
2 LBS	PORK SHOULDER CHOPS (ABOUT 1 INCH/2.5 CM THICK)	1 KG
	SALSA VERDE (PAGE 263)	

CRUSH THE SAGE AND ROSEMARY IN A MORTAR AND
PESTLE. IN A SMALL BOWL, COMBINE CRUSHED HERBS,
GARLIC, SALT, PEPPER AND OIL. RUB PASTE ONTO BOTH
SIDES OF CHOPS, COVER AND REFRIGERATE FOR AT LEAST
2 HOURS OR PREFERABLY ALL DAY.

PREHEAT BARBECUE GRILL TO MEDIUM-HIGH. GRILL
CHOPS FOR 3 MINUTES, THEN TURN THEM OVER AND
GRILL FOR ANOTHER 3 MINUTES. REDUCE HEAT TO
MEDIUM-LOW AND CONTINUE GRILLING UNTIL JUST A
HINT OF PINK REMAINS INSIDE PORK, ABOUT 2 TO 3 MORE
MINUTES ON EACH SIDE. CUT CHOPS INTO STRIPS AND
SERVE DRIZZLED WITH SALSA VERDE. SERVES 4.

GREEK-INSPIRED PORK SKEWERS

CERTAIN HUSBANDS OF OURS (DON'T WORRY, WE'VE ONLY GOT ONE APIECE!) WOULD EAT THESE SEVERAL TIMES A WEEK IF GIVEN THE OPTION. SERVE WRAPPED IN NAAN, WITH TZATZIKI AND TOMATOES.

3	GARLIC CLOVES, MINCED	3
3 TBSP	FINELY CHOPPED FRESH OREGANO	45 ML
3 TBSP	FINELY CHOPPED FRESH MINT	45 ML
2 TBSP	OLIVE OIL	30 ML
	GRATED ZEST OF $\frac{1}{2}$ LEMON	
I TBSP	LEMON JUICE	15 ML
	SALT AND BLACK PEPPER TO TASTE	
2 LBS	PORK SHOULDER CHOPS	I KG
$\frac{1}{2}$	LARGE ONION, SEPARATED INTO LAYERS AND CUT INTO ROUGHLY I-INCH (2.5 CM) SQUARES OR TRIANGLES	$\frac{1}{2}$

IN A LARGE BOWL, COMBINE GARLIC, OREGANO, MINT, OIL, LEMON ZEST, LEMON JUICE, SALT AND PEPPER. CUT PORK INTO CHUNKS ABOUT $1\frac{1}{4}$ INCHES (3 CM) SQUARE AND ADD TO THE BOWL; TOSS TO COMBINE. COVER AND REFRIGERATE OVERNIGHT OR FOR AT LEAST 2 HOURS (LONGER IS BETTER, IF YOU CAN).

PREHEAT BARBECUE GRILL TO MEDIUM-HIGH. REMOVE PORK FROM MARINADE, DISCARDING MARINADE. THREAD PORK AND ONION ONTO FLAT METAL SKEWERS (OR BAMBOO SKEWERS SOAKED FOR AT LEAST 30 MINUTES PRIOR), ALTERNATING BETWEEN THEM. GRILL, TURNING EVERY FEW MINUTES, UNTIL GRILL-MARKED ON ALL SIDES AND JUST A HINT OF PINK REMAINS INSIDE PORK, ABOUT 10 MINUTES. SERVES 4.

SOY GINGER FLANK STEAK

THIS IS THE ABSOLUTE EASIEST THING TO GRILL WHEN YOU HAVE A CROWD COMING OVER. JUST BE SURE TO PLAN FAR ENOUGH AHEAD TO LET THE STEAK MARINATE — YOU NEED TO LET THOSE FLAVORS MAKE THEIR WAY INTO THE MEAT.

1½ to 2 LB	BEEF FLANK STEAK	750 G to 1 KG
4	GARLIC CLOVES, MINCED	4
1	THUMB-SIZED PIECE FRESH GINGER, GRATED	1
⅓ CUP	SUGAR	75 ML
1 TSP	HOT PEPPER FLAKES	5 ML
¼ CUP	SOY SAUCE	60 ML
1 TBSP	VEGETABLE OIL	15 ML
1 TBSP	LIME JUICE	15 ML
	ADDITIONAL VEGETABLE OIL	

GIVE STEAK A QUICK RINSE IN COLD WATER AND PAT DRY. LIGHTLY SCORE MEAT IN A 2-INCH (5 CM) DIAMOND PATTERN. IN A SHALLOW GLASS BAKING DISH OR A HEAVY PLASTIC FREEZER BAG, COMBINE GARLIC, GINGER, SUGAR, HOT PEPPER FLAKES, SOY SAUCE, OIL AND LIME JUICE. ADD STEAK, TURNING TO COAT. COVER OR SEAL AND REFRIGERATE FOR AT LEAST 6 HOURS OR OVERNIGHT. IF YOU THINK OF IT, GIVE THE MEAT A TURN EVERY COUPLE HOURS OR SO, SO THAT THE MARINADE DOES ITS DUTY ON BOTH SIDES.

PREHEAT BARBECUE GRILL TO HIGH AND BRUSH GRILL WITH VEGETABLE OIL TO PREVENT STICKING. ONCE THE GRILL IS NICE AND HOT, PLACE STEAK ON THE GRILL AND

REDUCE HEAT TO MEDIUM. GRILL FOR 5 MINUTES PER SIDE FOR MEDIUM DONENESS (ADD A MINUTE OR TWO IF YOU LIKE YOUR MEAT WELL DONE). TRANSFER TO A PLATTER, COVER WITH FOIL AND LET REST FOR 10 MINUTES, THEN SLICE THINLY ACROSS THE GRAIN. SERVES 4 TO 6.

TIP: IF YOU HAVE A BIGGER GROUP OF PEOPLE (AND ENOUGH ROOM ON THE GRILL) MARINATE AND COOK 2 OR MORE STEAKS AT ONCE.

AS A TEENAGER YOU ARE AT THE LAST STAGE
IN YOUR LIFE WHEN YOU WILL BE HAPPY TO HEAR
THAT THE PHONE IS FOR YOU.
— FRAN LEBOWITZ

GRILLED STEAK BIBIMBAP

KOREAN RICE BOWLS, CALLED BIBIMBAP, ARE GREAT FOR GROUPS AND ARE A DIFFERENT WAY TO USE YOUR GRILL. USE WHATEVER VEGGIES ARE IN SEASON OR WHAT YOU'VE PLUCKED FROM THE GARDEN — IT ALL COOKS UP IN MINUTES ON THE HOT GRILL. IF YOU LIKE, TOP EACH BOWL WITH A FRIED EGG, AND PASS THE SRIRACHA.

1 LB	BEEF GRILLING STEAK (SUCH AS STRIP LOIN OR FLATIRON) OR FLANK STEAK	500 G
2	GREEN ONIONS, FINELY CHOPPED	2
2	GARLIC CLOVES, MINCED	2
1 TSP	GRATED FRESH GINGER	5 ML
2 TBSP	SUGAR OR LIQUID HONEY	30 ML
1/4 CUP	SOY SAUCE	60 ML
2 TBSP	RICE VINEGAR OR LIME JUICE	30 ML
1 TBSP	SESAME OIL	15 ML
	FRESH ASPARAGUS, ZUCCHINI, PEPPERS, TOMATOES, EGGPLANT OR ANY VEGGIES YOU LIKE	
	ADDITIONAL SESAME OIL	
	HOT STEAMED RICE	
	FRIED EGGS (OPTIONAL)	
	SRIRACHA	

THINLY SLICE STEAK ACROSS THE GRAIN AND PUT IT IN A SEALABLE PLASTIC BAG. ADD GREEN ONIONS, GARLIC, GINGER, SUGAR, SOY SAUCE, VINEGAR AND OIL; SEAL AND GENTLY MASSAGE THE BAG TO COAT EVERYTHING WELL. REFRIGERATE FOR A FEW HOURS (OR FREEZE FOR LONGER STORAGE — YOU CAN DO THIS PART AHEAD OF TIME).

PREHEAT BARBECUE GRILL TO MEDIUM-HIGH. PREPARE YOUR VEGGIES, SNAPPING THE ENDS OFF ASPARAGUS, CUTTING PEPPERS AND TOMATOES INTO THICK WEDGES, THICKLY SLICING ZUCCHINI AND EGGPLANT OR CUTTING THEM INTO RIBBONS, ETC., AND TOSS EVERYTHING WITH A DRIZZLE OF OIL TO COAT. REMOVE STEAK FROM MARINADE, DISCARDING MARINADE. LAY VEGGIES AND STEAK DIRECTLY ON THE GRILL AND COOK, TURNING WITH TONGS AS NEEDED, FOR 3 TO 4 MINUTES OR UNTIL MEAT IS COOKED THROUGH AND VEGGIES ARE TENDER-CRISP AND CHAR-MARKED. DIVIDE RICE AMONG BOWLS, ADD MEAT AND VEGETABLES AND, IF YOU LIKE, TOP EACH WITH A FRIED EGG. SERVE WITH SRIRACHA TO SPICE THINGS UP. SERVES 6.

CHEESEBURGERS ON THE GRILL

*THERE'S NOTHING LIKE A ROUND OF
JUICY BURGERS ON THE GRILL WHEN
THE FAMILY IS OVER. HERE ARE THE BASICS.*

1 1/2 LBS	LEAN OR REGULAR GROUND BEEF, GROUND CHUCK OR SIRLOIN	750 G
	SALT AND BLACK PEPPER TO TASTE	
	SLICED SHARP (OLD) CHEDDAR CHEESE OR PROCESSED CHEESE SLICES	
6	SOFT HAMBURGER BUNS, SPLIT	6
	CONDIMENTS OF YOUR CHOICE (LETTUCE, TOMATO, KETCHUP, MUSTARD, PICKLES, COOKED BACON, CARAMELIZED ONIONS, SLICED AVOCADO)	

PREHEAT BARBECUE GRILL TO MEDIUM-HIGH. SHAPE BEEF LOOSELY INTO 6 PATTIES SLIGHTLY LARGER THAN YOU'D LIKE THE FINISHED BURGERS TO BE (THE PATTIES WILL SHRINK AS THEY COOK), HANDLING THE MEAT AS LITTLE AS POSSIBLE. IF YOU LIKE, MAKE AN INDENTATION IN THE CENTER OF EACH PATTY TO KEEP THEM FROM BULGING IN THE MIDDLE AS THEY COOK. SPRINKLE WITH SALT AND PEPPER. GRILL PATTIES, WITHOUT CROWDING, FOR 4 TO 5 MINUTES ON THE FIRST SIDE, UNTIL A DEEP GOLDEN CRUST DEVELOPS ON THE BOTTOM. FLIP AND COOK FOR 3 TO 4 MINUTES OR UNTIL PATTIES ARE NO LONGER PINK INSIDE AND A MEAT THERMOMETER INSERTED SIDEWAYS INTO THE CENTER OF A PATTY REGISTERS 160°F (71°C). TURN OFF HEAT, ADD CHEESE AND CLOSE THE LID FOR A MINUTE, JUST UNTIL THE CHEESE MELTS. SLIDE PATTIES ONTO OPEN BUNS AND SERVE WITH YOUR FAVORITE CONDIMENTS. SERVES 6.

MEATLOAF BURGERS

FANCY UP A BACKYARD BARBECUE BY UPPING YOUR GRILL GAME WITH MEATLOAF BURGERS.

6	BACON STRIPS, COOKED AND CRUMBLED	6
1 LB	LEAN GROUND PORK	500 G
1 LB	LEAN GROUND BEEF	500 G
2	LARGE EGGS	2
1	LARGE ONION, GRATED	1
1/2 CUP	DRY BREAD CRUMBS	125 ML
2 TSP	DRIED PARSLEY	10 ML
2 TSP	DRIED OREGANO	10 ML
1 TSP	GROUND CORIANDER	5 ML
	SALT AND BLACK PEPPER TO TASTE	
1/2 CUP	BARBECUE SAUCE	125 ML
8	HAMBURGER BUNS, SPLIT	8
	HAMBURGER CONDIMENTS	

PREHEAT BARBECUE GRILL TO MEDIUM. IN A LARGE BOWL, COMBINE BACON, PORK AND BEEF. IN A SEPARATE BOWL, LIGHTLY BEAT EGGS, THEN WHISK IN ONION, BREAD CRUMBS, PARSLEY, OREGANO, CORIANDER, SALT, PEPPER AND BARBECUE SAUCE. ADD EGG MIXTURE TO MEAT MIXTURE AND COMBINE EVERYTHING WITH YOUR HANDS, BEING SURE TO EVENLY DISTRIBUTE PORK AND BEEF WITHOUT OVERHANDLING. SHAPE INTO 8 EQUAL PATTIES, ABOUT 1 INCH (2.5 CM) THICK. GRILL PATTIES FOR 12 TO 15 MINUTES, FLIPPING THEM OVER HALFWAY THROUGH, UNTIL PATTIES ARE NO LONGER PINK INSIDE AND A MEAT THERMOMETER INSERTED SIDEWAYS INTO THE CENTER OF A PATTY REGISTERS 160°F (71°C). SERVE WITH BUNS AND ALL OF YOUR FAVORITE BURGER FIXINGS. SERVES 8.

GRILLED LAMB CHOPS WITH GARLIC AND MINT

LAMB CHOPS ARE QUICK TO COOK ON THE GRILL. THEY CAN BE SIMPLY PREPARED WITH A SHOWER OF SALT AND PEPPER, BUT THIS SIMPLE MARINADE ADDS A TON OF FLAVOR.

1½ LBS	LAMB LOIN CHOPS (ABOUT ¾ INCH/2 CM THICK)	750 G
2	GARLIC CLOVES, MINCED	2
2 TBSP	CHOPPED FRESH MINT	30 ML
½ TSP	GROUND CUMIN	2 ML
	SALT AND BLACK PEPPER TO TASTE	
2 TBSP	VEGETABLE OIL	30 ML
2 TSP	BALSAMIC VINEGAR	10 ML
I TSP	LEMON JUICE	5 ML

PLACE LAMB CHOPS IN A HEAVY-DUTY SEALABLE PLASTIC BAG AND ADD THE REMAINING INGREDIENTS. SEAL AND REFRIGERATE FOR AT LEAST AN HOUR OR OVERNIGHT.

PREHEAT BARBECUE GRILL TO HIGH. REMOVE LAMB FROM MARINADE, DISCARDING MARINADE. GRILL LAMB FOR 2 MINUTES, THEN FLIP CHOPS OVER AND GRILL FOR 3 MINUTES FOR MEDIUM-RARE, OR CONTINUE TO COOK UNTIL DONE TO YOUR LIKING. TRANSFER TO A PLATE, COVER LOOSELY WITH FOIL AND LET REST FOR 5 TO 10 MINUTES BEFORE SERVING. SERVES 4.

STEWS & BRAISES

BEEF 'N' BEER STEW

AS OUR GRANDFATHERS WOULD SAY, NOTHING STICKS
TO YOUR RIBS LIKE A NICE HEARTY STEW. SERVE WITH
A PIECE OF CRUSTY BREAD OR OVER MASHED POTATOES.

	VEGETABLE OIL	
2 LBS	STEWING BEEF, CUT INTO 2-INCH (5 CM) CUBES	1 KG
3	CARROTS, SLICED	3
1	ONION, CHOPPED	1
2	GARLIC CLOVES, MINCED	2
2 TBSP	TOMATO PASTE	30 ML
1	CAN (12 OZ/341 ML) BEER (SEE TIP)	1
3 CUPS	READY-TO-USE BEEF BROTH (APPROX.)	750 ML
1 1/2 LBS	POTATOES, PEELED AND CUBED	750 G
1/2 TSP	DRIED THYME	2 ML
	SALT AND BLACK PEPPER TO TASTE	
1/2 CUP	FROZEN PEAS	125 ML

IN A DUTCH OVEN OR LARGE POT, HEAT A DRIZZLE OF
OIL OVER MEDIUM-HIGH HEAT. BROWN BEEF IN BATCHES,
WITHOUT CROWDING THE PAN, TRANSFERRING THE CUBES
TO A PLATE AS THEY'RE DONE AND ADDING MORE OIL AS
NECESSARY BETWEEN BATCHES. ADD SOME MORE OIL
TO THE POT IF NECESSARY AND SAUTÉ CARROTS AND
ONION FOR ABOUT 5 MINUTES, UNTIL ONION STARTS
TO SOFTEN. ADD GARLIC AND TOMATO PASTE; COOK,
STIRRING, FOR 1 MINUTE. POUR IN BEER AND BROTH.

RETURN BEEF AND ANY ACCUMULATED JUICES TO
THE POT AND STIR IN POTATOES, THYME, SALT AND
PEPPER. THE LIQUID SHOULD JUST COVER THE BEEF

AND POTATOES; IF IT DOESN'T, POUR IN SOME EXTRA BROTH OR WATER (BUT NOT TOO MUCH, SINCE THIS IS A STEW, NOT A SOUP, AND YOU DON'T WANT IT TO BE TOO WATERY). BRING TO A BOIL, THEN REDUCE HEAT, COVER AND SIMMER, STIRRING OCCASIONALLY, FOR ABOUT $1\frac{1}{2}$ HOURS OR UNTIL BEEF IS VERY TENDER, VEGETABLES ARE COOKED AND LIQUID HAS THICKENED. IF THE STEW IS NOT SAUCY ENOUGH, ADD A BIT OF BROTH TO THIN IT TO YOUR LIKING. STIR IN PEAS AND COOK FOR A FEW MORE MINUTES TO WARM THEM UP. SERVES 4 TO 6.

TIP: STOUT IS TRADITIONAL IN THIS KIND OF STEW (THINK OF THE IRISH!), BUT A LIGHTER BEER CAN ADD A NICE CRISP FLAVOR. EXPERIMENT WITH DIFFERENT BEERS OR JUST USE WHATEVER YOU HAPPEN TO HAVE IN THE FRIDGE.

HOW CAN YOU DELAY MILK TURNING SOUR?
ANSWER: KEEP IT IN THE COW.

STREAMLINED BEEF BOURGUIGNON

AN UPSCALE BEEF BRAISE, THIS CLASSIC FRENCH DISH WAS RECENTLY BROUGHT BACK INTO VOGUE BY THE RESURGENCE OF JULIA CHILD'S TOME MASTERING THE ART OF FRENCH COOKING. IT'S DELICIOUS, BUT THE PROCEDURE CAN BE LENGTHY. FORTUNATELY, IT REQUIRES LITTLE EFFORT AND CAN BE FAST-TRACKED WITH EQUALLY TASTY RESULTS. IF YOU LIKE, SERVE OVER MASHED POTATOES OR BUTTERED NOODLES.

	VEGETABLE OIL	
3 LBS	STEWING BEEF, CUT INTO 2-INCH (5 CM) CUBES	1.5 KG
1	LARGE ONION, HALVED AND SLICED	1
3	GARLIC CLOVES, MINCED	3
2 TBSP	ALL-PURPOSE FLOUR	30 ML
	SALT AND BLACK PEPPER TO TASTE	
2 CUPS	DRY RED WINE	500 ML
2 to 3 CUPS	READY-TO-USE BEEF BROTH	500 to 750 ML
2 TBSP	TOMATO PASTE	30 ML
2	FRESH THYME SPRIGS	2
2 TBSP	BUTTER	30 ML
20	SMALL WHITE PEARL ONIONS, PEELED	20
1 LB	MUSHROOMS, HALVED OR QUARTERED IF LARGE, LEFT WHOLE IF SMALL	500 G

PREHEAT OVEN TO 325°F (160°C). IN AN OVENPROOF DUTCH OVEN, HEAT A GENEROUS DRIZZLE OF OIL OVER MEDIUM-HIGH HEAT. BROWN BEEF IN BATCHES, WITHOUT CROWDING THE PAN, TRANSFERRING THE CUBES TO A PLATE AS THEY'RE DONE AND ADDING MORE OIL AS

NECESSARY BETWEEN BATCHES. ADD SLICED ONION TO THE PAN AND SAUTÉ FOR 3 TO 4 MINUTES OR UNTIL STARTING TO SOFTEN AND TURN GOLDEN. ADD GARLIC AND SAUTÉ FOR 1 MINUTE.

RETURN BEEF AND ANY ACCUMULATED JUICES TO THE PAN, SPRINKLE FLOUR OVER TOP AND TOSS TO COAT MEAT AND ONION. SPRINKLE WITH SALT AND PEPPER. POUR IN WINE AND ENOUGH BROTH TO COME HALFWAY UP THE MEAT MIXTURE, SCRAPING THE BOTTOM OF THE PAN TO LOOSEN ANY BROWNED BITS. STIR IN TOMATO PASTE. PULL THE LEAVES OFF THE THYME SPRIGS AND ADD THE LEAVES TO THE PAN. COVER, TRANSFER TO THE OVEN AND BAKE FOR $2\frac{1}{2}$ TO 3 HOURS OR UNTIL BEEF IS VERY TENDER.

TOWARD THE END OF THE COOKING TIME, HEAT ANOTHER DRIZZLE OF OIL IN A HEAVY SKILLET OVER MEDIUM HEAT. MELT BUTTER AND SAUTÉ PEARL ONIONS AND MUSHROOMS FOR 5 TO 8 MINUTES, UNTIL BOTH ARE SOFTENED AND TURNING GOLDEN. STIR INTO THE BEEF MIXTURE WHEN IT COMES OUT OF THE OVEN. SERVES 8 TO 10.

BRAISED BEEF SHORT RIBS WITH CRANBERRIES

CRANBERRIES CUT THE RICHNESS OF BEEF SHORT RIBS, WHICH LOOK LIKE MARBLED CHUNKS OF MEAT A COUPLE OF INCHES THICK BEFORE THEY'RE COOKED. A SLOW BRAISE CREATES A RICH SAUCE THAT'S PERFECT FOR DRAPING OVER MASHED POTATOES. TRY SUBSTITUTING LAMB SHANKS, WHICH BENEFIT FROM THE SAME LOW, SLOW COOKING METHOD.

	VEGETABLE OIL	
6	BEEF OR BISON SHORT RIBS (ABOUT 2 LBS/1 KG)	6
	SALT AND BLACK PEPPER TO TASTE	
2	CARROTS, CUT INTO 1-INCH (2.5 CM) PIECES	2
1	SMALL ONION, HALVED AND THINLY SLICED	1
2	GARLIC CLOVES, MINCED	2
1/4 CUP	BALSAMIC VINEGAR	60 ML
1 CUP	DRY RED WINE	250 ML
2 CUPS	FRESH OR FROZEN CRANBERRIES	500 ML
2	FRESH THYME SPRIGS	2
1	FRESH ROSEMARY SPRIG	1
2 to 3 CUPS	READY-TO-USE BEEF BROTH	500 to 750 ML
	MASHED POTATOES	

PREHEAT OVEN TO 325°F (160°C). IN AN OVENPROOF DUTCH OVEN, HEAT A DRIZZLE OF OIL OVER MEDIUM-HIGH HEAT. SEASON RIBS WITH SALT AND PEPPER. WORKING IN BATCHES, BROWN RIBS ON ALL SIDES, TRANSFERRING THEM TO A PLATE AS YOU GO. ADD CARROTS AND ONION

TO THE POT AND SAUTÉ FOR 4 TO 5 MINUTES OR UNTIL STARTING TO TURN GOLDEN ON THE EDGES. ADD GARLIC AND SAUTÉ FOR I MINUTE. ADD VINEGAR AND COOK FOR I MINUTE, SCRAPING UP ANY BROWNED BITS FROM THE BOTTOM OF THE PAN.

RETURN RIBS AND ANY ACCUMULATED JUICES TO THE POT AND STIR IN WINE, CRANBERRIES, THYME, ROSEMARY AND ENOUGH BROTH TO COME ABOUT HALFWAY UP THE SIDES OF THE RIBS. COVER, TRANSFER TO THE OVEN AND ROAST FOR 3 TO $3\frac{1}{2}$ HOURS OR UNTIL RIBS ARE VERY TENDER. DISCARD THYME AND ROSEMARY SPRIGS. SERVE RIBS OVER MASHED POTATOES, WITH THE BRAISING SAUCE. SERVES 6.

MIDDLE EASTERN LAMB STEW WITH CHICKPEAS

SCENTED WITH WARM SPICES, THIS THICK STEW IS DELICIOUS SERVED OVER COUSCOUS.

	VEGETABLE OIL	
1½ LB	BONELESS LEG OF LAMB, TRIMMED AND CUT INTO 1-INCH (2.5 CM) PIECES	750 G
3	LARGE ONIONS, HALVED AND THINLY SLICED	3
4	GARLIC CLOVES, MINCED	4
½ CUP	WATER	125 ML
1 TBSP	GRATED FRESH GINGER	15 ML
1 TSP	GROUND CUMIN	5 ML
¼ TSP	GROUND ALLSPICE	1 ML
1	CINNAMON STICK	1
3 CUPS	READY-TO-USE BEEF BROTH	750 ML
1	CAN (19 OZ/540 ML) CHICKPEAS, RINSED AND DRAINED (2 CUPS/500 ML)	1
2 CUPS	BABY CARROTS	500 ML
1 CUP	DRIED APRICOTS, SLICED	250 ML
	SALT AND BLACK PEPPER TO TASTE	
	CHOPPED FRESH MINT (OPTIONAL)	

IN A LARGE DUTCH OVEN, HEAT A DRIZZLE OF OIL OVER MEDIUM-HIGH HEAT. BROWN LAMB IN BATCHES, TRANSFERRING THE PIECES TO A PLATE AS THEY'RE DONE AND ADDING MORE OIL AS NECESSARY BETWEEN BATCHES. ADD ONIONS TO THE PAN AND SAUTÉ FOR 4 TO 5 MINUTES OR UNTIL SOFT. ADD GARLIC AND WATER; COOK, SCRAPING UP ANY BROWNED BITS FROM THE BOTTOM OF THE PAN, FOR 2 MINUTES.

RETURN LAMB AND ANY ACCUMULATED JUICES TO THE POT AND STIR IN GINGER, CUMIN, ALLSPICE AND CINNAMON STICK. STIR IN BROTH AND BRING TO A BOIL. REDUCE HEAT AND SIMMER, STIRRING OCCASIONALLY, FOR 2 HOURS OR UNTIL LAMB IS VERY TENDER. STIR IN CHICKPEAS, CARROTS AND APRICOTS; COVER AND SIMMER FOR 20 MINUTES OR UNTIL CARROTS ARE TENDER. SEASON WITH SALT AND PEPPER. IF DESIRED, STIR IN MINT JUST BEFORE SERVING OR SPRINKLE IT ON TOP OF EACH BOWL. SERVES 8.

*I COME FROM A FAMILY WHERE GRAVY
IS CONSIDERED A BEVERAGE.
— ERMA BOMBECK*

BRAISED LAMB SHANKS

LAMB SHANKS AREN'T PARTICULARLY INEXPENSIVE, BUT THEIR TOUGH CONNECTIVE TISSUES MAKE THEM INCREDIBLY FLAVORFUL AND A PERFECT CANDIDATE FOR BRAISING. IT'S A GOOD IDEA TO CHECK PARTWAY THROUGH TO MAKE SURE TOO MUCH LIQUID HASN'T COOKED OFF (YOU CAN ALWAYS ADD A BIT MORE), BUT DON'T OPEN THE OVEN TOO MANY TIMES OR YOU'LL SLOW THE COOKING PROCESS.

	VEGETABLE OIL	
4 to 6	LAMB SHANKS	4 to 6
	SALT AND BLACK PEPPER TO TASTE	
2	ONIONS, CHOPPED	2
2	CELERY STALKS, CHOPPED OR THINLY SLICED	2
2	CARROTS, CHOPPED	2
4	GARLIC CLOVES, MINCED	4
2	FRESH ROSEMARY SPRIGS	2
1	BAY LEAF	1
2 CUPS	READY-TO-USE BEEF BROTH, BASIC CHICKEN STOCK (PAGE 28) OR READY-TO-USE CHICKEN BROTH	500 ML
2 CUPS	DRY RED WINE (OR MORE BROTH)	500 ML
2 TBSP	BALSAMIC VINEGAR	30 ML
2 TBSP	TOMATO PASTE	30 ML
	MASHED POTATOES	

PREHEAT OVEN TO 300°F (150°C). IN A LARGE, HEAVY SKILLET, HEAT A DRIZZLE OF OIL OVER MEDIUM-HIGH HEAT. PAT LAMB DRY AND SPRINKLE WITH SALT AND PEPPER. WORKING IN BATCHES, BROWN LAMB ON ALL SIDES, TRANSFERRING THE SHANKS TO A ROASTING

PAN OR BAKING DISH AS THEY'RE DONE. ADD ANOTHER DRIZZLE OF OIL TO THE SKILLET AND SAUTÉ ONIONS, CELERY AND CARROTS FOR 5 TO 8 MINUTES OR UNTIL SOFT. TRANSFER TO THE ROASTING PAN AND STIR IN GARLIC, ROSEMARY, BAY LEAF, BROTH, WINE, VINEGAR AND TOMATO PASTE.

COVER TIGHTLY WITH A LID OR FOIL AND ROAST FOR 3 HOURS OR UNTIL LAMB IS VERY TENDER. DISCARD ROSEMARY SPRIGS AND BAY LEAF. IF YOU LIKE, REMOVE THE SHANKS AND PURÉE THE CHUNKY SAUCE IN A BLENDER OR FOOD PROCESSOR (OR USING AN IMMERSION BLENDER RIGHT IN THE POT), THEN RETURN THE PURÉE TO THE POT (IF NECESSARY) AND COOK OVER MEDIUM HEAT TO THICKEN. SERVE LAMB SHANKS TOPPED WITH SAUCE, WITH MASHED POTATOES TO CATCH ANY DRIPS. SERVES 4 TO 6.

ROASTED SQUASH COCONUT CURRY

CREAMY, SWEET AND TANGY, THIS SIMPLE CURRY IS FULL OF FLAVOR.

1/2	BUTTERNUT SQUASH, PEELED AND CUBED (ABOUT 2 CUPS/500 ML)	1/2
	OLIVE OIL	
	SALT AND BLACK PEPPER TO TASTE	
1	ONION, CHOPPED	1
3	GARLIC CLOVES, MINCED	3
1	CAN (19 OZ/540 ML) CHICKPEAS, RINSED AND DRAINED (2 CUPS/500 ML)	1
1/4 CUP	DRAINED OIL-PACKED SUN-DRIED TOMATOES, CHOPPED	60 ML
1 TBSP	GRATED FRESH GINGER	15 ML
PINCH	HOT PEPPER FLAKES	PINCH
2 TSP	MILD CURRY PASTE	10 ML
1	CAN (14 OZ/400 ML) COCONUT MILK	1
1 1/2 CUPS	TRIMMED SPINACH LEAVES	375 ML
2 TBSP	LEMON JUICE	30 ML
	HOT COOKED RICE OR NAAN (PAGE 244)	

PREHEAT OVEN TO 400°F (200°C). IN A BOWL, TOSS SQUASH WITH A SPLASH OF OIL AND SEASON WITH SALT AND PEPPER. SPREAD OUT ON A RIMMED BAKING SHEET LINED WITH FOIL. ROAST FOR 25 TO 30 MINUTES OR UNTIL TENDER BUT NOT MUSHY. (WE USUALLY ROAST THE WHOLE SQUASH HERE AND SAVE THE SECOND HALF FOR LUNCH THE NEXT DAY.)

HEAT ANOTHER SPLASH OF OIL IN A LARGE SAUCEPAN OVER MEDIUM HEAT. SAUTÉ ONION UNTIL VERY SOFT,

ABOUT 10 MINUTES. ADD GARLIC, CHICKPEAS, TOMATOES, GINGER, HOT PEPPER FLAKES AND CURRY PASTE; SAUTÉ FOR 2 TO 3 MINUTES OR UNTIL FRAGRANT. ADD COCONUT MILK AND BRING TO A SIMMER. ADD SQUASH, SPINACH AND LEMON JUICE; COOK FOR 10 MINUTES OR UNTIL SAUCE HAS THICKENED TO YOUR LIKING. SERVE OVER RICE OR WITH NAAN. SERVES 4.

IN REAL LIFE, I ASSURE YOU, THERE IS
NO SUCH THING AS ALGEBRA.
— FRAN LEBOWITZ

MOROCCAN-INSPIRED CHICKEN STEW

CHICKPEAS, WALNUTS AND A BLEND OF SPICES MAKE THIS SIMPLE STEW AN EASY DINNER. VEGETARIANS CAN USE TOFU IN PLACE OF THE CHICKEN OR JUST LEAVE IT OUT ALTOGETHER.

	VEGETABLE OIL	
2	BONELESS SKINLESS CHICKEN BREASTS, CUT INTO 1-INCH (2.5 CM) PIECES	2
2	GARLIC CLOVES, MINCED	2
1	LARGE ONION, CHOPPED	1
1 CUP	SLICED MUSHROOMS	250 ML
2	LARGE CARROTS, SLICED	2
2	CELERY STALKS, SLICED	2
1	CAN (14 OZ/398 ML) CHICKPEAS, RINSED AND DRAINED (1$\frac{1}{2}$ CUPS/ 375 ML)	1
$\frac{1}{2}$ CUP	CHOPPED WALNUTS	125 ML
2 TSP	GROUND CUMIN	10 ML
1 TSP	GROUND CORIANDER	5 ML
1 TSP	PAPRIKA	5 ML
$\frac{1}{4}$ TSP	CAYENNE PEPPER	1 ML
	SALT TO TASTE	
1	CAN (14 OZ/398 ML) TOMATO SAUCE	1
1$\frac{1}{2}$ CUPS	WATER	375 ML
	JUICE OF $\frac{1}{2}$ LEMON	
	HOT COOKED COUSCOUS	

IN A LARGE SAUCEPAN OR A DUTCH OVEN, HEAT A DRIZZLE OF OIL OVER MEDIUM-HIGH HEAT. ADD CHICKEN AND COOK, STIRRING, UNTIL BROWNED ON ALL SIDES.

USING A SLOTTED SPOON, TRANSFER CHICKEN TO A PLATE. ADD GARLIC, ONION AND MUSHROOMS TO THE PAN AND SAUTÉ FOR ABOUT 5 MINUTES, UNTIL MUSHROOMS AND ONIONS START TO SOFTEN. STIR IN CARROTS, CELERY, CHICKPEAS, WALNUTS, CUMIN, CORIANDER, PAPRIKA, CAYENNE, SALT, TOMATO SAUCE AND WATER; INCREASE HEAT AND BRING TO A BOIL.

RETURN CHICKEN AND ANY ACCUMULATED JUICES TO THE PAN, REDUCE HEAT TO LOW, COVER AND SIMMER FOR 40 MINUTES OR UNTIL VEGETABLES ARE TENDER, CHICKEN IS NO LONGER PINK INSIDE AND ALL THE FLAVORS HAVE MINGLED. STIR IN LEMON JUICE AND ADJUST THE SEASONING. SERVE OVER COUSCOUS. SERVES 4 TO 6.

AFRICAN-STYLE CHICKEN PEANUT STEW

THIS RICH AND EARTHY CHICKEN STEW ISN'T AUTHENTICALLY AFRICAN, BUT IT DOES THE TRICK ON A CHILLY NIGHT.

	VEGETABLE OIL	
2 LBS	BONELESS SKINLESS CHICKEN THIGHS, CUT INTO QUARTERS	1 KG
1	LARGE ONION, CHOPPED	1
3	GARLIC CLOVES, MINCED	3
1	LARGE SWEET POTATO, PEELED AND CUBED	1
1	RED BELL PEPPER, CHOPPED	1
1	THUMB-SIZED PIECE OF FRESH GINGER, GRATED	1
1	CAN (28 OZ/796 ML) CRUSHED TOMATOES	1
1	CAN (19 OZ/540) CHICKPEAS, RINSED AND DRAINED (2 CUPS/500 ML)	1
2 1/2 CUPS	BASIC CHICKEN STOCK (PAGE 28) OR READY-TO-USE CHICKEN BROTH (APPROX.)	625 ML
1 CUP	PEANUT BUTTER	250 ML
1 TBSP	GROUND CORIANDER	15 ML
2 TSP	GROUND CUMIN	10 ML
1 TSP	GROUND TURMERIC	5 ML
1/4 TSP	GROUND CINNAMON	1 ML
1/4 TSP	CAYENNE PEPPER	1 ML
2	BAY LEAVES	2
	SALT AND BLACK PEPPER TO TASTE	
	HOT COOKED COUSCOUS OR RICE	
	CHOPPED FRESH CILANTRO	

CONTINUED ON PAGE 145...

Grilled Mussels with Lemon (page 115)

Soy Ginger Flank Steak (page 122)

Braised Beef Short Ribs with Cranberries (page 134)

Middle Eastern Lamb Stew with Chickpeas (page 136)

IN A LARGE POT OR DUTCH OVEN, HEAT A DRIZZLE OF OIL OVER MEDIUM-HIGH HEAT. WORKING IN BATCHES, ADD CHICKEN AND COOK, STIRRING, UNTIL BROWNED ON ALL SIDES, TRANSFERRING THE PIECES TO A PLATE AS THEY'RE DONE AND ADDING MORE OIL AS NECESSARY BETWEEN BATCHES. ADD SOME MORE OIL TO THE POT, IF NECESSARY, THEN SAUTÉ ONION UNTIL IT STARTS TO SOFTEN, ABOUT 5 MINUTES. ADD GARLIC, SWEET POTATO, RED PEPPER AND GINGER; SAUTÉ FOR A COUPLE OF MINUTES.

RETURN CHICKEN AND ANY ACCUMULATED JUICES TO THE POT, THEN STIR IN TOMATOES, CHICKPEAS, STOCK, PEANUT BUTTER, CORIANDER, CUMIN, TURMERIC, CINNAMON, CAYENNE, BAY LEAVES, SALT AND BLACK PEPPER; BRING TO A BOIL. REDUCE HEAT TO LOW, COVER AND SIMMER FOR ABOUT 1 HOUR OR UNTIL JUICES RUN CLEAR WHEN CHICKEN IS PIERCED, SWEET POTATO IS TENDER AND FLAVORS HAVE MINGLED. DISCARD BAY LEAVES. ADJUST THE SEASONING WITH SALT AND PEPPER (AND CAYENNE, IF IT'S NOT HOT ENOUGH) AND THIN WITH MORE STOCK IF IT'S TOO THICK. SERVE OVER COUSCOUS, GARNISHED WITH CILANTRO. SERVES 8.

TIP: THIS G-RATED VERSION GOES LIGHT ON THE SPICE, BUT FEEL FREE TO UP THE CAYENNE (OR ADD A CHOPPED CHILE PEPPER OR TWO) IF YOU LIKE IT HOT.

CHICKEN AND CHICKEN SAUSAGE STEW WITH GOUDA

THIS SAVORY, CHEESY AND SLIGHTLY SWEET STEW WILL BECOME A FAMILY FAVORITE.

2 LBS	BONELESS SKINLESS CHICKEN BREASTS OR THIGHS	1 KG
	VEGETABLE OIL	
1 LB	CHICKEN SAUSAGES (SEE TIP)	500 G
2	CELERY STALKS, CHOPPED	2
2	CARROTS, CHOPPED	2
1	LARGE ONION, CHOPPED	1
	SALT AND BLACK PEPPER TO TASTE	
	WATER	
2	GARLIC CLOVES, MINCED	2
2 TBSP	ALL-PURPOSE FLOUR	30 ML
2 CUPS	BASIC CHICKEN STOCK (PAGE 28) OR READY-TO-USE CHICKEN BROTH	500 ML
2	SMALL FRESH THYME SPRIGS	2
1	LARGE SWEET APPLE (SUCH AS GALA), CHOPPED (NO NEED TO PEEL)	1
1 TSP	LEMON JUICE	5 ML
1 CUP	SHREDDED GOUDA CHEESE	250 ML
1/4 CUP	HEAVY OR WHIPPING (35%) CREAM OR HALF-AND-HALF (10%) CREAM	60 ML

CUT THE CHICKEN INTO 2-INCH (5 CM) CHUNKS. IN A LARGE DUTCH OVEN, HEAT A SKIFF OF OIL OVER MEDIUM HEAT. WORKING IN BATCHES, ADD CHICKEN AND COOK, STIRRING, UNTIL BROWNED ON ALL SIDES, TRANSFERRING THE PIECES TO A PLATE AS THEY'RE DONE AND ADDING MORE OIL AS NECESSARY BETWEEN BATCHES. BROWN SAUSAGES, THEN TRANSFER TO A PLATE AND CUT

EACH SAUSAGE INTO 4 OR 5 PIECES. (NEITHER CHICKEN
NOR SAUSAGE NEEDS TO BE COOKED THROUGH AT
THIS POINT.)

ADD CELERY, CARROT, ONION, SALT, PEPPER AND A
DRIZZLE OF WATER TO THE POT; COVER AND SWEAT
VEGETABLES FOR 3 MINUTES. REMOVE LID AND SCRAPE UP
BROWNED BITS, THEN LET ANY LIQUID BOIL AWAY. BROWN
VEGETABLES SLIGHTLY, ADDING A LITTLE OIL IF NEEDED.
ADD GARLIC AND FLOUR; COOK, STIRRING, FOR 2 MINUTES.

RETURN CHICKEN, SAUSAGE AND ANY ACCUMULATED
JUICES TO THE PAN, ADD STOCK AND BRING TO A SIMMER.
STIR IN THYME SPRIGS, REDUCE HEAT AND SIMMER,
UNCOVERED, FOR 20 MINUTES, STIRRING OCCASIONALLY.
ADD APPLE AND COOK, STIRRING OCCASIONALLY, FOR 15 TO
20 MINUTES OR UNTIL APPLE IS SOFTENED AND SAUCE
IS THICKENED. DISCARD THYME SPRIGS, THEN STIR IN
LEMON JUICE. REMOVE FROM HEAT AND STIR IN CHEESE
AND CREAM. SERVES 8.

TIP: CHICKEN APPLE SAUSAGE WORKS BRILLIANTLY IN THIS
RECIPE, BUT IF YOU WISH, YOU CAN SUBSTITUTE A MILD
PORK SAUSAGE.

CHICKEN AND HAM STEW WITH BUTTERMILK DUMPLINGS

THIS IS CLASSIC COMFORT FOOD!

STEW

	VEGETABLE OIL	
1 1/2 LBS	BONELESS SKINLESS CHICKEN THIGHS, CUT IN HALF IF LARGE	750 G
	SALT AND BLACK PEPPER TO TASTE	
1	LEEK (WHITE AND PALE GREEN PARTS ONLY), CUT IN HALF LENGTHWISE, THEN THINLY SLICED	1
1	CELERY STALK, CHOPPED	1
1	CARROT, CHOPPED	1
1	GARLIC CLOVE, MINCED	1
1 1/2 TBSP	ALL-PURPOSE FLOUR	22 ML
4 OZ	HAM, CUT INTO 1/2-INCH (1 CM) PIECES	125 G
1/2 TSP	DRIED SAGE	2 ML
1/4 TSP	DRIED ROSEMARY	1 ML
4 CUPS	BASIC CHICKEN STOCK (PAGE 28) OR READY-TO-USE CHICKEN BROTH	1 L
1/4 CUP	SHREDDED SHARP (OLD) CHEDDAR CHEESE	60 ML
1/2 CUP	FROZEN PEAS	125 ML

BUTTERMILK DUMPLINGS

1 1/2 CUPS	ALL-PURPOSE FLOUR	375 ML
1 1/2 TSP	BAKING POWDER	7 ML
1/8 TSP	BAKING SODA	0.5 ML
1/4 TSP	SALT	1 ML
1 1/2 TBSP	BUTTER, MELTED	22 ML
1/2 CUP + 2 TBSP	BUTTERMILK, AT ROOM TEMPERATURE	155 ML
3 TBSP	FINELY CHOPPED FRESH PARSLEY	45 ML

STEW: IN A LARGE SAUTÉ PAN OR DUTCH OVEN, HEAT A DRIZZLE OF OIL OVER MEDIUM HEAT. SEASON CHICKEN WITH SALT AND PEPPER. WORKING IN BATCHES, COOK CHICKEN, TURNING, UNTIL BROWNED ON ALL SIDES. TRANSFER CHICKEN TO A PLATE. ADD LEEK, CELERY, CARROT AND A DRIZZLE OF WATER TO THE PAN; COVER AND SWEAT FOR 3 MINUTES. SCRAPE UP BROWNED BITS AND COOK, UNCOVERED, UNTIL VEGETABLES ARE NEARLY SOFTENED, ABOUT 3 MINUTES. STIR IN GARLIC AND FLOUR; COOK, STIRRING, FOR 2 MINUTES.

RETURN CHICKEN TO PAN AND STIR IN HAM, SAGE, ROSEMARY AND STOCK; BRING TO A SIMMER. REDUCE HEAT AND SIMMER, STIRRING OCCASIONALLY, FOR 30 OR 40 MINUTES OR UNTIL LIQUID IN PAN HAS REDUCED BY ABOUT A QUARTER AND EVERYTHING IS COOKED THROUGH. TRANSFER CHICKEN TO A PLATE AND PULL EACH PIECE INTO 2 OR 3 PIECES WITH TWO FORKS. RETURN CHICKEN TO STEW AND STIR IN CHEESE.

DUMPLINGS: MEANWHILE, IN A MEDIUM BOWL, STIR TOGETHER FLOUR, BAKING POWDER, BAKING SODA AND SALT. STIR BUTTER INTO BUTTERMILK, THEN POUR INTO FLOUR MIXTURE. ADD PARSLEY AND STIR UNTIL JUST COMBINED. DROP BATTER IN SPOONFULS ON TOP OF COOKED STEW, COVER AND COOK (WITHOUT PEEKING!) FOR 15 MINUTES. USE A TESTER TO SEE IF DUMPLINGS ARE COOKED THROUGH; IF NOT, COVER AND COOK FOR ANOTHER FEW MINUTES.

WHEN THE DUMPLINGS ARE DONE, SPRINKLE PEAS OVER THE STEW, COVER AND COOK FOR 2 MINUTES. SERVES 6.

PEANUT BUTTER CURRY CHICKEN

THIS THAI-STYLE CURRY IS MILD ENOUGH FOR KIDS
TO ENJOY. SERVE OVER RICE.

	VEGETABLE OIL	
2	BONELESS SKINLESS CHICKEN BREASTS, CUT INTO 1-INCH (2.5 CM) CUBES	2
1	LARGE ONION, CHOPPED	1
2	GARLIC CLOVES, MINCED	2
1 TBSP	GRATED FRESH GINGER	15 ML
1 TBSP	THAI RED CURRY PASTE	15 ML
1	RED BELL PEPPER, CHOPPED	1
1	CAN (14 OZ/400 ML) COCONUT MILK	1
1/3 CUP	PEANUT BUTTER	75 ML
1 TSP	FISH SAUCE	5 ML
PINCH	HOT PEPPER FLAKES	PINCH
2 TBSP	LIME JUICE	30 ML

IN A LARGE SKILLET, HEAT A DRIZZLE OF OIL OVER MEDIUM
HEAT. ADD CHICKEN AND COOK, STIRRING, UNTIL BROWNED
ON ALL SIDES. TRANSFER CHICKEN TO A PLATE. ADD
A LITTLE MORE OIL TO THE PAN IF NECESSARY, THEN
ADD ONION AND SAUTÉ FOR 5 TO 10 MINUTES OR UNTIL
SOFT. ADD GARLIC, GINGER AND CURRY PASTE; SAUTÉ FOR
1 MINUTE. ADD RED PEPPER AND SAUTÉ FOR 2 MINUTES.
POUR IN COCONUT MILK, THEN STIR IN PEANUT BUTTER,
FISH SAUCE AND HOT PEPPER FLAKES.

RETURN CHICKEN AND ANY ACCUMULATED JUICES TO
THE PAN AND BRING TO A BOIL. REDUCE HEAT AND SIMMER,
STIRRING OCCASIONALLY, FOR 10 TO 15 MINUTES OR UNTIL
CHICKEN IS NO LONGER PINK INSIDE AND RED PEPPER IS
SOFT. STIR IN LIME JUICE. SERVES 4 TO 6.

CASSEROLES & SAVORY PIES

CAROL'S GREEN ENCHILADAS

ELIZABETH'S MOM MAKES A COUPLE OF BATCHES OF THESE ENCHILADAS WHENEVER HER SEVEN GRANDCHILDREN ARE OVER. SURE TO SATISFY EVEN THE PICKIEST OF EATERS (AND THEIR PARENTS, TOO).

2	BONELESS SKINLESS CHICKEN BREASTS	2
	SALT TO TASTE	
	COLD WATER	
	NONSTICK COOKING SPRAY	
2	GARLIC CLOVES	2
1/3 CUP	FRESH CILANTRO LEAVES	75 ML
1/3 CUP	FRESH PARSLEY LEAVES	75 ML
1 1/2 CUPS	SALSA VERDE (SEE TIP)	375 ML
1 TBSP	LIME JUICE	15 ML
1 CUP	SHREDDED MOZZARELLA CHEESE, DIVIDED	250 ML
6	10- TO 12-INCH (25 TO 30 CM) FLOUR TORTILLAS	6

ARRANGE CHICKEN IN A SINGLE LAYER IN A LARGE SKILLET OR POT. SEASON WITH SALT AND POUR IN ENOUGH COLD WATER TO COVER THE CHICKEN BY ABOUT 1 INCH (2.5 CM). BRING TO A BOIL OVER MEDIUM-HIGH HEAT. REDUCE HEAT AND SIMMER FOR 15 MINUTES OR UNTIL CHICKEN IS NO LONGER PINK INSIDE. REMOVE CHICKEN FROM THE POT, PAT DRY AND ROUGHLY CHOP OR SHRED INTO A LARGE BOWL.

PREHEAT OVEN TO 350°F (180°C) AND SPRAY A 13- BY 9-INCH (33 BY 23 CM) CASSEROLE DISH WITH NONSTICK COOKING SPRAY. IN A FOOD PROCESSOR, COMBINE GARLIC, CILANTRO, PARSLEY, SALSA AND LIME JUICE; BLITZ UNTIL

SMOOTH. ADD HALF THE SAUCE AND $\frac{1}{4}$ CUP (60 ML) CHEESE TO THE CHICKEN AND TOSS TO COAT. DISTRIBUTE CHICKEN MIXTURE EVENLY ALONG THE CENTER OF EACH TORTILLA AND ROLL CLOSED, TUCKING IN THE ENDS. ARRANGE ROLLED ENCHILADAS IN PREPARED CASSEROLE DISH. POUR THE REMAINING SAUCE OVER THE ENCHILADAS AND SPRINKLE THE REMAINING CHEESE ON TOP. BAKE FOR 25 MINUTES OR UNTIL CHEESE IS MELTED AND GOOEY. SERVES 4 TO 6.

TIP: SALSA VERDE (GREEN SALSA) IS AVAILABLE IN MOST GROCERY STORES. THE SALSA VERDE IN THIS BOOK HAS A DIFFERENT CONSISTENCY AND FLAVOR, AND WON'T WORK FOR THIS RECIPE.

I DON'T BELIEVE IN EATING ON AN EMPTY STOMACH.

JOHANNA'S QUINOA-STUFFED BUTTERNUT SQUASH

OUR FRIEND JOHANNA SHOWED UP AT A POTLUCK WITH A DELICIOUS STUFFED SQUASH TOPPED WITH CANDIED CASHEWS. SHE MADE IT OFF-THE-CUFF, WITHOUT A RECIPE, SO WE HAD TO TRY TO RECREATE IT TO SHARE.

1	MEDIUM BUTTERNUT SQUASH	1
	OLIVE OIL	
1/2 CUP	QUINOA, RINSED	125 ML
	WATER	
	SALT	
1/2 CUP	CASHEWS	125 ML
1/4 CUP	SUGAR	60 ML
1/4 TSP	GROUND CORIANDER	1 ML
PINCH	GROUND ALLSPICE	PINCH
PINCH	CAYENNE PEPPER	PINCH
1	APPLE, PEELED AND CHOPPED	1
1/2 CUP	CRUMBLED FETA CHEESE	125 ML
2 TBSP	CHOPPED FRESH PARSLEY	30 ML
	JUICE OF 1/2 LEMON	
	BLACK PEPPER TO TASTE	

PREHEAT OVEN TO 375°F (190°C). CUT SQUASH IN HALF LENGTHWISE AND SCOOP OUT SEEDS. PLACE BOTH HALVES, CUT SIDE UP, ON A BAKING SHEET AND DRIZZLE WITH OIL. BAKE FOR 40 MINUTES OR UNTIL SOFT BUT NOT MUSHY. REMOVE FROM OVEN, LEAVING OVEN ON.

MEANWHILE, IN A MEDIUM SAUCEPAN, COMBINE QUINOA, 1 CUP (250 ML) WATER AND A PINCH OF SALT. BRING TO A BOIL OVER MEDIUM-HIGH HEAT, THEN REDUCE HEAT AND SIMMER, PARTIALLY COVERED, UNTIL WATER IS ABSORBED

AND QUINOA IS TENDER BUT NOT MUSHY, ABOUT 15 MINUTES. REMOVE PAN FROM HEAT. PLACE A FOLDED CLEAN TEA TOWEL UNDER LID AND LET STEAM FOR 10 MINUTES. REMOVE LID AND LET COOL COMPLETELY.

IN A MEDIUM SKILLET, COMBINE CASHEWS, SUGAR AND 2 TBSP (30 ML) WATER. BRING TO A BOIL OVER HIGH HEAT. REDUCE HEAT TO MEDIUM-LOW AND COOK, STIRRING OCCASIONALLY, FOR ABOUT 5 MINUTES OR UNTIL SUGAR GETS CRUSTY AROUND THE CASHEWS. STIR IN CORIANDER, ALLSPICE AND CAYENNE; INCREASE HEAT TO MEDIUM AND COOK FOR A COUPLE OF MINUTES SO THAT THE SUGAR MELTS AND CARAMELIZES, STIRRING CONSTANTLY TO LIFT THE MELTED SUGAR FROM THE BOTTOM OF THE PAN TO COAT THE CASHEWS. ONCE THE SUGAR HAS TURNED INTO A STICKY AMBER-COLORED SYRUP, REMOVE THE CASHEWS FROM THE PAN AND SPREAD OUT ON A BAKING SHEET LINED WITH PARCHMENT PAPER TO COOL.

STIR APPLE, FETA, PARSLEY AND LEMON JUICE INTO QUINOA AND SEASON WITH SALT AND BLACK PEPPER. IF THE CAVITIES OF THE SQUASH DON'T LOOK LARGE ENOUGH TO HOLD ALL OF THE QUINOA MIXTURE, HOLLOW THEM OUT A BIT. FILL EACH SQUASH CAVITY WITH HALF THE QUINOA MIXTURE, THEN TOP WITH CANDIED CASHEWS. RETURN TO THE OVEN AND BAKE FOR 20 MINUTES. SCOOP THE SQUASH AND QUINOA MIXTURE OUT OF THE SQUASH PEEL DIRECTLY ONTO GUESTS' PLATES TO SERVE.

SERVES 4.

DINNER FRITTATA

FRITTATA CAN BE MADE WITH ALMOST ANYTHING YOU HAVE IN THE FRIDGE AND WANT TO USE UP, SUCH AS ONIONS, SAUSAGE OR ASPARAGUS. JUST ENSURE THE INGREDIENTS ARE COOKED BEFORE COMBINING THEM WITH THE EGG MIXTURE.

6	LARGE EGGS	6
1/2 CUP	GRATED OR SHREDDED CHEESE (ANY KIND YOU HAVE ON HAND), DIVIDED	125 ML
1/4 CUP	CREAM (ANY KIND YOU HAVE ON HAND)	60 ML
	SALT AND BLACK PEPPER TO TASTE	
5	BACON SLICES, CHOPPED	5
2	SMALL POTATOES, COOKED AND CHOPPED	2
1 1/2 CUPS	SLICED MUSHROOMS	375 ML
1/2	BELL PEPPER (ANY COLOR) OR POBLANO PEPPER, CHOPPED	1/2
	OLIVE OIL	
1 1/2 CUPS	PACKED SLICED SWISS CHARD LEAVES	375 ML
2	GARLIC CLOVES, MINCED	2

PREHEAT OVEN TO 350°F (180°C). IN A LARGE BOWL, USE A FORK TO STIR TOGETHER EGGS, HALF THE CHEESE, CREAM, SALT AND PEPPER. DON'T OVERMIX; THE EGGS SHOULD BE COMBINED BUT STILL VERY THICK. SET ASIDE.

IN A LARGE OVENPROOF SKILLET (CAST-IRON IS PERFECT), COOK BACON OVER MEDIUM HEAT UNTIL CRISP. USING A SLOTTED SPOON, TRANSFER BACON TO A MEDIUM BOWL. DRAIN ALL BUT 1 TBSP (15 ML) FAT FROM PAN AND ADD POTATOES, MUSHROOMS, BELL PEPPER, SALT AND PEPPER. COOK, STIRRING, FOR 5 TO 10 MINUTES,

ADDING OIL IF NEEDED, UNTIL MOISTURE RELEASED FROM VEGETABLES HAS EVAPORATED AND VEGETABLES ARE BROWNED. TRANSFER TO THE BOWL WITH THE BACON. ADD CHARD TO THE PAN WITH A LITTLE MORE OIL AND COOK, STIRRING, UNTIL WILTED AND MOISTURE HAS EVAPORATED. ADD GARLIC AND COOK, STIRRING, FOR I MINUTE. RETURN BACON AND VEGETABLES TO PAN. ADD A LITTLE MORE OIL TO THE PAN IF IT'S DRY, THEN POUR IN EGG MIXTURE. COOK, WITHOUT STIRRING, UNTIL THE BOTTOM IS SET, ABOUT 5 MINUTES. SPRINKLE THE REMAINING CHEESE OVER TOP.

PLACE SKILLET IN OVEN AND BAKE UNTIL EGG IS BARELY SET, ABOUT IO MINUTES. CUT INTO WEDGES AND SERVE. SERVES 4.

BOXING DAY SEAFOOD CASSEROLE

THIS SAVORY SEAFOOD BAKE APPEARS AT ELIZABETH'S PARENTS' HOUSE EVERY YEAR FOR THEIR BOXING DAY FAMILY FEAST, BUT IT WORKS FOR A BUFFET DINNER ANY DAY OF THE YEAR.

2 TBSP	BUTTER	30 ML
	VEGETABLE OIL	
I LB	FROZEN RAW MEDIUM SHRIMP, THAWED AND DRAINED	500 G
I LB	FROZEN RAW BAY SCALLOPS, THAWED AND DRAINED	500 G
2	GARLIC CLOVES, MINCED	2
I	LARGE ONION, CHOPPED	I
I CUP	SLICED MUSHROOMS	250 ML
I 1/2 CUPS	LONG-GRAIN WHITE RICE	375 ML
I	CAN (28 OZ/796 ML) DICED TOMATOES, WITH JUICE	I
3 CUPS	BASIC CHICKEN STOCK (PAGE 28) OR READY-TO-USE CHICKEN BROTH	750 ML
2 TSP	WORCESTERSHIRE SAUCE	10 ML
1/2 TSP	GROUND TURMERIC	2 ML
1/2 TSP	CURRY POWDER	2 ML
PINCH	SAFFRON	PINCH
	SALT AND BLACK PEPPER TO TASTE	
I CUP	FROZEN PEAS	250 ML
2 TSP	LEMON JUICE	10 ML

IN AN OVENPROOF DUTCH OVEN OR A LARGE SAUCEPAN, MELT BUTTER WITH A DRIZZLE OF OIL OVER MEDIUM HEAT. SAUTÉ SHRIMP AND SCALLOPS FOR 4 TO 5 MINUTES OR UNTIL FIRM AND OPAQUE. USING A SLOTTED SPOON, TRANSFER SEAFOOD TO A PLATE AND LET COOL, THEN

COVER AND REFRIGERATE UNTIL READY TO RETURN TO THE POT.

DRAIN OFF ANY EXCESS LIQUID FROM THE POT. RETURN TO THE HEAT AND ADD ANOTHER DRIZZLE OF OIL. SAUTÉ GARLIC, ONION AND MUSHROOMS FOR 5 TO 10 MINUTES OR UNTIL ONION AND MUSHROOMS ARE SOFT. STIR IN RICE UNTIL COATED. STIR IN TOMATOES, STOCK, WORCESTERSHIRE SAUCE, TURMERIC, CURRY POWDER, SAFFRON, SALT AND PEPPER UNTIL EVENLY COMBINED. INCREASE HEAT AND BRING TO A BOIL. REDUCE HEAT, COVER AND SIMMER FOR 25 TO 30 MINUTES OR UNTIL RICE IS JUST TENDER BUT STILL HAS SOME BITE.

MEANWHILE, PREHEAT OVEN TO 350°F (180°C). REMOVE RICE MIXTURE FROM HEAT AND STIR IN SHRIMP, SCALLOPS, PEAS AND LEMON JUICE. COVER, PLACE IN THE OVEN AND BAKE FOR 30 MINUTES. SERVE IMMEDIATELY. SERVES 8 TO 10.

I LOVE YOU THE WAY YOU ARE.
BUT DON'T GET ANY WORSE.

BASIC BUTTER PIE PASTRY

THIS BASIC PIE PASTRY CAN BE USED IN ANY OF THE SAVORY OR SWEET PIES IN THE BOOK THAT CALL FOR A PASTRY CRUST.

1¼ CUPS	ALL-PURPOSE FLOUR	300 ML
1 TSP	SUGAR	5 ML
½ CUP	COLD BUTTER, CUT INTO BITS	125 ML
3 TBSP	ICE WATER (APPROX.)	45 ML
1 TSP	WHITE VINEGAR OR LEMON JUICE (OPTIONAL)	5 ML

IN A LARGE BOWL, COMBINE FLOUR AND SUGAR. USING YOUR HANDS OR A PASTRY CUTTER, WORK IN BUTTER UNTIL THE MIXTURE IS CRUMB-LIKE, WITH PEA-SIZE CHUNKS OF BUTTER SCATTERED THROUGHOUT. ADD ICE WATER AND VINEGAR (IF USING) AND STIR INTO FLOUR. ADD MORE ICE WATER AS NEEDED (NO MORE THAN AN EXTRA 1 TO 2 TBSP/15 TO 30 ML) AND STIR UNTIL THE DOUGH COMES TOGETHER, BEING CAREFUL NOT TO OVERWORK IT. PAT DOUGH INTO A FLAT DISC, WRAP IN PLASTIC WRAP AND REFRIGERATE FOR AT LEAST 30 MINUTES OR UP TO 3 DAYS. LET WARM AT ROOM TEMPERATURE FOR 20 TO 30 MINUTES BEFORE ROLLING OUT, TO MAKE IT EASIER TO HANDLE. UNBAKED DISCS OF DOUGH CAN ALSO BE FROZEN FOR UP TO 1 MONTH. MAKES PASTRY FOR A SINGLE PIE CRUST.

TIP: THIS RECIPE CAN EASILY BE DOUBLED IF YOU'RE MAKING A DOUBLE-CRUST PIE, OR CAN BE TRIPLED OR QUADRUPLED IF YOU WANT TO STOCKPILE PASTRY IN THE FREEZER FOR THE NEXT TIME YOU'RE CRAVING PIE.

LEEK, CHARD AND GRUYÈRE QUICHE

A VEGETARIAN QUICHE MAKES A NICE LIGHT MEAL WITH A WELL-DRESSED GREEN SALAD, OR SERVE IT IN SLIVERS ALONGSIDE A ROASTED CHICKEN OR BAKED HAM.

	BASIC BUTTER PIE PASTRY (OPPOSITE)	
2 TBSP	VEGETABLE OIL	30 ML
2 TBSP	BUTTER	30 ML
2	LARGE LEEKS (WHITE AND PALE GREEN PARTS ONLY), HALVED LENGTHWISE AND THINLY SLICED	2
3 CUPS	CHOPPED OR TORN SWISS CHARD (TENDER STEMS, TOO)	750 ML
I CUP	SHREDDED GRUYÈRE OR SHARP (OLD) WHITE CHEDDAR CHEESE	250 ML
3	LARGE EGGS	3
I CUP	HALF-AND-HALF (10%) CREAM	250 ML
	SALT AND BLACK PEPPER TO TASTE	

PREHEAT OVEN TO 350°F (180°C). ON A LIGHTLY FLOURED SURFACE, ROLL PASTRY OUT INTO A 10-INCH (25 CM) CIRCLE AND TRANSFER IT TO A 9-INCH (23 CM) PIE PLATE. TRIM THE OVERHANG AND CHILL WHILE YOU MAKE THE FILLING.

IN A LARGE SKILLET, HEAT OIL AND BUTTER OVER MEDIUM-HIGH HEAT. SAUTÉ LEEKS UNTIL SOFT. ADD CHARD AND SAUTÉ UNTIL WILTED. REMOVE FROM HEAT AND LET COOL SLIGHTLY, THEN SCRAPE INTO PASTRY SHELL AND TOP WITH CHEESE.

IN A MEDIUM BOWL, WHISK TOGETHER EGGS, CREAM, SALT AND PEPPER. POUR OVER LEEK MIXTURE. BAKE FOR 30 MINUTES OR UNTIL FILLING IS PUFFED, GOLDEN AND SET. SERVE WARM, AT ROOM TEMPERATURE OR COLD.

SERVES 8.

BRITISH FISH PIE

FISH PIE IS A U.K. CLASSIC. IT HAS AS MANY VERSIONS AS THERE ARE COOKS MAKING IT — SOME INCLUDE SHELLFISH AND CREAM, SOME SLICED HARD-COOKED EGGS. WE FIND THIS VERSION DELICIOUSLY COMFORTING AND PLENTY RICH.

MASHED POTATOES

2 LBS	RUSSET POTATOES, PEELED AND CUT INTO 1-INCH (2.5 CM) PIECES	1 KG
1/8 TSP	SALT	0.5 ML
2 TBSP	MILK	30 ML
2 TBSP	BUTTER	30 ML

FILLING

12 OZ	SMOKED WHITE FISH (SUCH AS COD OR HADDOCK)	375 G
	COLD WATER	
2 CUPS	MILK	500 ML
1	ONION, PEELED AND CUT INTO EIGHTHS (KEEP ATTACHED AT ROOT END)	1
2	FRESH PARSLEY SPRIGS	2
2	BAY LEAVES	2
1/8 TSP	WHOLE BLACK PEPPERCORNS	0.5 ML
1 1/4 LBS	SKINLESS WHITE FISH (SUCH AS TILAPIA OR ROCKFISH)	625 G
3 TBSP	BUTTER	45 ML
2 1/2 TBSP	ALL-PURPOSE FLOUR	37 ML
1/4 CUP	DRY WHITE WINE	60 ML

TOPPING

1/4 CUP	PANKO OR OTHER FINE BREAD CRUMBS	60 ML
3 TBSP	GRATED PARMESAN CHEESE	45 ML

MASHED POTATOES: PLACE POTATOES IN A LARGE SAUCEPAN WITH SALT AND ENOUGH WATER TO COVER BY 1 INCH (2.5 CM). BRING TO A BOIL OVER HIGH HEAT. REDUCE HEAT TO MEDIUM AND BOIL GENTLY UNTIL FORK-TENDER, ABOUT 15 MINUTES. DRAIN, THEN MASH WHILE STILL WARM. MASH IN MILK AND BUTTER. SET ASIDE.

FILLING: SOAK SMOKED FISH IN ENOUGH COLD WATER TO COVER FOR 5 MINUTES, THEN DRAIN. PREHEAT OVEN TO 375°F (190°C). POUR MILK INTO A LARGE SAUCEPAN. ADD ONION, PARSLEY, BAY LEAVES AND PEPPERCORNS; BRING TO A SIMMER OVER MEDIUM HEAT. ADD BOTH SMOKED AND RAW FISH (FISH MAY NOT BE COMPLETELY SUBMERGED) AND COOK, PARTIALLY COVERED, FOR ABOUT 10 MINUTES OR UNTIL FISH FLAKES EASILY WHEN TESTED WITH A FORK. USING A SLOTTED SPOON, TRANSFER FISH TO A 12-CUP (3 L) DEEP-DISH CASSEROLE DISH AND FLAKE INTO BITE-SIZE PIECES. POUR POACHING MILK THROUGH A SIEVE AND RESERVE, DISCARDING SOLIDS.

IN SAME SAUCEPAN (GIVE IT A QUICK SCRUB), STIR TOGETHER BUTTER AND FLOUR; COOK, STIRRING, FOR 2 MINUTES OVER MEDIUM HEAT. WHISK IN 1½ CUPS (375 ML) POACHING MILK AND BRING TO A BOIL. BOIL FOR 1 MINUTE OR UNTIL THICKENED, THEN STIR IN WINE. POUR OVER FISH AND STIR GENTLY. SPOON MASHED POTATOES OVER FISH.

TOPPING: IN A SMALL BOWL, COMBINE PANKO AND PARMESAN. SPRINKLE OVER MASHED POTATOES.

BAKE FOR 30 TO 40 MINUTES OR UNTIL HEATED THROUGH AND BUBBLING AT THE EDGES. SERVES 6.

ANNE'S HAM AND MUSHROOM TART WITH ROSEMARY AND GRUYÈRE

JULIE'S SISTER ANNE MAKES THIS SAVORY TART FOR EVERY CELEBRATORY MEAL — IT'S PERFECT AS AN APPETIZER OR ALONGSIDE THE MAIN EVENT.

	BASIC BUTTER PIE PASTRY (PAGE 160)	
2 TBSP	OLIVE OIL	30 ML
2 TBSP	BUTTER	30 ML
I	SMALL ONION, FINELY CHOPPED	I
8 OZ	CREMINI OR BUTTON MUSHROOMS, THINLY SLICED	250 G
I TBSP	CHOPPED FRESH ROSEMARY AND/OR THYME	15 ML
	SALT AND BLACK PEPPER TO TASTE	
2 TBSP	SHERRY (OPTIONAL)	30 ML
$1/2$ CUP	FINELY DICED HAM	125 ML
I CUP	SHREDDED GRUYÈRE, AGED GOUDA OR WHITE CHEDDAR CHEESE, DIVIDED	250 ML
2	LARGE EGG YOLKS	2
I	LARGE EGG	I
$3/4$ CUP	HEAVY OR WHIPPING (35%) CREAM	175 ML

ON A LIGHTLY FLOURED SURFACE, ROLL PASTRY OUT INTO A 10- TO II-INCH (25 TO 28 CM) CIRCLE — JUST BIGGER THAN A 9- OR 10-INCH (23 OR 25 CM) TART PAN WITH A REMOVABLE BOTTOM. FIT IT INTO THE PAN AND FOLD THE EDGES OVER INWARD, MAKING A DOUBLE-THICK CRUST AROUND THE SIDES OF THE PAN; TRIM TO ABOUT $1/8$ INCH (3 MM) ABOVE THE EDGE OF THE PAN. CHILL CRUST FOR 30 MINUTES. MEANWHILE, PREHEAT OVEN TO 375°F (190°C).

LINE CRUST WITH FOIL AND FILL WITH DRIED BEANS OR PIE WEIGHTS. BAKE FOR 12 TO 15 MINUTES OR UNTIL PALE GOLDEN. REMOVE WEIGHTS AND FOIL.

MEANWHILE, IN A HEAVY SKILLET, HEAT OIL AND BUTTER SET OVER MEDIUM-HIGH HEAT. SAUTÉ ONION AND MUSHROOMS FOR 7 TO 8 MINUTES OR UNTIL SOFT. ADD ROSEMARY, SALT AND PEPPER; SAUTÉ UNTIL ALL THE LIQUID HAS COOKED OFF AND MUSHROOMS ARE STARTING TO TURN GOLDEN. ADD SHERRY (IF USING) AND COOK UNTIL EVAPORATED. STIR IN HAM.

SPRINKLE HALF THE CHEESE OVER THE BOTTOM OF THE CRUST. COVER WITH MUSHROOM MIXTURE. IN A SMALL BOWL, WHISK TOGETHER EGG YOLKS, EGG AND CREAM (ADD A FEW EXTRA SNIPPETS OF THYME, IF YOU LIKE). POUR CUSTARD OVER MUSHROOM MIXTURE. SCATTER WITH THE REMAINING CHEESE. BAKE FOR 30 MINUTES, UNTIL SET AND GOLDEN. SERVE WARM, AT ROOM TEMPERATURE OR COLD. SERVES 8.

BEEF AND GUINNESS PIE

*THIS IS A NO-NONSENSE CLASSIC POT PIE,
SIMMERED WITH A CAN OR TWO OF DARK STOUT.
THIS PIE TAKES TIME, BUT ONCE YOU DIG IN,
YOU'LL REALIZE IT'S WORTH THE EFFORT.*

	VEGETABLE OIL	
1	LARGE ONION, CHOPPED	1
3	GARLIC CLOVES, MINCED	3
2	CARROTS, CHOPPED	2
2	CELERY STALKS, CHOPPED	2
1 CUP	SLICED MUSHROOMS	250 ML
2 LBS	STEWING BEEF, CUT INTO CHUNKS	1 KG
2 TBSP	ALL-PURPOSE FLOUR	30 ML
1 TBSP	FINELY CHOPPED FRESH ROSEMARY	15 ML
1 TSP	DRY MUSTARD	5 ML
2	BAY LEAVES	2
1 to 2	CANS (EACH 15 OZ/440 ML) GUINNESS OR A SIMILAR DARK STOUT	1 to 2
	BASIC BUTTER PIE PASTRY (PAGE 160)	
1	LARGE EGG, LIGHTLY BEATEN	1

PREHEAT OVEN TO 375°F (190°C). IN A LARGE OVENPROOF
SKILLET OR DUTCH OVEN, HEAT A DRIZZLE OF OIL
OVER MEDIUM HEAT. SAUTÉ ONION UNTIL SOFT,
ABOUT 5 MINUTES. ADD GARLIC, CARROTS, CELERY AND
MUSHROOMS; SAUTÉ FOR ABOUT 5 MINUTES, UNTIL
MUSHROOMS START TO SOFTEN. ADD BEEF AND COOK,
STIRRING, FOR 4 TO 5 MINUTES TO GET A BIT OF COLOR
ON THE MEAT. STIR IN FLOUR, ROSEMARY, MUSTARD
AND BAY LEAVES. POUR IN ENOUGH GUINNESS TO JUST
COVER THE BEEF AND BRING TO A BOIL. COVER, PLACE IN

THE OVEN AND COOK FOR 2½ HOURS OR UNTIL BEEF IS VERY TENDER.

ON A LIGHTLY FLOURED SURFACE, ROLL OUT PASTRY SO THAT IT'S SLIGHTLY LARGER THAN YOUR BAKING DISH (A 9-INCH/23 CM SQUARE SHALLOW BAKING DISH WILL WORK, OR A DEEP-DISH PIE PLATE — ANYTHING THAT WILL COMFORTABLY HOUSE THE STEW WITHOUT LEAVING TOO MUCH ROOM AT THE TOP ONCE FILLED). REMOVE STEW FROM OVEN, LEAVING OVEN ON, DISCARD BAY LEAVES AND TRANSFER STEW TO BAKING DISH. IF THERE IS A LOT OF EXCESS LIQUID IN THE STEW, LEAVE IT BEHIND IN THE PAN, AS YOU DON'T WANT YOUR PIE TO BE TOO SOUPY. PLACE PASTRY ON TOP AND PINCH THE EDGES AGAINST THE SIDE OF THE DISH TO SEAL, TRIMMING THE PASTRY AS NECESSARY. BRUSH THE TOP WITH EGG AND CUT A FEW SLITS WITH A KNIFE. BAKE FOR ABOUT 45 MINUTES OR UNTIL CRUST IS GOLDEN AND FILLING IS BUBBLING. SERVES 6.

MY SPOUSE AND I OFTEN LAUGH ABOUT HOW COMPETITIVE WE ARE. BUT I LAUGH MORE.

EASY TOURTIÈRE

THIS FRENCH CANADIAN CLASSIC IS TRADITIONALLY SERVED DURING THE HOLIDAYS, BUT IT'S PERFECT FOR FAMILY-STYLE MEALS YEAR ROUND. WE LIKE THE SIMPLICITY OF USING FROZEN PUFF PASTRY AS A LID, AND THE FACT THAT, ALTHOUGH IT SEEMS LIKE A CELEBRATORY DISH, IT'S MADE WITH INEXPENSIVE GROUND PORK AND BEEF.

	VEGETABLE OIL	
1	ONION, FINELY CHOPPED	1
1	CELERY STALK, CHOPPED	1
1	CARROT, CHOPPED	1
2	GARLIC CLOVES, MINCED	2
1 LB	GROUND PORK	500 G
8 OZ	LEAN GROUND BEEF	250 G
1 TSP	DRIED THYME	5 ML
1/2 TSP	DRIED SAGE	2 ML
	SALT AND BLACK PEPPER TO TASTE	
1/4 CUP	BASIC CHICKEN STOCK (PAGE 28), READY-TO-USE CHICKEN OR BEEF BROTH, OR WATER	60 ML
1/2	PACKAGE FROZEN PUFF PASTRY, THAWED	1/2
1	LARGE EGG, LIGHTLY BEATEN	1

PREHEAT OVEN TO 400°F (200°C). IN A LARGE SKILLET, HEAT A DRIZZLE OF OIL OVER MEDIUM-HIGH HEAT. SAUTÉ ONION, CELERY AND CARROT FOR 4 TO 5 MINUTES OR UNTIL SOFT. ADD GARLIC, PORK AND BEEF; COOK, BREAKING MEAT UP WITH A SPOON, FOR 5 TO 7 MINUTES OR UNTIL MEAT IS NO LONGER PINK. AS IT COOKS, SPRINKLE THE MEAT WITH THYME, SAGE, SALT AND

PEPPER. POUR IN STOCK AND COOK, SCRAPING UP ANY
BROWNED BITS FROM THE BOTTOM OF THE PAN, UNTIL
MOST OF THE MOISTURE HAS COOKED OFF. REMOVE
FROM HEAT. (THIS PART CAN BE DONE AHEAD OF TIME,
IF YOU LIKE; REFRIGERATE THE MIXTURE FOR UP TO
3 DAYS OR FREEZE FOR UP TO 6 MONTHS.)

SCRAPE THE MEAT MIXTURE INTO A PIE PLATE OR
OTHER BAKING DISH THAT WILL ACCOMMODATE IT. ON
A LIGHTLY FLOURED SURFACE, ROLL OUT PUFF PASTRY
SO THAT IT'S SLIGHTLY LARGER THAN THE BAKING DISH.
DRAPE PASTRY OVER THE FILLING, LETTING IT HANG OVER
THE EDGE OF THE DISH OR TUCKING IT IN AROUND THE
SIDES. BRUSH THE TOP WITH EGG AND CUT A FEW SLITS
WITH A KNIFE. BAKE FOR 25 TO 30 MINUTES OR UNTIL
PASTRY IS PUFFED AND GOLDEN. SERVES 4 TO 6.

TACO PIE

ALL THE COMFORT OF SHEPHERD'S PIE, BUT WITH SOME EXTRA ZIP AND A CORNBREAD CRUST. WE TOOK AN EXTRA 5 MINUTES TO MAKE THE CRUST FROM SCRATCH INSTEAD OF USING A PACKAGED CORNBREAD MIX.

1½ LBS	LEAN GROUND BEEF	750 G
2	GARLIC CLOVES, MINCED	2
1	GREEN BELL PEPPER, CHOPPED	1
1	ONION, CHOPPED	1
1	CAN (14 OZ/398 ML) TOMATO SAUCE	1
2 TSP	CHILI POWDER	10 ML
1 TSP	GROUND CUMIN	5 ML
½ TSP	PAPRIKA	2 ML
1 TSP	SALT	5 ML
PINCH	HOT PEPPER FLAKES	PINCH
⅔ CUP	ALL-PURPOSE FLOUR	150 ML
½ CUP	YELLOW CORNMEAL	125 ML
⅓ CUP	SUGAR	75 ML
1 TBSP	BAKING POWDER	15 ML
1	LARGE EGG, LIGHTLY BEATEN	1
⅓ CUP	MILK	75 ML
1	CAN (4½ OZ/127 G) CHOPPED GREEN CHILES	1
½ CUP	SHREDDED CHEDDAR CHEESE	125 ML

PREHEAT OVEN TO 375°F (190°C). IN A LARGE SKILLET OVER MEDIUM HEAT, COOK BEEF, BREAKING IT UP WITH A SPOON, FOR ABOUT 10 MINUTES OR UNTIL JUST A BIT OF PINK REMAINS. ADD GARLIC, GREEN PEPPER AND ONION; COOK, STIRRING, UNTIL BEEF IS NO LONGER PINK AND VEGETABLES ARE STARTING TO SOFTEN. ADD TOMATO

SAUCE, CHILI POWDER, CUMIN, PAPRIKA, SALT AND HOT PEPPER FLAKES; COOK, STIRRING OCCASIONALLY, UNTIL SAUCE BEGINS TO BUBBLE, THEN REMOVE FROM HEAT.

IN A LARGE BOWL, WHISK TOGETHER FLOUR, CORNMEAL, SUGAR AND BAKING POWDER. STIR IN EGG AND MILK UNTIL AN EVEN BATTER FORMS, THEN STIR IN CHILES.

SCRAPE BEEF MIXTURE INTO AN 8-CUP (2 L) BAKING DISH. SPOON CORNMEAL MIXTURE OVER TOP, THEN SPREAD TO EVENLY COVER THE BEEF MIXTURE. BAKE FOR 20 MINUTES OR UNTIL A TESTER INSERTED IN THE CENTER OF THE CRUST COMES OUT CLEAN. SPRINKLE WITH CHEESE AND BAKE FOR 3 MINUTES OR UNTIL CHEESE HAS MELTED. SERVES 4 TO 6.

SANDY'S MEAT PIES

SUE'S MUM, SANDY, HAS MADE THESE HAND PIES FOR YEARS. CHILLED, THEY MAKE EXCELLENT PICNIC FARE – THE TRICK IS TO NOT EAT THEM ALL WHILE THEY'RE FRESH OUT OF THE OVEN!

PASTRY

3 1/3 CUPS	ALL-PURPOSE FLOUR	825 ML
1/8 TSP	SALT (SEE TIP)	0.5 ML
1 1/4 CUPS	COLD BUTTER, CUT INTO BITS	300 ML
1/2 CUP	ICE WATER (APPROX.)	125 ML

FILLING

	VEGETABLE OIL	
2	ONIONS, FINELY CHOPPED	2
4	PLUM (ROMA) TOMATOES (ABOUT 10 OZ/300 G TOTAL)	4
2	GARLIC CLOVES, MINCED	2
1 LB	LEAN GROUND BEEF	500 G
1 TSP	SUGAR	5 ML
1/2 TSP	GROUND CORIANDER	2 ML
1/4 TSP	GROUND GINGER	1 ML
	SALT AND BLACK PEPPER TO TASTE	
2 TBSP	FINELY CHOPPED FRESH PARSLEY	30 ML
1/3 CUP	CHOPPED PIMENTO-STUFFED GREEN OLIVES	75 ML
1	LARGE EGG	1
1 TSP	WATER	5 ML

PASTRY: IN A LARGE BOWL, COMBINE FLOUR AND SALT. USING YOUR HANDS OR A PASTRY CUTTER, WORK IN BUTTER UNTIL LUMPS ARE ABOUT THE SIZE OF PEAS.

DRIZZLE ICE WATER OVER FLOUR MIXTURE AND TOSS TOGETHER. GATHER DOUGH WITH YOUR HANDS UNTIL IT JUST CLUMPS TOGETHER — IF NEEDED, DRIZZLE SMALL AMOUNTS OF EXTRA ICE WATER ONTO DRY AREAS. FORM INTO 2 EQUAL DISCS, WRAP IN PLASTIC WRAP AND REFRIGERATE FOR AT LEAST 30 MINUTES OR UP TO 3 DAYS. LET WARM TO ROOM TEMPERATURE BEFORE ROLLING OUT.

FILLING: IN A VERY LARGE SKILLET, HEAT A DRIZZLE OF OIL OVER MEDIUM HEAT. SAUTÉ ONION UNTIL SOFTENED AND BROWNED, ABOUT 7 MINUTES. MEANWHILE, CUT TOMATOES IN HALF AND SQUEEZE OUT SOME MOISTURE AND SEEDS (NO NEED TO BE THOROUGH). FINELY CHOP TOMATOES. ADD TOMATOES TO THE PAN AND COOK, STIRRING OCCASIONALLY, FOR 5 TO 10 MINUTES OR UNTIL MOST OF THE MOISTURE HAS EVAPORATED. ADD GARLIC, BEEF, SUGAR, CORIANDER, GINGER, SALT AND PEPPER. INCREASE HEAT TO MEDIUM-HIGH AND COOK, BREAKING BEEF UP WITH A SPOON, UNTIL BEEF IS NO LONGER PINK. STIR IN PARSLEY AND OLIVES. REMOVE FROM HEAT AND LET COOL TO ROOM TEMPERATURE.

PREHEAT OVEN TO 375°F (190°C), WITH ONE RACK PLACED IN THE UPPER THIRD AND ONE IN THE LOWER THIRD. CUT EACH DISC OF DOUGH IN HALF, THEN CUT EACH HALF INTO 5 EQUAL PORTIONS (MAKING 20 IN TOTAL). ROLL DOUGH PORTIONS INTO BALLS, EVENING THEM OUT IN SIZE. ROLL OUT 1 BALL INTO A 6-INCH (15 CM) CIRCLE. PLACE 2 TBSP (30 ML) FILLING SLIGHTLY OFF-CENTER,

CONTINUED...

THEN FOLD PASTRY OVER FILLING TO MAKE A HALF-MOON SHAPE. STARTING AT ONE CORNER, ROLL THE SEAM OVER ITSELF AND PINCH CLOSED. PLACE ON A BAKING SHEET LINED WITH PARCHMENT PAPER. REPEAT WITH THE REMAINING DOUGH BALLS AND FILLING, DIVIDING PIES BETWEEN 2 BAKING SHEETS, SPACING THEM EVENLY.

IN A SMALL BOWL, WHISK TOGETHER EGG AND WATER. BRUSH PIES WITH EGG WASH AND CUT 3 SMALL SLITS IN EACH PIE TO LET STEAM ESCAPE. BAKE FOR 40 TO 50 MINUTES, SWITCHING BAKING SHEETS HALFWAY THROUGH, UNTIL PIES ARE GOLDEN AND CRISP. SERVE IMMEDIATELY OR LET COOL AND REFRIGERATE IN AN AIRTIGHT CONTAINER FOR UP TO 3 DAYS. MAKES 20 MEAT PIES. ALLOW 2 TO 3 PER PERSON.

TIP: IF USING UNSALTED BUTTER TO MAKE THE PASTRY, INCREASE THE SALT TO $3/4$ TSP (3 ML).

PIZZAS & PASTAS

PLANNING YOUR PIZZA NIGHT

WE HAVE A FEW DIFFERENT TYPES OF PIZZA HERE, AND SOME, LIKE BUTTER CHICKEN PIZZA (PAGE 186) AND STEAK AND BLUE CHEESE PIZZA (PAGE 190), REQUIRE A FAIR BIT OF COOKING AND PREP WORK BEFORE THEY GO IN THE OVEN. THESE RECIPES MAKE TWO LARGE PIZZAS. OTHERS ARE LESS INVOLVED, SO YOU CAN PLAY AROUND WITH SEVERAL DIFFERENT RECIPES AND GUESTS CAN SAMPLE THEM ALL. THESE RECIPES YIELD ONE PIZZA EACH.

WITH DOUGH AND TOPPINGS AND PIZZAS COMING OUT OF THE OVEN, THE EVENING USUALLY BECOMES ONE BIG KITCHEN PARTY — SOMETHING KIDS AND ADULTS CAN GET INTO TOGETHER. YAHOO!

TIP: SINCE SOME OVENS WON'T GO ANY HOTTER THAN 450°F (230°C), WE'VE TESTED ALL THE PIZZAS AT THAT TEMPERATURE. IF YOU CAN GO TO 550°F (290°C), BY ALL MEANS DO SO. COOKING TIMES WILL BE SHORTENED — START CHECKING AT ABOUT 7 MINUTES.

BASIC PIZZA DOUGH

EVERYONE SHOULD BE ABLE TO MIX TOGETHER A BATCH OF PIZZA DOUGH FROM SCRATCH — HOMEMADE PIZZA NIGHT IS A GREAT REASON TO GATHER, ANY NIGHT OF THE WEEK.

I CUP	WARM WATER	250 ML
2 TSP	ACTIVE DRY YEAST	10 ML
I TSP	SUGAR	5 ML
2½ to 3 CUPS	ALL-PURPOSE FLOUR	625 to 750 ML
2 TBSP	OLIVE OIL	30 ML
I TSP	SALT	5 ML
	ADDITIONAL OLIVE OIL	

POUR WARM WATER INTO A LARGE BOWL AND SPRINKLE WITH YEAST AND SUGAR; LET STAND FOR 3 TO 5 MINUTES, OR UNTIL FOAMY. (IF IT DOESN'T DO ANYTHING, TOSS IT OUT AND BUY SOME FRESH YEAST!)

ADD 2½ CUPS (625 ML) FLOUR, ALONG WITH THE OIL AND SALT, AND STIR UNTIL THE DOUGH COMES TOGETHER. ADD A LITTLE MORE FLOUR IF THE DOUGH IS TOO STICKY — IT SHOULD BE JUST TACKY. ON A LIGHTLY FLOURED SURFACE, KNEAD DOUGH FOR ABOUT 8 MINUTES, UNTIL SMOOTH AND ELASTIC. RETURN DOUGH TO THE BOWL, DRIZZLE WITH OIL AND TURN IT ALL OVER TO COAT. COVER WITH A TEA TOWEL AND SET ASIDE IN A WARM PLACE FOR AN HOUR OR UNTIL DOUBLED IN BULK.

MAKES ABOUT 1¼ LBS (625 G) OF DOUGH, ENOUGH FOR TWO 10- TO 12-INCH (25 TO 30 CM) PIZZAS.

BASIC PIZZA SAUCE AND GARLIC OLIVE OIL

THINK OF THESE AS YOUR PIZZA TOOL KIT. THE SAUCE WILL GIVE TOMATOEY RICHNESS, BUT LET THE MAIN INGREDIENTS DO THE TALKING. GARLIC OIL IS BRUSHED ONTO THE CRUST EITHER BEFORE OR AFTER BAKING, AND SOMETIMES TAKES THE PLACE OF THE TOMATO SAUCE ALTOGETHER.

BASIC PIZZA SAUCE

1	CAN (28 OZ/796 ML) WHOLE OR DICED TOMATOES	1
1/4 CUP	TOMATO PASTE	60 ML

PLACE TOMATOES IN A FINE-MESH SIEVE SET OVER A BOWL, BREAKING APART ANY WHOLE TOMATOES. GENTLY PRESS DOWN ON SOLIDS (USE JUICE FOR ANOTHER PURPOSE). LET STAND FOR 10 MINUTES, THEN TRANSFER SOLIDS TO A LARGE GLASS MEASURING CUP, ADD TOMATO PASTE AND USE AN IMMERSION BLENDER TO COMBINE. LEFTOVERS CAN BE FROZEN FOR A FEW MONTHS. MAKES ABOUT 3 CUPS (750 ML).

GARLIC OLIVE OIL

1/4 CUP	OLIVE OIL	60 ML
3	GARLIC CLOVES, MINCED	3

IN A SMALL SAUCEPAN, HEAT OIL OVER MEDIUM HEAT. ADD GARLIC AND COOK, STIRRING, UNTIL SIZZLING BUT NOT BROWNED, ABOUT 3 MINUTES. REMOVE FROM HEAT AND LET COOL. MAKES 1/4 CUP (60 ML), ENOUGH FOR 3 OR 4 PIZZAS. STORE LEFTOVERS IN AN AIRTIGHT CONTAINER IN THE FRIDGE FOR UP TO 3 DAYS.

RED SAUCE

WELL-LOVED ITALIAN FOOD WRITER MARCELLA HAZAN ORIGINALLY SHARED THIS SIMPLE (AND NOW ICONIC) FORMULA FOR A POT OF RED SAUCE — A SIMPLE STAPLE YOU CAN USE ON PIZZA OR PASTA, OR IN PASTA DISHES LIKE LASAGNA. WE'VE TWEAKED IT A BIT AND OFTEN MAKE IT IN THE SLOW COOKER.

2	CANS (EACH 28 OZ/796 ML) GOOD-QUALITY WHOLE TOMATOES (PREFERABLY SAN MARZANO-STYLE), WITH JUICE	2
1/3 CUP	BUTTER	75 ML
1	SMALL ONION, HALVED	1
	SALT TO TASTE	

IN A MEDIUM POT, COMBINE TOMATOES, BUTTER AND ONION. BRING TO A SIMMER OVER MEDIUM HEAT. REDUCE HEAT AND SIMMER FOR 45 MINUTES OR UNTIL TOMATOES AND ONION ARE VERY SOFT AND SAUCE HAS THICKENED. (PUT A LID ON IF YOU DON'T WANT ANY RED SPATTERS IN THE VICINITY OF THE POT.) STIR OCCASIONALLY, BREAKING UP THE TOMATOES AGAINST THE SIDE OF THE POT WITH YOUR SPOON. (ALTERNATIVELY, PUT EVERYTHING IN A SLOW COOKER, COVER AND COOK ON LOW FOR 4 TO 6 HOURS.)

FISH OUT THE ONION HALVES (OR LEAVE THEM IN AND PURÉE ALONG WITH THE TOMATOES) AND, IF YOU LIKE, BLEND UNTIL SMOOTH WITH AN IMMERSION BLENDER. MAKES ABOUT 4 CUPS (1 L).

TIP: SAN MARZANO-STYLE CANNED TOMATOES ARE PACKED IN TOMATO PURÉE INSTEAD OF WATER. IF YOU CAN'T FIND THEM, SWAP IN ANY JAR OF GOOD TOMATOES, PLAIN OR FIRE-ROASTED.

MARINATED TOMATO AND FETA PIZZA

THIS VEGETARIAN PIZZA USES MARINATED FRESH TOMATOES RATHER THAN PIZZA SAUCE.

	CORNMEAL OR ALL-PURPOSE FLOUR	
3 OR 4	PLUM (ROMA) TOMATOES (ABOUT 1 LB/500 G TOTAL)	3 OR 4
1 TBSP	RED WINE VINEGAR	15 ML
PINCH	DRIED OREGANO	PINCH
	SALT AND BLACK PEPPER TO TASTE	
	BASIC PIZZA DOUGH (PAGE 177) FOR 1 PIZZA	
	GARLIC OLIVE OIL (PAGE 178)	
1/2 CUP	CRUMBLED FETA CHEESE	125 ML
3/4 CUP	SHREDDED MOZZARELLA CHEESE	175 ML
	SLIVERED FRESH BASIL LEAVES	

IF YOU HAVE A PIZZA STONE, PLACE IT ON THE BOTTOM RACK OF THE OVEN. REMOVE THE UPPER RACK AND PREHEAT OVEN TO 450°F (230°C) OR AS HOT AS IT WILL GO (SEE TIP, PAGE 176). SCATTER A GENEROUS LAYER OF CORNMEAL OR FLOUR ON A METAL PIZZA PAN AND SET ASIDE.

CUT TOMATOES IN HALF AND SQUEEZE OUT JUICE AND SEEDS. SLICE AND PLACE IN A MEDIUM BOWL WITH VINEGAR, OREGANO, SALT AND PEPPER. LET MARINATE FOR 20 MINUTES, THEN DRAIN.

CONTINUED ON PAGE 181...

Roasted Squash Coconut Curry (page 140)
and Naan (page 244)

Leek, Chard and Gruyère Quiche (page 161)

Beef and Guinness Pie (page 166)

Sandy's Meat Pies (page 172)

ROLL DOUGH OUT INTO A 10- TO 12-INCH (25 TO 30 CM) CIRCLE AND TRANSFER TO PREPARED PAN. BRUSH WITH GARLIC OIL, THEN SCATTER TOMATOES OVER DOUGH. USING A RIGID METAL SPATULA, SLIDE THE PIZZA FROM THE PAN ONTO THE STONE (IF YOU DON'T HAVE A STONE, LEAVE THE PIZZA ON THE PAN AND PLACE ON THE LOWER RACK). BAKE FOR 5 TO 8 MINUTES OR UNTIL MOST OF THE MOISTURE FROM THE TOMATOES HAS EVAPORATED. REMOVE PIZZA FROM THE OVEN (USE THE SPATULA TO TRANSFER THE PIZZA BACK ONTO THE PAN) AND SCATTER FETA AND MOZZARELLA OVER TOP. RETURN TO THE OVEN AND BAKE FOR 7 TO 10 MINUTES OR UNTIL CHEESE IS MELTED AND BUBBLING. TRANSFER PIZZA FROM THE OVEN TO A WIRE RACK AND LET COOL FOR 1 MINUTE. TOP WITH BASIL. TRANSFER TO A CUTTING BOARD AND CUT INTO WEDGES. MAKES 1 PIZZA, SERVING 2.

THE BEST WAY TO GET RID OF KITCHEN ODORS?
EAT OUT.

ROASTED VEGETABLE PIZZA

WE WERE UNSURE WHERE A QUEST FOR A VEGAN
PIZZA WOULD TAKE US, BUT WE WERE GRATIFIED
TO FIND THIS BOTH EASY AND DELICIOUS.

1	RED BELL PEPPER	1
1	ONION, CUT IN HALF AND SLICED	1
2 TBSP	VEGETABLE OIL	30 ML
	SALT AND BLACK PEPPER TO TASTE	
2 TBSP	PINE NUTS, FINELY CHOPPED	30 ML
1 TSP	NUTRITIONAL YEAST (OPTIONAL)	5 ML
PINCH	GARLIC POWDER	PINCH
	CORNMEAL OR ALL-PURPOSE FLOUR	
	BASIC PIZZA DOUGH (PAGE 177) FOR 1 PIZZA	
	GARLIC OLIVE OIL (PAGE 178)	
3 TBSP	BASIC PIZZA SAUCE (PAGE 178)	45 ML

IF YOU HAVE A PIZZA STONE, PLACE IT ON THE BOTTOM
RACK OF THE OVEN AND PLACE THE UPPER RACK IN THE
MIDDLE OF THE OVEN. PREHEAT OVEN TO 400°F (200°C).
CUT RED PEPPER INTO STRIPS ABOUT 2 BY $\frac{1}{4}$ INCHES
(5 BY 0.5 CM). PLACE ON A RIMMED BAKING SHEET LINED
WITH PARCHMENT PAPER, ALONG WITH ONION, VEGETABLE
OIL, SALT AND PEPPER; TOSS TO COMBINE, THEN SPREAD
OUT IN A SINGLE LAYER. ROAST ON THE UPPER RACK
FOR 25 TO 30 MINUTES, STIRRING OCCASIONALLY, UNTIL
MOISTURE RELEASED FROM VEGETABLES HAS EVAPORATED
AND VEGGIES ARE QUITE BROWNED. LET COOL.

IN A SMALL BOWL, COMBINE PINE NUTS, YEAST (IF
USING), GARLIC POWDER AND A PINCH OF SALT. SET ASIDE.

REMOVE THE UPPER RACK AND INCREASE THE OVEN TEMPERATURE TO 450°F (230°C) OR AS HOT AS IT WILL GO (SEE TIP, PAGE 176). SCATTER A GENEROUS LAYER OF CORNMEAL OR FLOUR ON A METAL PIZZA PAN.

ROLL DOUGH OUT INTO A 10- TO 12-INCH (25 TO 30 CM) CIRCLE AND TRANSFER TO PREPARED PAN. BRUSH WITH GARLIC OIL, THEN SPREAD PIZZA SAUCE OVER DOUGH TO WITHIN $\frac{1}{2}$ INCH (1 CM) OF EDGE. SCATTER ROASTED VEGETABLES OVER SAUCE. USING A RIGID METAL SPATULA, SLIDE THE PIZZA FROM THE PAN ONTO THE STONE (IF YOU DON'T HAVE A STONE, LEAVE THE PIZZA ON THE PAN AND PLACE ON THE LOWER RACK). BAKE FOR 12 TO 15 MINUTES OR UNTIL CRUST IS SET AND BROWNED. USE THE SPATULA TO TRANSFER THE PIZZA BACK ONTO THE PAN (IF NECESSARY) AND ONTO A WIRE RACK; LET COOL FOR 1 MINUTE. SPRINKLE PINE NUT MIXTURE OVER PIZZA. TRANSFER TO A CUTTING BOARD AND CUT INTO WEDGES. MAKES 1 PIZZA, SERVING 2.

PIZZA BIANCA WITH SAUTÉED KALE AND CHICKEN

A WHITE PIZZA, OR PIZZA BIANCA, IS ONE MADE WITHOUT A TOMATO BASE. THE KEY IN THIS RECIPE IS TO KEEP THE CHICKEN A LITTLE UNDERDONE WHEN YOU SAUTÉ IT — IT WILL FINISH COOKING WHEN THE PIZZA IS IN THE OVEN.

	CORNMEAL OR ALL-PURPOSE FLOUR	
	VEGETABLE OIL	
6	LARGE KALE LEAVES, CHOPPED (RIBS DISCARDED)	6
	SALT AND BLACK PEPPER TO TASTE	
	WATER	
8 OZ	BONELESS SKINLESS CHICKEN BREAST, CUT INTO BITE-SIZE PIECES	250 G
1/4 TSP	DRIED ITALIAN SEASONING	1 ML
1	GARLIC CLOVE, MINCED	1
	BASIC PIZZA DOUGH (PAGE 177) FOR 1 PIZZA	
	GARLIC OLIVE OIL (PAGE 178)	
1 1/4 CUPS	SHREDDED MOZZARELLA CHEESE	300 ML

IF YOU HAVE A PIZZA STONE, PLACE IT ON THE BOTTOM RACK OF THE OVEN. REMOVE THE UPPER RACK AND PREHEAT OVEN TO 450°F (230°C) OR AS HOT AS IT WILL GO (SEE TIP, PAGE 176). SCATTER A GENEROUS LAYER OF CORNMEAL OR FLOUR ON A METAL PIZZA PAN AND SET ASIDE.

IN A LARGE SKILLET, HEAT A DRIZZLE OF OIL OVER MEDIUM HEAT. ADD KALE, SALT, PEPPER AND A DRIZZLE OF WATER; COVER AND COOK UNTIL KALE IS WILTED,

ABOUT 3 MINUTES. REMOVE LID AND COOK FOR 5 TO 8 MINUTES OR UNTIL LIQUID IS EVAPORATED AND KALE IS VERY TENDER. TRANSFER KALE TO A BOWL. INCREASE HEAT TO HIGH AND ADD A LITTLE MORE OIL TO THE PAN. ADD CHICKEN, ITALIAN SEASONING, SALT AND PEPPER; SAUTÉ UNTIL CHICKEN IS BROWNED ON ALL SIDES, ABOUT 5 MINUTES. ADD GARLIC AND COOK, STIRRING, FOR 1 MINUTE. REMOVE FROM HEAT.

ROLL DOUGH OUT INTO A 10- TO 12-INCH (25 TO 30 CM) CIRCLE AND TRANSFER TO PREPARED PAN. BRUSH GENEROUSLY WITH GARLIC OIL, THEN SCATTER KALE OVER DOUGH. DISTRIBUTE CHICKEN OVER KALE AND TOP WITH CHEESE. USING A RIGID METAL SPATULA, SLIDE THE PIZZA FROM THE PAN ONTO THE STONE (IF YOU DON'T HAVE A STONE, LEAVE THE PIZZA ON THE PAN AND PLACE ON THE LOWER RACK). BAKE FOR 12 TO 15 MINUTES OR UNTIL CRUST IS SET AND BROWNED AND CHEESE IS BUBBLING. USE THE SPATULA TO TRANSFER THE PIZZA BACK ONTO THE PAN (IF NECESSARY) AND ONTO A WIRE RACK; LET COOL FOR 1 MINUTE. TRANSFER TO A CUTTING BOARD AND CUT INTO WEDGES. MAKES 1 PIZZA, SERVING 2.

BUTTER CHICKEN PIZZA

YOU ALREADY LOVE BUTTER CHICKEN. YOU ALREADY LOVE PIZZA. BRINGING THE TWO TOGETHER JUST MAKES SENSE.

	VEGETABLE OIL	
4	BONELESS SKINLESS CHICKEN THIGHS, CUT INTO BITE-SIZE PIECES	4
1/2	ONION, FINELY CHOPPED	1/2
2	GARLIC CLOVES, MINCED	2
2 TBSP	CURRY PASTE	30 ML
I CUP	TOMATO SAUCE	250 ML
3/4 CUP	HALF-AND-HALF (10%) CREAM	175 ML
1/3 CUP	BUTTER	75 ML
PINCH	CAYENNE PEPPER	PINCH
	SALT TO TASTE	
	CORNMEAL OR ALL-PURPOSE FLOUR	
	BASIC PIZZA DOUGH (PAGE 177) FOR 2 PIZZAS	
2 CUPS	SHREDDED MOZZARELLA CHEESE, DIVIDED	500 ML
	FINELY CHOPPED BANANA PEPPERS OR BELL PEPPERS (OPTIONAL), DIVIDED	
	CHOPPED FRESH CILANTRO (OPTIONAL), DIVIDED	

IN A LARGE SKILLET, HEAT A DRIZZLE OF OIL OVER MEDIUM HEAT. SAUTÉ CHICKEN UNTIL BROWNED ON ALL SIDES, ABOUT 5 MINUTES. USING A SLOTTED SPOON, TRANSFER CHICKEN TO A PLATE. ADD MORE OIL TO THE PAN IF NECESSARY. SAUTÉ ONION UNTIL SOFT, ABOUT 5 MINUTES. ADD GARLIC AND CURRY PASTE; COOK, STIRRING, FOR I MINUTE. RETURN CHICKEN AND ANY

ACCUMULATED JUICES TO THE PAN, ALONG WITH TOMATO SAUCE, CREAM, BUTTER, CAYENNE AND SALT; BRING TO A BOIL. REDUCE HEAT AND SIMMER FOR 30 MINUTES OR UNTIL SAUCE HAS THICKENED. TRY TO SAVE THE BUTTER CHICKEN FOR THE PIZZA RATHER THAN EATING IT DIRECTLY OUT OF THE PAN (THIS WILL BE CHALLENGING).

MEANWHILE, IF YOU HAVE A PIZZA STONE, PLACE IT ON THE BOTTOM RACK OF THE OVEN. REMOVE THE UPPER RACK AND PREHEAT OVEN TO 450°F (230°C) OR AS HOT AS IT WILL GO (SEE TIP, PAGE 176). SCATTER A GENEROUS LAYER OF CORNMEAL OR FLOUR ON A METAL PIZZA PAN.

ROLL DOUGH OUT INTO TWO 10- TO 12-INCH (25 TO 30 CM) CIRCLES AND TRANSFER ONE CRUST TO PREPARED PAN. SPREAD HALF THE BUTTER CHICKEN OVER DOUGH, THEN SPRINKLE WITH HALF THE CHEESE AND, IF DESIRED, BANANA PEPPERS AND CILANTRO. USING A RIGID METAL SPATULA, SLIDE THE PIZZA FROM THE PAN ONTO THE STONE (IF YOU DON'T HAVE A STONE, LEAVE THE PIZZA ON THE PAN AND PLACE ON THE LOWER RACK). BAKE FOR 12 TO 15 MINUTES OR UNTIL CRUST IS SET AND BROWNED. USE THE SPATULA TO TRANSFER THE PIZZA BACK ONTO THE PAN (IF NECESSARY) AND ONTO A WIRE RACK; LET COOL FOR 1 MINUTE. TRANSFER TO A CUTTING BOARD AND CUT INTO WEDGES. REPEAT WITH THE REMAINING DOUGH, BUTTER CHICKEN AND TOPPINGS. MAKES 2 PIZZAS, SERVING 4 TO 6.

NEW-SCHOOL MEAT LOVER'S PIZZA

RIGHT, SO IN OUR BOOKS A NEW-SCHOOL MEAT LOVER IS A PERSON WHO LOVES THEIR MEAT ON THE HIGHBROW SIDE, WITH A SMATTERING OF BITTER GREENS FOR BALANCE. VOILA!

	CORNMEAL OR ALL-PURPOSE FLOUR	
	BASIC PIZZA DOUGH (PAGE 177) FOR 1 PIZZA	
1/4 CUP	BASIC PIZZA SAUCE (PAGE 178) OR RED SAUCE (PAGE 179)	60 ML
2 OZ	CALABRESE SALAMI, THINLY SLICED	60 G
1 CUP	SHREDDED MOZZARELLA CHEESE	250 G
	GARLIC OLIVE OIL (PAGE 178)	
	HANDFUL OF ARUGULA	
2 OZ	PROSCIUTTO SLICES, CUT INTO QUARTERS	60 G

IF YOU HAVE A PIZZA STONE, PLACE IT ON THE BOTTOM RACK OF THE OVEN. REMOVE THE UPPER RACK AND PREHEAT OVEN TO 450°F (230°C) OR AS HOT AS IT WILL GO (SEE TIP, PAGE 176). SCATTER A GENEROUS LAYER OF CORNMEAL OR FLOUR ON A METAL PIZZA PAN AND SET ASIDE.

ROLL DOUGH OUT INTO A 10- TO 12-INCH (25 TO 30 CM) CIRCLE AND TRANSFER TO PREPARED PAN. SPREAD PIZZA SAUCE OVER DOUGH TO WITHIN 1/2 INCH (1 CM) OF THE EDGE. DISTRIBUTE SALAMI EVENLY OVER SAUCE. TOP WITH CHEESE. USING A RIGID METAL SPATULA, SLIDE THE PIZZA FROM THE PAN ONTO THE STONE (IF YOU DON'T HAVE A STONE, LEAVE THE PIZZA ON THE PAN AND PLACE ON THE LOWER RACK). BAKE FOR 12 TO 15 MINUTES OR

UNTIL CRUST IS SET AND BROWNED AND THE CHEESE IS BUBBLING. USE THE SPATULA TO TRANSFER THE PIZZA BACK ONTO THE PAN (IF NECESSARY) AND ONTO A WIRE RACK. BRUSH EXPOSED CRUST WITH GARLIC OIL. SCATTER ARUGULA OVER HOT PIZZA, THEN PROSCIUTTO (PIECES CAN BE BALLED UP RATHER THAN FLAT) ON TOP OF ARUGULA. TRANSFER TO A CUTTING BOARD AND CUT INTO WEDGES. MAKES 1 PIZZA, SERVING 2.

TIP: YOU CAN USE MORE SAUCE IF YOU LIKE YOUR PIZZA SAUCY.

BECOMING VEGAN IS A BIG MISSED STEAK.

STEAK AND BLUE CHEESE PIZZA

STEAK, BLUE CHEESE AND CARAMELIZED ONIONS GO
TOGETHER PERFECTLY. PUT THEM ON A PIZZA AND
YOU ONLY HAVE TO SPRING FOR A SINGLE STEAK
TO FEED FOUR TO SIX PEOPLE!

2 TBSP	BUTTER, DIVIDED	30 ML
1 TBSP	OLIVE OIL	15 ML
2	LARGE ONIONS, HALVED AND SLICED	2
2 TBSP	BALSAMIC VINEGAR	30 ML
	SALT AND BLACK PEPPER TO TASTE	
12 OZ	BEEF STRIP LOIN (NEW YORK) STEAK	375 G
	CORNMEAL OR ALL-PURPOSE FLOUR	
	BASIC PIZZA DOUGH (PAGE 177) FOR 2 PIZZAS	
1 CUP	TRIMMED SPINACH LEAVES	250 ML
1/2 CUP	CRUMBLED BLUE CHEESE	125 ML
1 CUP	SHREDDED MOZZARELLA CHEESE	250 ML

IN A LARGE SKILLET, MELT 1 TBSP (15 ML) BUTTER ALONG
WITH OIL OVER MEDIUM HEAT. ADD ONIONS AND COOK,
STIRRING OCCASIONALLY, FOR ABOUT 45 MINUTES OR
UNTIL CARAMELIZED. WATCH THE HEAT AND REDUCE IT AS
NECESSARY — YOU WANT THE ONIONS TO TURN BROWN
FROM THE CARAMELIZATION PROCESS, NOT FROM THE
HEAT OF THE PAN. ONCE THE ONIONS ARE INCREDIBLY
SOFT, GOLDEN AND STICKY, ADD VINEGAR AND SCRAPE
ANY BROWN GOOEY BITS FROM THE BOTTOM OF THE
PAN. SEASON WITH SALT AND PEPPER AND REMOVE
FROM HEAT.

MEANWHILE, SEASON BOTH SIDES OF STEAK WITH SALT
AND PEPPER. HEAT ANOTHER SKILLET OVER HIGH HEAT,

THEN DROP IN THE REMAINING BUTTER. AS SOON AS THE BUTTER IS MELTED, ADD STEAK AND COOK, WITHOUT MOVING IT, FOR 3 MINUTES SO THAT A CRUST FORMS. FLIP THE STEAK OVER AND COOK FOR 3 TO 4 MINUTES OR UNTIL A CRUST FORMS ON THE OTHER SIDE. REMOVE STEAK FROM PAN AND LET REST FOR 10 MINUTES, THEN THINLY SLICE.

MEANWHILE, IF YOU HAVE A PIZZA STONE, PLACE IT ON THE BOTTOM RACK OF THE OVEN. REMOVE THE UPPER RACK AND PREHEAT OVEN TO 450°F (230°C) OR AS HOT AS IT WILL GO (SEE TIP, PAGE 176). SCATTER A GENEROUS LAYER OF CORNMEAL OR FLOUR ON A METAL PIZZA PAN.

ROLL DOUGH OUT INTO TWO 10- TO 12-INCH (25 TO 30 CM) CIRCLES AND TRANSFER ONE CRUST TO PREPARED PAN. DISTRIBUTE HALF THE CARAMELIZED ONIONS OVER DOUGH, FOLLOWED BY HALF THE STEAK SLICES, SPINACH, BLUE CHEESE AND MOZZARELLA. USING A RIGID METAL SPATULA, SLIDE THE PIZZA FROM THE PAN ONTO THE STONE (IF YOU DON'T HAVE A STONE, LEAVE THE PIZZA ON THE PAN AND PLACE ON THE LOWER RACK). BAKE FOR 12 TO 15 MINUTES OR UNTIL CRUST IS SET AND BROWNED. USE THE SPATULA TO TRANSFER THE PIZZA BACK ONTO THE PAN (IF NECESSARY) AND ONTO A WIRE RACK; LET COOL FOR 1 MINUTE. TRANSFER TO A CUTTING BOARD AND CUT INTO WEDGES. REPEAT WITH THE REMAINING DOUGH AND TOPPINGS. MAKES 2 PIZZAS, SERVING 4 TO 6.

QUICK TORTILLA PIZZAS

WHENEVER YOU GET HOME LATE AFTER A LONG DAY OUT, THESE ARE THE PIZZAS YOU'RE LOOKING FOR! THEY COME TOGETHER IN NO TIME (MUCH FASTER THAN ORDERING IN) AND STILL TASTE GREAT.

8	10-INCH (25 CM) FLOUR TORTILLAS	8
1/4 CUP	GRATED PARMESAN CHEESE	60 ML
1 CUP	BASIC PIZZA SAUCE (PAGE 178) OR RED SAUCE (PAGE 179)	250 ML
	PIZZA TOPPINGS OF YOUR CHOICE, SUCH AS PEPPERONI SLICES, SLICED MUSHROOMS, SPINACH, ETC.	
3 CUPS	SHREDDED MOZZARELLA CHEESE	750 ML

PREHEAT OVEN TO 400°F (200°C). PLACE 1 TORTILLA ON A BAKING SHEET. SCATTER 1 TBSP (15 ML) PARMESAN ON TOP, THEN TOP WITH A SECOND TORTILLA. SPREAD WITH 1/4 CUP (60 ML) PIZZA SAUCE, THEN ADD A FEW PIZZA TOPPINGS (SEE TIP). SCATTER WITH ONE-QUARTER OF THE MOZZARELLA. BAKE FOR 6 TO 10 MINUTES OR UNTIL CHEESE IS MELTED AND STARTING TO BUBBLE. REPEAT WITH THE REMAINING TORTILLAS, SAUCE AND TOPPINGS. MAKES 4 PIZZAS, SERVING 4 TO 6.

TIP: YOU CAN USE MORE SAUCE IF YOU LIKE YOUR PIZZA SAUCY.

TIP: IT'S IMPORTANT NOT TO OVERLOAD THESE PIZZAS WITH TOPPINGS, AS TORTILLAS ARE NOT AS STRUCTURALLY SOUND AS CONVENTIONAL PIZZA DOUGH.

VARIATIONS: USE 4 PITAS IN PLACE OF THE TORTILLAS, AND/OR USE SPINACH AND WALNUT PESTO (PAGE 265) IN PLACE OF THE TOMATO SAUCE.

QUICK AND DIRTY SPAGHETTI WITH GARLIC AND ANCHOVIES

THIS FLAVORFUL PASTA TAKES MINUTES TO MAKE — MAKE IT SUNDAY SUPPER-WORTHY BY BUYING THE VERY BEST OLIVE OIL, PARMESAN CHEESE AND ANCHOVIES YOU CAN FIND.

1 LB	DRIED SPAGHETTI	500 G
	SALT TO TASTE	
1/4 CUP	OLIVE OIL	60 ML
8	GARLIC CLOVES, THINLY SLICED	8
1	TIN (1.7 OZ/50 G) ANCHOVIES	1
PINCH	HOT PEPPER FLAKES	PINCH
1/2 CUP	GRATED PARMESAN CHEESE	125 ML

IN A LARGE POT OF BOILING GENEROUSLY SALTED WATER, COOK SPAGHETTI ACCORDING TO PACKAGE DIRECTIONS UNTIL AL DENTE.

MEANWHILE, IN A SMALL SAUCEPAN, HEAT OIL OVER MEDIUM HEAT. ADD GARLIC, ANCHOVIES AND HOT PEPPER FLAKES. REDUCE HEAT TO MEDIUM-LOW AND WATCH THE HEAT — YOU WANT THE SAUCE TO SIZZLE A BIT, BUT YOU NEED TO BE CAREFUL NOT TO BURN THE GARLIC. COOK, STIRRING REGULARLY WITH A WOODEN SPOON AND BREAKING UP THE ANCHOVIES UNTIL THEY MELT INTO THE OIL.

ONCE THE PASTA IS READY, POUR A LADLEFUL OF COOKING LIQUID INTO THE SAUCE, THEN DRAIN PASTA. RETURN PASTA TO ITS POT, POUR IN SAUCE AND STIR UNTIL PASTA IS EVENLY COATED. STIR IN PARMESAN AND SERVE IMMEDIATELY. *SERVES 4 TO 6.*

BAKED MAC AND CHEESE
(WITH BACON OR NOT)

HOMEMADE MAC AND CHEESE IS SPECIAL ENOUGH FOR THE MAIN EVENT, BUT ALSO MAKES A GREAT SIDE FOR ANYTHING FROM BAKED HAM TO CHILI (SERVE ONE OVER THE OTHER — REALLY). BAKE IT IN A LARGE CASSEROLE DISH OR DIVIDE IT AMONG SMALL BAKING DISHES FOR SINGLE SERVINGS.

12 OZ	DRIED ELBOW MACARONI	375 G
8	BACON SLICES, CHOPPED (OPTIONAL)	8
	VEGETABLE OIL (IF NOT USING BACON)	
1	SMALL ONION, FINELY CHOPPED	1
2	GARLIC CLOVES, MINCED	2
1/4 CUP	BUTTER	60 ML
1/4 CUP	ALL-PURPOSE FLOUR	60 ML
3 CUPS	MILK	750 ML
3 CUPS	SHREDDED SHARP (OLD) CHEDDAR CHEESE, AGED GOUDA CHEESE OR A COMBINATION	750 ML
	SALT AND BLACK PEPPER TO TASTE	

CRUMB TOPPING

2	SLICES WHITE SANDWICH BREAD, TORN INTO CHUNKS	2
1/4 CUP	GRATED PARMESAN CHEESE	60 ML
2 TBSP	BUTTER, MELTED	30 ML

IN A LARGE POT OF BOILING SALTED WATER, COOK PASTA ACCORDING TO PACKAGE DIRECTIONS UNTIL AL DENTE. DRAIN AND RETURN TO THE POT. SET ASIDE.

MEANWHILE, IN A HEAVY SKILLET OR MEDIUM SAUCEPAN, COOK BACON (IF USING) AND ONION OVER

MEDIUM-HIGH HEAT FOR 7 TO 8 MINUTES OR UNTIL BACON IS CRISP AND ONION IS STARTING TO TURN GOLDEN. (IF NOT USING BACON, SIMPLY SAUTÉ THE ONION IN OIL.) ADD GARLIC AND COOK FOR 1 MINUTE. DRAIN OFF ANY EXCESS FAT AND ADD ONION MIXTURE TO THE PASTA.

RETURN SKILLET TO MEDIUM HEAT AND ADD BUTTER. WHEN THE FOAM SUBSIDES, ADD FLOUR AND COOK, STIRRING, FOR 1 MINUTE. WHISK IN MILK AND BRING TO A BOIL, WHISKING OFTEN. REDUCE HEAT AND SIMMER GENTLY, STIRRING CONSTANTLY, FOR 1 TO 2 MINUTES OR UNTIL THICKENED. STIR IN CHEESE, REMOVE FROM HEAT AND STIR UNTIL CHEESE MELTS AND SAUCE IS SMOOTH. SEASON WITH SALT AND PEPPER. ADD CHEESE SAUCE TO THE PASTA MIXTURE, STIRRING TO COMBINE.

TOPPING: PREHEAT OVEN TO 350°F (180°C). IN A FOOD PROCESSOR, PULSE BREAD TO CRUMBS. ADD PARMESAN AND BUTTER; PULSE TO BLEND WELL.

POUR PASTA MIXTURE INTO A 13- BY 9-INCH (33 BY 23 CM) OR SIMILAR BAKING DISH AND SCATTER WITH TOPPING. BAKE FOR 45 MINUTES, UNTIL GOLDEN AND BUBBLY AROUND THE EDGES. SERVES 6.

ROASTED SQUASH AND RICOTTA RAVIOLI

RAVIOLI IS SIMPLE TO MAKE USING WONTON WRAPPERS, AND FILLING AND PINCHING THEM CLOSED IS A GREAT ACTIVITY FOR KIDS TO TAKE ON IN THE KITCHEN.

1	SMALL BUTTERNUT SQUASH	1
	VEGETABLE OIL	
1 CUP	RICOTTA CHEESE	250 ML
1 TBSP	PURE MAPLE SYRUP	15 ML
	SALT AND BLACK PEPPER TO TASTE	
1/2	PACKAGE (1 LB/500 G) WONTON WRAPPERS, THAWED IF FROZEN	1/2
	SMALL DISH OF WATER	
	TOMATO SAUCE OR MELTED BUTTER	

PREHEAT OVEN TO 400°F (200°C). TRIM STEM OFF SQUASH AND CUT SQUASH IN HALF LENGTHWISE. SCOOP OUT SEEDS, PLACE SQUASH, CUT SIDE UP, ON A RIMMED BAKING SHEET OR IN A BAKING DISH AND DRIZZLE WITH OIL. BAKE FOR 45 TO 60 MINUTES OR UNTIL SOFT. SET ASIDE UNTIL COOL ENOUGH TO HANDLE.

SCOOP COOLED ROASTED SQUASH INTO A BOWL AND MASH IT, THEN STIR IN RICOTTA, MAPLE SYRUP, SALT AND PEPPER. PLACE A WONTON WRAPPER ON THE COUNTER AND PUT A SMALL SPOONFUL OF FILLING IN THE MIDDLE. DIP YOUR FINGER IN WATER AND RUN IT AROUND THE EDGES OF THE WRAPPER, THEN FOLD WRAPPER OVER, FORMING A TRIANGLE. PRESS DOWN TO SEAL THE EDGES, PRESSING OUT ANY AIR BUBBLES AROUND THE FILLING.

BRING A MEDIUM POT OF WATER TO A GENTLE BOIL OVER MEDIUM-HIGH HEAT. WORKING IN BATCHES, ADD RAVIOLI AND BOIL GENTLY FOR 3 TO 4 MINUTES OR UNTIL THEY FLOAT TO THE SURFACE. REMOVE RAVIOLI WITH A SLOTTED SPOON AND SERVE WITH TOMATO SAUCE OR MELTED BUTTER. SERVES 6.

TIP: TO MAKE RAVIOLI AHEAD, FREEZE IN A SINGLE LAYER ON A BAKING SHEET, THEN TRANSFER TO FREEZER BAGS. COOK THEM STRAIGHT FROM FROZEN.

I THINK IT'S WRONG THAT ONLY ONE COMPANY MAKES THE GAME MONOPOLY.
— STEVEN WRIGHT

SUNDAY NIGHT BOLOGNESE

THIS DELICIOUS WINE-SPIKED MEAT SAUCE ISN'T
DIFFICULT TO MAKE, BUT IT'S PERFECT FOR SUNDAYS
BECAUSE THE FLAVOR DEEPENS AS IT BUBBLES AWAY
ON THE STOVE.

	VEGETABLE OIL	
I LB	LEAN GROUND BEEF	500 G
3	GARLIC CLOVES, MINCED	3
I	ONION, CHOPPED	I
2	CARROTS, DICED	2
2	CELERY STALKS, DICED	2
I	CAN (28 OZ/796 ML) SAN MARZANO-STYLE TOMATOES (SEE TIP), WITH JUICE	I
1/2 CUP	DRY RED WINE (SEE TIP)	125 ML
1/2 CUP	WATER (APPROX.)	125 ML
I TSP	DRIED OREGANO	5 ML
PINCH	SUGAR	PINCH
PINCH	HOT PEPPER FLAKES	PINCH
	SALT AND BLACK PEPPER TO TASTE	
I LB	DRIED PASTA (SPAGHETTI OR RIGATONI ARE GOOD CHOICES)	500 G
	GRATED PARMESAN CHEESE	

IN A LARGE POT OR DUTCH OVEN, HEAT A DRIZZLE OF
OIL OVER MEDIUM-HIGH HEAT. COOK BEEF, BREAKING
IT UP WITH A SPOON, FOR 7 TO 10 MINUTES OR UNTIL
BEEF IS NO LONGER PINK. ADD GARLIC AND ONION; COOK,
STIRRING, FOR ABOUT 5 MINUTES, UNTIL ONION STARTS
TO SOFTEN. ADD CARROTS AND CELERY; COOK, STIRRING,
FOR ABOUT 5 MINUTES, UNTIL VEGETABLES START TO
SOFTEN. STIR IN TOMATOES, WINE, WATER, OREGANO,

SUGAR, HOT PEPPER FLAKES, SALT AND BLACK PEPPER; BRING TO A BOIL. REDUCE HEAT, COVER AND SIMMER, STIRRING OCCASIONALLY, FOR 1 HOUR. IF THE SAUCE IS TOO THICK, ADD SOME MORE WATER TO THIN IT OUT.

MEANWHILE, IN A LARGE POT OF BOILING SALTED WATER, COOK PASTA ACCORDING TO PACKAGE DIRECTIONS UNTIL AL DENTE. DRAIN PASTA AND SERVE WITH BOLOGNESE SAUCE OVER TOP. PASS THE PARMESAN AT THE TABLE. SERVES 4 TO 6.

TIP: SAN MARZANO-STYLE TOMATOES ARE HIGH-QUALITY TOMATOES PACKED IN TOMATO PURÉE — IF YOU CAN'T FIND THEM, USE A CAN OF REGULAR WHOLE TOMATOES AND ADD 1 TBSP (15 ML) TOMATO PASTE TO THICKEN YOUR SAUCE A BIT.

TIP: IF YOU DON'T WANT TO USE WINE IN THIS RECIPE, REPLACE IT WITH AN ADDITIONAL 1/2 CUP (125 ML) WATER AND A SPLASH OF RED WINE VINEGAR (OR TO TASTE).

TIP: BOLOGNESE SAUCE WAS MADE FOR FREEZING! DOUBLE THE RECIPE FOR A SECOND MEAL ON A BUSY WEEKNIGHT.

BAKED PASTA WITH MEATBALLS

MEATBALLS ARE JUST BETTER WHEN THEY'RE COVERED
WITH GOOEY CHEESE AND BUBBLING MARINARA SAUCE.

I LB	LEAN GROUND BEEF	500 G
12 OZ	BULK SAUSAGE (OR REMOVED FROM CASINGS)	375 G
1/4 CUP	DRY BREAD CRUMBS	60 ML
1/4 CUP	GRATED PARMESAN CHEESE	60 ML
1/2 TSP	DRIED OREGANO	2 ML
	SALT AND BLACK PEPPER TO TASTE	
I	LARGE EGG, LIGHTLY BEATEN	I
I TBSP	MILK	15 ML
	VEGETABLE OIL	
I	CAN (28 OZ/796 ML) SAN MARZANO-STYLE TOMATOES (SEE TIP, PAGE 199), WITH JUICE	I
3 TBSP	OLIVE OIL	45 ML
6	GARLIC CLOVES, THINLY SLICED	6
I CUP	WATER	250 ML
3 TBSP	TOMATO PASTE	45 ML
I TBSP	BALSAMIC VINEGAR	15 ML
I	FRESH BASIL SPRIG	I
I LB	DRIED PASTA (PENNE, RIGATONI OR OTHER SHORT PASTA)	500 G
12 OZ	MOZZARELLA CHEESE, ROUGHLY TORN OR CHOPPED, DIVIDED	375 G

IN A LARGE BOWL, COMBINE BEEF AND SAUSAGE, BREAKING
THEM UP WITH A SPOON. ADD BREAD CRUMBS, PARMESAN,
OREGANO, SALT, PEPPER, EGG AND MILK. MIX TOGETHER
WITH YOUR HANDS (MAKE SURE THEY'RE CLEAN!) SO
THAT EVERYTHING IS EVENLY COMBINED. FORM INTO

SMALLISH ($1\frac{1}{2}$- TO 2-INCH/4 TO 5 CM) MEATBALLS. IN A LARGE SKILLET, HEAT A GENEROUS DRIZZLE OF VEGETABLE OIL OVER MEDIUM HEAT. WORKING IN BATCHES AND REPLENISHING OIL AS NEEDED, BROWN MEATBALLS, TURNING THEM GENTLY WITH A FORK TO BROWN ON ALL SIDES. TRANSFER TO PLATES LINED WITH PAPER TOWELS TO ABSORB SOME OF THE OIL.

PREHEAT OVEN TO 350°F (180°C). POUR TOMATOES INTO A LARGE BOWL AND SQUISH THEM UP WITH YOUR HANDS; SET ASIDE. IN A LARGE SAUCEPAN OR SKILLET, HEAT OLIVE OIL OVER MEDIUM HEAT. ADD GARLIC AND COOK, STIRRING, UNTIL FRAGRANT — IT SHOULD SIZZLE, BUT BE CAREFUL NOT TO LET IT BROWN OR BURN. STIR IN TOMATOES, WATER, TOMATO PASTE AND VINEGAR. SEASON GENEROUSLY WITH SALT. NESTLE MEATBALLS IN THE SAUCE, MAKING SURE THEY'RE FULLY SUBMERGED. BRING TO A GOOD BUBBLE, THEN PLACE BASIL SPRIG ON TOP OF SAUCE AND LET IT WILT. REDUCE HEAT AND SIMMER FOR 20 MINUTES OR UNTIL SAUCE HAS THICKENED AND MEATBALLS ARE COOKED THROUGH. DISCARD BASIL.

MEANWHILE, IN A LARGE POT OF BOILING SALTED WATER, COOK PASTA ACCORDING TO PACKAGE DIRECTIONS UNTIL AL DENTE. DRAIN AND RETURN PASTA TO THE POT.

ADD SAUCE AND MEATBALLS TO THE PASTA AND STIR IN HALF THE MOZZARELLA. POUR INTO A 13- BY 9-INCH (33 BY 23 CM) GLASS BAKING DISH AND SCATTER THE REMAINING CHEESE ON TOP. BAKE FOR 30 TO 40 MINUTES OR UNTIL SAUCE IS BUBBLING AND CHEESE ON TOP IS GOOEY AND GOLDEN. SERVES 8 TO 10.

ALANA-ISH BAKED ZITI

OUR FRIEND ALANA MAKES THE BEST BAKED ZITI. WHILE SHE WOULDN'T GIVE US THE RECIPE FOR HER SECRET MEAT SAUCE (MAKING THIS RECIPE ONLY "ALANA-ISH"), SHE DID GIVE US A FEW TIPS ON MAKING A PERFECT VERSION OF THIS ITALIAN COMFORT FOOD: USE LOTS OF SAUCE, DON'T SKIMP ON THE FULL-FAT CHEESE AND LET IT BAKE LONG ENOUGH TO GET SOME NICE CRISPY BITS ON TOP.

	VEGETABLE OIL	
I LB	LEAN GROUND BEEF	500 G
13 OZ	BULK ITALIAN SAUSAGE (OR REMOVED FROM CASINGS)	400 G
2	GARLIC CLOVES, MINCED	2
I	LARGE ONION, FINELY CHOPPED	I
5 CUPS	TOMATO SAUCE	1.25 L
I TSP	DRIED OREGANO	5 ML
PINCH	HOT PEPPER FLAKES	PINCH
	SALT TO TASTE	
1/2 CUP	DRY RED WINE	125 ML
I TBSP	BUTTER	15 ML
I LB	DRIED ZITI OR PENNE PASTA	500 G
I CUP	RICOTTA CHEESE	250 ML
1/2 CUP	GRATED PARMESAN CHEESE, DIVIDED	125 ML
2 CUPS	SHREDDED MOZZARELLA CHEESE, DIVIDED	500 ML

PREHEAT OVEN TO 375°F (190°C). IN A LARGE SAUCEPAN OR DUTCH OVEN, HEAT A DRIZZLE OF OIL OVER MEDIUM HEAT. ADD BEEF AND SAUSAGE; COOK, BREAKING THE MEAT UP WITH A SPOON, FOR 7 TO 10 MINUTES OR UNTIL NO LONGER PINK. ADD GARLIC AND ONION; COOK, STIRRING,

FOR 2 MINUTES, UNTIL ONION STARTS TO SOFTEN. ADD TOMATO SAUCE AND STIR TO EVENLY COAT THE MEAT. STIR IN OREGANO, HOT PEPPER FLAKES, SALT, WINE AND BUTTER; INCREASE HEAT AND BRING TO A BOIL. REDUCE HEAT AND LET THE SAUCE GENTLY BUBBLE AWAY, STIRRING OCCASIONALLY, WHILE YOU COOK THE PASTA.

MEANWHILE, IN A LARGE POT OF BOILING SALTED WATER, COOK ZITI ACCORDING TO PACKAGE DIRECTIONS UNTIL AL DENTE. DRAIN PASTA AND RETURN TO THE POT.

TURN OFF HEAT UNDER SAUCE AND LADLE HALF THE SAUCE OVER THE PASTA, STIRRING TO EVENLY COAT. IN A BOWL, COMBINE RICOTTA, HALF THE PARMESAN AND A PINCH OF SALT. FOLD RICOTTA MIXTURE INTO PASTA (YOU DON'T WANT TO FULLY INCORPORATE IT; THERE SHOULD BE SOME NICE VISIBLE GLOBS OF RICOTTA THROUGHOUT).

SPREAD HALF THE PASTA MIXTURE ALONG THE BOTTOM OF A 13- BY 9-INCH (33 BY 23 CM) GLASS BAKING DISH, PRESSING DOWN ON THE PASTA WITH A SPATULA TO SQUEEZE SOME OF THE AIR OUT. SPRINKLE WITH HALF THE MOZZARELLA AND TOP WITH THE REMAINING PASTA, ONCE AGAIN PRESSING EVERYTHING DOWN. POUR THE REMAINING SAUCE EVENLY OVER THE PASTA, THEN TOP WITH THE REMAINING MOZZARELLA AND PARMESAN. BAKE FOR 30 MINUTES OR UNTIL CHEESE IS BUBBLING AND BEGINNING TO GET CRUSTY ALONG THE EDGES. LET STAND FOR 15 MINUTES BEFORE SERVING. SERVES 8 TO 10.

TIP: FOR A VEGETARIAN VERSION, SIMPLY SKIP THE GROUND BEEF AND SAUSAGE (OR, IF YOU DON'T EAT RED MEAT, TRY USING GROUND CHICKEN OR TURKEY).

CHEESY SEAFOOD LASAGNA

FOR A TRULY SPECTACULAR DINNER, THIS
INDULGENTLY CREAMY, CHEESY LASAGNA IS
A SEAFOOD LOVER'S DREAM.

12	DRIED LASAGNA NOODLES	12
1/4 CUP	BUTTER	60 ML
1 TBSP	VEGETABLE OIL	15 ML
1	SMALL ONION, FINELY CHOPPED	1
2	GARLIC CLOVES, MINCED	2
1/4 CUP	ALL-PURPOSE FLOUR	60 ML
4 CUPS	HALF-AND-HALF (10%) CREAM OR 2% MILK	1 L
8 OZ	SKINLESS COD, HALIBUT OR OTHER WHITE FISH, CUT INTO BITE-SIZE PIECES	250 G
8 OZ	BAY SCALLOPS, TRIMMED OF HARD SIDE MUSCLES AND HALVED OR QUARTERED IF LARGE	250 G
8 OZ	SMALL SHRIMP, PEELED AND DEVEINED	250 G
1 CUP	GRATED PARMESAN CHEESE	250 ML
1/2 TSP	BLACK PEPPER	2 ML
3 CUPS	SHREDDED SHARP (OLD) WHITE CHEDDAR CHEESE, AGED GOUDA CHEESE OR A COMBINATION	750 ML

IN A LARGE POT OF BOILING SALTED WATER, COOK
LASAGNA NOODLES ACCORDING TO PACKAGE DIRECTIONS
UNTIL AL DENTE. DRAIN WELL.

IN A LARGE, HEAVY SKILLET, HEAT BUTTER AND OIL
OVER MEDIUM-HIGH HEAT. ONCE THE FOAMING SUBSIDES,
SAUTÉ ONION FOR 5 MINUTES OR UNTIL SOFT. ADD GARLIC
AND COOK, STIRRING, FOR 1 MINUTE. STIR IN FLOUR. WHISK

IN CREAM AND BRING TO A SIMMER. REDUCE HEAT AND COOK, WHISKING CONSTANTLY, FOR 1 TO 2 MINUTES OR UNTIL SAUCE HAS THICKENED. ADD FISH, SCALLOPS AND SHRIMP; COOK FOR 2 TO 3 MINUTES OR UNTIL SEAFOOD IS OPAQUE. STIR IN PARMESAN AND PEPPER. REMOVE FROM HEAT.

PREHEAT OVEN TO 350°F (180°C). BUTTER A 13- BY 9-INCH (33 BY 23 CM) GLASS BAKING DISH OR SIMILAR-SIZE CASSEROLE DISH — ONE THAT WILL ACCOMMODATE 4 LASAGNA NOODLES IN A SINGLE LAYER. SPREAD ABOUT $\frac{1}{2}$ CUP (125 ML) OF THE SAUCE (TRY TO LEAVE OUT CHUNKS OF SEAFOOD) OVER THE BOTTOM OF THE DISH. PLACE 4 LASAGNA NOODLES ON TOP. SPREAD ABOUT HALF THE SEAFOOD MIXTURE OVER THE NOODLES. PLACE ANOTHER 4 NOODLES ON TOP, THEN ADD MOST OF THE REMAINING SEAFOOD MIXTURE, HOLDING BACK ABOUT $\frac{1}{2}$ CUP (125 ML) SAUCE (AGAIN, WITHOUT MUCH IN THE WAY OF SEAFOOD). LAY THE FINAL 4 NOODLES ON TOP AND SPREAD WITH THE RESERVED SAUCE. SPRINKLE WITH SHREDDED CHEESE. BAKE FOR 1 HOUR OR UNTIL BUBBLY AND GOLDEN. LET STAND FOR 10 MINUTES BEFORE CUTTING AND SERVING. SERVES 8.

LEENA'S LASAGNA

ALTHOUGH SHE'S NOT ITALIAN, ELIZABETH'S MOTHER-IN-LAW, LEENA, LEARNED HOW TO MAKE THIS LASAGNA BY CAREFULLY WATCHING HER FAMILY FRIEND PIERINA COOK ONE AFTERNOON IN ROME MANY MOONS AGO — IN FACT, THIS IS THE FIRST TIME LEENA HAS SEEN THE RECIPE WRITTEN DOWN, SINCE SHE'S ALWAYS MADE IT BY MEMORY! FOR THIS CLASSIC ITALIAN LASAGNA, WE SKIP ADD-INS LIKE COTTAGE CHEESE OR MOZZARELLA AND GO STRAIGHT FOR AN ULTRA-RICH BÉCHAMEL SAUCE.

1	CAN (28 OZ/796 ML) WHOLE TOMATOES, WITH JUICE	1
	OLIVE OIL	
1	SMALL ONION, CHOPPED	1
2	GARLIC CLOVES, MINCED	2
1	CELERY STALK, DICED	1
1	RED BELL PEPPER, FINELY CHOPPED	1
1 LB	LEAN GROUND BEEF	500 G
1 CUP	SLICED MUSHROOMS	250 ML
1	CAN (5$\frac{1}{2}$ OZ/156 ML) TOMATO PASTE	1
1 TSP	DRIED OREGANO	5 ML
PINCH	HOT PEPPER FLAKES	PINCH
	SALT AND BLACK PEPPER TO TASTE	
	WATER OR DRY RED WINE (OPTIONAL)	
12	DRIED LASAGNA NOODLES	12
2 CUPS	MILK	500 ML
2$\frac{1}{2}$ TBSP	BUTTER	37 ML
2 TBSP	ALL-PURPOSE FLOUR	30 ML
$\frac{1}{4}$ TSP	GROUND NUTMEG	1 ML
$\frac{1}{2}$ CUP	GRATED PARMESAN CHEESE	125 ML

POUR TOMATOES INTO A LARGE BOWL AND SQUISH THEM UP WITH YOUR HANDS; SET ASIDE. IN A LARGE SAUCEPAN, HEAT A DRIZZLE OF OIL OVER MEDIUM HEAT. SAUTÉ ONION FOR ABOUT 5 MINUTES, UNTIL STARTING TO SOFTEN. ADD GARLIC, CELERY AND RED PEPPER; SAUTÉ FOR 1 TO 2 MINUTES OR UNTIL JUST STARTING TO SOFTEN. ADD BEEF AND COOK, BREAKING IT UP WITH A SPOON, UNTIL NO LONGER PINK. ADD MUSHROOMS AND COOK, STIRRING, FOR 2 TO 3 MINUTES OR UNTIL STARTING TO SOFTEN. STIR IN TOMATOES WITH JUICE, TOMATO PASTE, OREGANO, HOT PEPPER FLAKES, SALT AND BLACK PEPPER; BRING TO A BOIL. REDUCE HEAT, COVER AND SIMMER FOR 1 HOUR. IF THE SAUCE GETS TOO THICK, THIN WITH WATER OR WINE.

PREHEAT OVEN TO 350°F (180°C). IN A LARGE POT OF BOILING SALTED WATER, COOK LASAGNA NOODLES ACCORDING TO PACKAGE DIRECTIONS UNTIL AL DENTE. DRAIN WELL.

IN A SMALL SAUCEPAN, HEAT MILK OVER MEDIUM HEAT UNTIL STEAMING, WITHOUT BRINGING IT TO A BOIL. IN A MEDIUM SAUCEPAN, MELT BUTTER OVER MEDIUM HEAT. WHISK IN FLOUR AND COOK, WHISKING, FOR 3 TO 5 MINUTES OR UNTIL THE MIXTURE HAS A LITTLE BIT OF COLOR BUT ISN'T BROWN. GRADUALLY WHISK IN HOT MILK AND COOK, WHISKING CONSTANTLY, FOR ABOUT 10 MINUTES OR UNTIL THICKENED. STIR IN NUTMEG AND REMOVE FROM HEAT.

CONTINUED...

LEENA'S LASAGNA (continued)

SPREAD A SCANT LAYER OF TOMATO SAUCE IN THE BOTTOM OF A 13- BY 9-INCH (33 BY 23 CM) GLASS BAKING DISH OR A SIMILAR-SIZE CASSEROLE DISH. OVERLAP 4 NOODLES ON TOP. LAYER WITH ONE-THIRD OF THE TOMATO SAUCE, THEN ONE-THIRD OF THE BÉCHAMEL AND A GENEROUS SPRINKLE OF PARMESAN. REPEAT LAYERS TWO MORE TIMES, ENDING WITH PARMESAN. BAKE FOR 30 TO 45 MINUTES OR UNTIL LASAGNA IS BUBBLING. LET STAND FOR ABOUT 10 MINUTES BEFORE CUTTING AND SERVING. SERVES 6 TO 8.

TIP: THE TOMATO SAUCE CAN BE MADE A DAY IN ADVANCE AND STORED IN THE FRIDGE, AND AN UNBAKED LASAGNA CAN BE FROZEN AFTER ASSEMBLY. JUST MAKE SURE TO THAW IT SLIGHTLY BEFORE BAKING.

THE TROUBLE WITH BEING PUNCTUAL IS THAT
NO ONE IS THERE TO APPRECIATE IT.

SIDES

ASPARAGUS WITH LEMON BUTTER

THE LEMON BUTTER HERE IS VERY TANGY; IF YOU PREFER THINGS ON THE MILD SIDE, REDUCE THE LEMON JUICE BY HALF.

	GRATED ZEST OF 1/2 LEMON	
	GRATED ZEST OF 1/2 LEMON	
2 TBSP	LEMON JUICE	30 ML
1/4 CUP	BUTTER, DIVIDED	60 ML
	VEGETABLE OIL	
1 LB	ASPARAGUS, WOODY ENDS TRIMMED	500 G
	WATER	
	SALT TO TASTE (SEE TIP)	

IN A VERY SMALL SAUCEPAN SET OVER MEDIUM HEAT, BOIL LEMON JUICE FOR 5 TO 8 MINUTES, UNTIL IT FORMS A THICK SYRUP. LET COOL SLIGHTLY. ADD HALF THE BUTTER AND STIR WITH A HEATPROOF SPATULA, SCRAPING UP ANY GELLED BITS OF LEMON JUICE UNTIL BLENDED. LET COOL COMPLETELY. TRANSFER TO A SMALL BOWL, AND ADD LEMON ZEST AND THE REMAINING BUTTER. MASH WITH A FORK TO COMBINE.

IN A LARGE SKILLET, HEAT A LITTLE OIL OVER MEDIUM HEAT. ADD ASPARAGUS AND A DRIZZLE OF WATER, COVER AND COOK UNTIL NEARLY TENDER, ABOUT 4 MINUTES. REMOVE LID AND COOK UNTIL WATER HAS EVAPORATED. SPRINKLE WITH SALT AND SERVE WITH A PAT OF LEMON BUTTER. SERVES 4.

TIP: FLAKY SALT WORKS WELL, IF YOU HAVE IT ON HAND.

ROASTED BROCCOLI WITH GARLIC AND PARMESAN

WE LOVE EATING OUR VEGGIES WHEN THEY TASTE THIS GOOD! THIS RECIPE HAS MADE BROCCOLI CONVERTS OUT OF A FEW DOUBTERS IN OUR LIVES.

I LB	BROCCOLI CROWN	500 G
2 TBSP	VEGETABLE OIL	30 ML
1/8 TSP	HOT PEPPER FLAKES (OR TO TASTE)	0.5 ML
	SALT AND BLACK PEPPER TO TASTE	
3	GARLIC CLOVES, MINCED	3
1/2 CUP	PANKO	125 ML
1/2 CUP	GRATED PARMESAN CHEESE	125 ML
I TBSP	BUTTER, MELTED	15 ML

PREHEAT OVEN TO 375°F (190°C). CUT BROCCOLI INTO LARGE FLORETS (ABOUT 3 TO 4 BITES EACH), WITH STEMS ON. PLACE BROCCOLI ON A RIMMED BAKING SHEET LINED WITH PARCHMENT PAPER. DRIZZLE WITH OIL AND TOSS WITH YOUR HANDS TO COAT WELL. SPRINKLE WITH HOT PEPPER FLAKES, SALT AND BLACK PEPPER, THEN TOSS AGAIN AND SPREAD OUT IN A SINGLE LAYER. BAKE FOR ABOUT 20 MINUTES OR UNTIL FLORET ENDS ARE TENDER BUT THICKER STEMS ARE STILL FIRM.

MEANWHILE, IN A SMALL BOWL, COMBINE GARLIC, PANKO, CHEESE AND BUTTER. REDUCE OVEN TEMPERATURE TO 350°F (180°C). SPOON CRUMB MIXTURE ONTO BROCCOLI. BAKE FOR 15 TO 20 MINUTES OR UNTIL BROCCOLI IS TENDER AND CRUMB TOPPING IS GOLDEN BROWN.

SERVES 4 TO 6.

TRIPLE-B RED CABBAGE

BALSAMIC. BACON. BRAISED. STICKY, TANGY AND SWEET, THIS IS CABBAGE FOR PEOPLE WHO THINK THEY HATE CABBAGE.

6	BACON SLICES, CUT INTO 1-INCH (2.5 CM) PIECES	6
1	ONION, HALVED AND THINLY SLICED	1
2	APPLES, PEELED AND CHOPPED	2
1	MEDIUM HEAD RED CABBAGE, CHOPPED	1
1/2 CUP	BALSAMIC VINEGAR	125 ML
1/4 CUP	WATER	60 ML
1 TSP	MUSTARD SEEDS	5 ML
	SALT AND BLACK PEPPER TO TASTE	
2 TBSP	BUTTER	30 ML

IN A LARGE POT OR DUTCH OVEN, COOK BACON OVER MEDIUM HEAT UNTIL STARTING TO BROWN. ADD ONION AND COOK, STIRRING REGULARLY, FOR 8 TO 10 MINUTES OR UNTIL ONION IS SOFT AND GOLDEN AND BACON IS STARTING TO GET CRISPY. ADD APPLES, CABBAGE, VINEGAR, WATER, MUSTARD SEEDS, SALT AND PEPPER, STIRRING CAREFULLY TO DISPERSE THE BACON AND ONIONS (BE CAREFUL, THE POT WILL BE PRETTY FULL). COOK, STIRRING OCCASIONALLY, FOR 5 TO 10 MINUTES OR UNTIL THE LIQUID STARTS TO BUBBLE. PLACE BUTTER ON TOP OF CABBAGE, COVER AND REDUCE HEAT TO LOW. COOK, STIRRING OCCASIONALLY SO THAT NOTHING CATCHES ON THE BOTTOM OF THE POT, FOR 45 TO 60 MINUTES OR UNTIL CABBAGE IS SOFT AND STICKY AND LIQUID IS MOSTLY ABSORBED. SERVES 6 TO 8.

CHEESY BRUSSELS SPROUTS

MOST VEGETABLES MAKE A DELICIOUS CREAMY, CHEESY GRATIN. IF YOU LIKE, RESURRECT LEFTOVER STEAMED OR ROASTED VEGETABLES BY PREPARING THEM THE SAME WAY, STARTING AT THE POINT WHERE YOU COMBINE THEM WITH THE FLOUR AND CREAM.

1 LB	BRUSSELS SPROUTS	500 G
1 TBSP	VEGETABLE OIL	15 ML
1 TBSP	BUTTER	15 ML
	SALT AND BLACK PEPPER TO TASTE	
1/4 CUP	WATER	60 ML
1 TBSP	ALL-PURPOSE FLOUR	15 ML
1 CUP	HALF-AND-HALF (10%) CREAM OR HEAVY OR WHIPPING (35%) CREAM	250 ML
1 CUP	FRESH BREAD CRUMBS	250 ML
1/2 CUP	GRATED PARMESAN CHEESE	125 ML
2 TBSP	BUTTER, MELTED	30 ML

PREHEAT OVEN TO 350°F (180°C). TRIM SPROUTS AND CUT IN HALF THROUGH THE STEM END. SET A LARGE SKILLET OVER MEDIUM-HIGH HEAT AND ADD OIL AND 1 TBSP (15 ML) BUTTER. WHEN THE FOAM SUBSIDES, ADD SPROUTS, SEASON WITH SALT AND PEPPER, AND COOK, STIRRING OFTEN, FOR 5 MINUTES OR UNTIL TURNING GOLDEN. ADD WATER, COVER AND COOK FOR 10 MINUTES OR UNTIL TENDER. SPRINKLE WITH FLOUR AND STIR TO COAT, THEN STIR IN CREAM. BRING TO A SIMMER AND COOK, STIRRING, UNTIL THICKENED. POUR INTO A BAKING DISH. IN A SMALL BOWL, STIR TOGETHER BREAD CRUMBS, CHEESE AND MELTED BUTTER; SPRINKLE OVER SPROUTS. BAKE FOR 20 MINUTES OR UNTIL GOLDEN. SERVES 4 TO 6.

CUMIN-ROASTED BRUSSELS SPROUTS

SPROUTS ARE THE NEW COOL THING ON RESTAURANT MENUS EVERYWHERE. IF YOU HAVE A FANCY FLAKY SALT IN THE HOUSE, THE EXTRA CRUNCH GOES BEAUTIFULLY HERE (BUT NO NEED TO GO BUY SOME — TABLE SALT IS JUST FINE TOO).

2 TSP	CUMIN SEEDS	10 ML
2 LBS	BRUSSELS SPROUTS	1 KG
3	LARGE SHALLOTS, CUT IN HALF AND THINLY SLICED	3
2	GARLIC CLOVES, MINCED	2
1/4 CUP	VEGETABLE OIL (APPROX.)	60 ML
	SALT AND BLACK PEPPER TO TASTE	

PREHEAT OVEN TO 425°F (220°C). IN A SMALL SAUCEPAN, TOAST CUMIN SEEDS OVER MEDIUM HEAT FOR 3 TO 5 MINUTES OR UNTIL FRAGRANT. SPREAD SEEDS OUT ON A PLATE AND LET COOL, THEN LIGHTLY CRUSH IN A MORTAR AND PESTLE (SEE TIP).

TRIM SPROUTS AND CUT IN HALF THROUGH THE STEM END. PLACE IN A LARGE BOWL AND ADD CRUSHED CUMIN SEEDS, SHALLOTS, GARLIC, OIL, SALT AND PEPPER. TOSS UNTIL SPROUTS ARE WELL COATED, ADDING A LITTLE MORE OIL IF NEEDED. SPREAD SPROUTS OUT IN A SINGLE LAYER ON A RIMMED BAKING SHEET LINED WITH PARCHMENT PAPER. ROAST, STIRRING ONCE OR TWICE, FOR 25 TO 30 MINUTES OR UNTIL TENDER AND WELL BROWNED IN PLACES. SERVES 6 TO 8.

TIP: IF YOU DON'T HAVE A MORTAR AND PESTLE, PLACE THE TOASTED CUMIN SEEDS BETWEEN TWO LAYERS OF

PARCHMENT PAPER ON A CUTTING BOARD AND ROLL OVER THEM WITH A ROLLING PIN OR EVEN A STRAIGHT-SIDED WINE BOTTLE. (THE PARCHMENT WILL ENSURE THAT YOUR NEXT PASTRY WON'T BE CUMIN-FLAVORED!)

SPICED ROASTED CAULIFLOWER

ROASTING IS A DELICIOUS WAY TO COOK CAULIFLOWER. IF YOU LIKE, OMIT THE CURRY POWDER AND ROAST THE FLORETS SIMPLY WITH SALT AND PEPPER, THEN FINISH THEM OFF WITH A SHOWER OF FRESHLY GRATED PARMESAN CHEESE.

1/4 CUP	VEGETABLE OIL	60 ML
1 TSP	CURRY POWDER OR PASTE	5 ML
1	MEDIUM CAULIFLOWER, SEPARATED INTO FLORETS	1
	SALT TO TASTE	

PREHEAT OVEN TO 425°F (220°C). IN A SMALL BOWL, STIR TOGETHER OIL AND CURRY POWDER. PLACE CAULIFLOWER IN A LARGE BOWL, DRIZZLE WITH CURRIED OIL AND TOSS TO COAT. SPREAD OUT IN A SINGLE LAYER ON A RIMMED BAKING SHEET LINED WITH PARCHMENT PAPER AND SPRINKLE WITH SALT. ROAST FOR 25 TO 30 MINUTES, STIRRING ONCE OR TWICE, UNTIL TENDER AND GOLDEN ON THE EDGES. *SERVES 4 TO 6.*

STICKY CARROTS

BE PATIENT WITH THESE CARROTS — IF YOU WAIT LONG ENOUGH, YOU'LL END UP WITH A PERFECT STICKY COOKED-ON GLAZE.

2 TBSP	BUTTER	30 ML
I TBSP	LIQUID HONEY	15 ML
I TSP	DRIED ROSEMARY	5 ML
I LB	CARROTS, CUT INTO 2-INCH (5 CM) PIECES	500 G
I CUP	WATER	250 ML
	SALT AND BLACK PEPPER TO TASTE	

CHOOSE A SAUCEPAN IN WHICH THE CARROTS CAN SIT SNUGLY IN A SINGLE LAYER ALONG THE BOTTOM (BUT DON'T PUT THEM IN THE PAN QUITE YET). PLACE THE PAN OVER MEDIUM HEAT AND MELT BUTTER WITH HONEY AND ROSEMARY. ADD CARROTS AND WATER, AND SEASON WITH SALT AND PEPPER. INCREASE HEAT AND BRING TO A BOIL. REDUCE HEAT TO LOW AND SIMMER UNTIL THE LIQUID HAS BOILED OFF, ABOUT 40 MINUTES. THERE SHOULD BE A THIN LAYER OF STICKY GOO AT THE BOTTOM OF THE PAN; CONTINUE COOKING, WITHOUT STIRRING, UNTIL CARROTS ARE BROWN AND STICKY, BUT NOT BURNT. TIP CARROTS AND ANY REMAINING GOO INTO A BOWL. SERVES 4 TO 6.

HOW CAN YOU TELL WHEN SOUR CREAM GOES BAD?

Roasted Squash and Ricotta Ravioli (page 196)

Sunday Night Bolognese (page 198)

Alana-ish Baked Ziti (page 202)

Cumin-Roasted Brussels Sprouts (page 214)

BROWN-BUTTERED CORN

BROWN BUTTER IS MAGIC — IT TRANSFORMS
EVERYTHING IT TOUCHES INTO FOOD GOLD. ALL YOU
HAVE TO DO IS HEAT BUTTER IN A PAN A LITTLE BIT
LONGER THAN YOU WOULD IF YOU WERE JUST MELTING
IT, AND IT TURNS INTO A DEEP, NUTTY SAUCE.

3	EARS CORN	3
1/4 CUP	BUTTER	60 ML
PINCH	CAYENNE PEPPER	PINCH
	SALT TO TASTE	

STRIP CORN KERNELS OFF THE EARS BY STANDING EACH
EAR UPRIGHT IN A SHALLOW BOWL AND SAWING THEM
OFF WITH A SHARP KNIFE. SET KERNELS ASIDE. IN A
MEDIUM SAUCEPAN, MELT BUTTER OVER MEDIUM HEAT
AND CONTINUE COOKING, STIRRING OFTEN, UNTIL BUTTER
IS A DEEP AMBER COLOR — IT SHOULD START TO SMELL
NUTTY, BUT NOT BURNT. ADD CORN, CAYENNE AND SALT.
(BE GENEROUS WITH THE SALT; IT'S WHAT MAKES THIS
DELICIOUS!) COVER, REDUCE HEAT TO MEDIUM-LOW AND
COOK FOR ABOUT 5 MINUTES OR UNTIL CORN IS TENDER.
SERVE HOT AND TRY NOT TO LICK THE EXCESS BUTTER
RIGHT OUT OF THE POT (OR AT LEAST WAIT UNTIL IT
COOLS). SERVES 6 TO 8.

FANCY-PANTS CAULIFLOWER AND CHEESE

CAULIFLOWER WITH MELTY CHEESE SAUCE IS A FAVORITE FOR MANY, BUT IT FEELS SO MUCH MORE GROWN-UP WHEN YOU DITCH THE PROCESSED CHEESE PRODUCT AND MAKE A FROM-SCRATCH MORNAY SAUCE. YOU DON'T EVEN HAVE TO LET YOUR GUESTS KNOW HOW EASY IT IS TO DO.

I	LARGE HEAD CAULIFLOWER, CUT INTO FLORETS	I
2 CUPS	MILK (APPROX.)	500 ML
6 TBSP	BUTTER, DIVIDED	90 ML
1/4 CUP	ALL-PURPOSE FLOUR	60 ML
I CUP	SHREDDED SWISS, WHITE CHEDDAR OR GOUDA CHEESE	250 ML
I TBSP	GRAINY MUSTARD	15 ML
1/4 TSP	CAYENNE PEPPER	I ML
I TSP	WORCESTERSHIRE SAUCE	5 ML
	SALT TO TASTE	
1/4 CUP	DRY BREAD CRUMBS	60 ML

PREHEAT OVEN TO 350°F (180°C). IN A LARGE POT OF BOILING SALTED WATER, COOK CAULIFLOWER FOR 5 TO 6 MINUTES OR UNTIL STARTING TO BECOME TENDER BUT NOT YET FULLY COOKED. DRAIN AND SET ASIDE.

MEANWHILE, IN A SMALL SAUCEPAN, HEAT MILK OVER MEDIUM HEAT. YOU DON'T WANT TO BRING IT TO A BOIL, JUST GET IT NICE AND WARM.

WHILE THE MILK IS WARMING, MELT 1/4 CUP (60 ML) BUTTER IN A SEPARATE, SLIGHTLY LARGER SAUCEPAN. REDUCE HEAT TO MEDIUM-LOW AND GRADUALLY WHISK

IN FLOUR. COOK FOR A MINUTE OR TWO, WHISKING CONSTANTLY (DON'T LET IT BROWN), UNTIL THICK AND SMOOTH. GRADUALLY WHISK IN WARM MILK AND COOK, WHISKING CONSTANTLY, UNTIL THE SAUCE HAS THICKENED AND HAS A CONSISTENT TEXTURE. IF IT IS TOO THICK TO EASILY WHISK, ADD A LITTLE MORE MILK. REMOVE FROM HEAT AND WHISK IN CHEESE UNTIL MELTED, THEN WHISK IN MUSTARD, CAYENNE AND WORCESTERSHIRE SAUCE. SEASON WITH SALT.

ARRANGE CAULIFLOWER IN A SINGLE LAYER IN A 13- BY 9-INCH (33 BY 23 CM) BAKING DISH. POUR CHEESE SAUCE OVER TOP (DEPENDING ON THE SIZE OF YOUR CAULIFLOWER HEAD, YOU MAY NOT WANT TO USE ALL OF THE SAUCE — BUT THE MORE SAUCE THE BETTER, IN OUR OPINION). SPRINKLE EVENLY WITH BREAD CRUMBS. MELT THE REMAINING BUTTER AND DRIZZLE OVER BREAD CRUMBS. BAKE FOR 25 TO 30 MINUTES OR UNTIL SAUCE IS BUBBLING AND CRUMBS ARE BROWNED. SERVES 4 TO 6.

GLAZED MAPLE GREEN BEANS

GREEN BEANS ARE GOOD. SWEET AND STICKY GREEN
BEANS WITH BACON AND WALNUTS ARE BETTER.

I LB	GREEN BEANS, STEM ENDS TRIMMED	500 G
	ICE WATER	
3	BACON SLICES, CUT INTO I-INCH (2.5 CM) PIECES	3
2	LARGE SHALLOTS, FINELY CHOPPED	2
I	GARLIC CLOVE, MINCED	I
1/4 CUP	PURE MAPLE SYRUP	60 ML
I TBSP	GRAINY MUSTARD	15 ML
PINCH	HOT PEPPER FLAKES	PINCH
1/4 CUP	CHOPPED WALNUTS	60 ML
	SALT AND BLACK PEPPER TO TASTE	

FILL A LARGE SAUCEPAN HALFWAY WITH WATER AND BRING
IT TO A BOIL. ADD GREEN BEANS AND COOK FOR 3 TO
4 MINUTES OR UNTIL SLIGHTLY TENDER WITH A BIT OF
CRUNCH. USING A SLOTTED SPOON, TRANSFER BEANS TO
A BOWL OF ICE WATER AND LET STAND FOR A COUPLE OF
MINUTES, THEN DRAIN AND SET ASIDE.

IN A SKILLET, COOK BACON OVER MEDIUM HEAT UNTIL
CRISPY. TRANSFER BACON TO A PLATE LINED WITH PAPER
TOWEL. POUR OFF ALL BUT I TBSP (15 ML) FAT AND RETURN
SKILLET TO THE STOVE. SAUTÉ SHALLOTS AND GARLIC
UNTIL SOFTENED. ADD MAPLE SYRUP, MUSTARD AND HOT
PEPPER FLAKES; LET BUBBLE UNTIL SLIGHTLY THICKENED.
ADD GREEN BEANS, STIRRING TO COAT WITH SYRUP, AND
COOK UNTIL BEANS ARE WARMED THROUGH. ADD WALNUTS
AND TOSS TO COAT. SEASON WITH SALT AND PEPPER.
SERVE IMMEDIATELY. SERVES 6 TO 8.

SICHUAN GREEN BEANS

THIS QUICK SIDE DISH IS SPICY AND ADDICTIVE —
A DIFFERENT WAY TO TREAT YOUR GREEN BEANS.

	VEGETABLE OIL	
	SESAME OIL (OPTIONAL)	
8 OZ	GREEN BEANS, STEM ENDS TRIMMED	250 G
4	GARLIC CLOVES, THINLY SLICED	4
2	GREEN ONIONS, CHOPPED	2
2 TSP	GRATED FRESH GINGER	10 ML
1 TSP	SUGAR	5 ML
1 TBSP	SOY SAUCE	15 ML
1/2 TSP	SRIRACHA (OR TO TASTE)	2 ML
	TOASTED SESAME SEEDS	

IN A HEAVY SKILLET, HEAT A DRIZZLE OF VEGETABLE OIL
AND SESAME OIL (IF USING) OVER MEDIUM-HIGH HEAT. ADD
GREEN BEANS AND COOK, STIRRING, FOR 3 TO 4 MINUTES
OR UNTIL STARTING TO TURN GOLDEN. ADD GARLIC, GREEN
ONIONS, GINGER, SUGAR, SOY SAUCE AND SRIRACHA; COOK
FOR 2 TO 3 MINUTES, TOSSING IN THE PAN, UNTIL GARLIC
IS GOLDEN AND BEANS ARE DEEP GOLDEN AND STICKY.
SERVE SPRINKLED WITH SESAME SEEDS. SERVES 4.

CLASSIC SCALLOPED POTATOES

SCALLOPED POTATOES ARE A SUNDAY DINNER CLASSIC.

1/4 CUP	BUTTER	60 ML
1/4 CUP	ALL-PURPOSE FLOUR	60 ML
3 CUPS	MILK	750 ML
1/2 TSP	DRIED THYME	2 ML
	SALT AND BLACK PEPPER TO TASTE	
4	MEDIUM RUSSET OR LARGE YELLOW POTATOES (ABOUT 3 LBS/1.5 KG), PEELED IF YOU LIKE AND THINLY SLICED	4
1	SMALL ONION, THINLY SLICED	1
1 CUP	SHREDDED CHEDDAR, GOUDA OR GRUYÈRE CHEESE	250 ML

PREHEAT OVEN TO 350°F (180°C). IN A MEDIUM SAUCEPAN, MELT BUTTER AND WHISK IN FLOUR UNTIL A THICK PASTE FORMS. WHISK IN MILK, THYME, SALT AND PEPPER. BRING TO A SIMMER AND COOK, STIRRING, FOR A MINUTE OR TWO, UNTIL THICKENED.

LAYER POTATOES AND ONION IN A BUTTERED 13- BY 9-INCH (33 BY 23 CM) BAKING DISH OR 8-CUP (2 L) CASSEROLE DISH, MAKING THREE LAYERS OF POTATOES AND TWO OF ONION. POUR SAUCE OVER TOP AND MOVE POTATOES AROUND WITH THE TIP OF A KNIFE TO LET SOME OF THE SAUCE OOZE BETWEEN THE LAYERS. COVER WITH FOIL AND BAKE FOR 45 TO 60 MINUTES (DEPENDING ON DISH SIZE). UNCOVER, SCATTER WITH CHEESE AND BAKE FOR 15 TO 20 MINUTES OR UNTIL CHEESE IS GOLDEN AND POTATOES ARE TENDER. LET STAND FOR 5 MINUTES BEFORE SERVING. SERVES 6.

TWICE-BAKED POTATOES

BAKE 'EM ONCE, STUFF 'EM WITH CHEESE AND SOUR CREAM, AND BAKE 'EM AGAIN.

4	LARGE BAKING POTATOES	4
	OLIVE OIL	
	SALT AND BLACK PEPPER TO TASTE	
4 OZ	CREAM CHEESE, SOFTENED AND CUT INTO CHUNKS	125 G
1 CUP	SHREDDED CHEDDAR CHEESE, DIVIDED	250 ML
1/3 CUP	SOUR CREAM	75 ML

PREHEAT OVEN TO 425°F (220°C). SCRUB POTATOES AND PAT DRY, THEN LIGHTLY RUB WITH OIL AND SEASON WITH SALT AND PEPPER. PRICK THE SKIN OF EACH POTATO A FEW TIMES WITH A FORK. ARRANGE POTATOES ON A BAKING SHEET AND BAKE FOR 45 TO 60 MINUTES OR UNTIL SOFT. REMOVE FROM OVEN AND REDUCE OVEN TEMPERATURE TO 350°F (180°C). LET POTATOES COOL ENOUGH TO HANDLE. CUT EACH IN HALF LENGTHWISE, THEN CAREFULLY SCOOP THE INSIDES INTO A LARGE BOWL, BEING CAREFUL NOT TO TEAR THE SKIN.

ADD CREAM CHEESE, HALF THE CHEDDAR AND SOUR CREAM TO THE POTATO. SEASON WITH SALT AND PEPPER. USING A POTATO MASHER, MASH CHEESES AND SOUR CREAM INTO THE POTATOES. STIR UNTIL EVENLY COMBINED. SPOON POTATO MIXTURE BACK INTO POTATO SKINS AND SPRINKLE THE REMAINING CHEDDAR OVER TOP. PLACE POTATOES ON THE BAKING SHEET. BAKE FOR 20 MINUTES OR UNTIL POTATOES ARE HEATED THROUGH AND CHEESE IS BUBBLING. SERVES 4 TO 8.

SUPER MASHED POTATOES

THIS IS A VARIATION ON THE VERY POPULAR CLASSIC BRIDGE RECIPE CALLED ELSIE'S POTATOES — MASHED POTATOES FORTIFIED WITH CREAM CHEESE AND SOUR CREAM (THE ADDITION OF WHICH MAKES THEM MAGICALLY FREEZER-FRIENDLY). WE GAVE ELSIE SOME EXTRA SUPERPOWERS IN THE FORM OF GARLIC, BACON AND GREEN ONIONS FOR A FULLY LOADED MASH.

5 LBS	POTATOES, PEELED AND CHOPPED	2.5 KG
1	GARLIC BULB, CLOVES SEPARATED AND PEELED	1
1	PACKAGE (8 OZ/250 G) CREAM CHEESE, SOFTENED AND CUT INTO CHUNKS	1
6	BACON SLICES, COOKED CRISP AND CRUMBLED OR CHOPPED	6
4	GREEN ONIONS (LIGHT GREEN AND WHITE PARTS ONLY), THINLY SLICED	4
1 CUP	SOUR CREAM	250 ML
	SALT AND BLACK PEPPER TO TASTE	
2 TBSP	BUTTER	30 ML

PREHEAT OVEN TO 350°F (180°C). SET A LARGE POT OF COLD WATER OVER HIGH HEAT AND ADD POTATOES AND GARLIC; BRING TO A BOIL. BOIL UNTIL POTATOES ARE TENDER, ABOUT 20 MINUTES. REMOVE FROM HEAT, DRAIN AND RETURN TO THE POT, ALONG WITH CREAM CHEESE. MASH POTATOES, GARLIC AND CHEESE UNTIL SMOOTH. STIR IN BACON, GREEN ONIONS AND SOUR CREAM, THEN SEASON WITH SALT AND PEPPER. SCRAPE POTATO MIXTURE INTO A 10-CUP (2.5 L) CASSEROLE DISH AND DOT WITH BUTTER. BAKE FOR 30 MINUTES OR UNTIL THE TOP IS JUST STARTING TO BROWN. SERVES 8 TO 10.

JACKI'S LATKES

JACKI MAKES THE BEST LATKES — GOLDEN AND
CRISP, PERFECT FOR SERVING WITH HER BRISKET
(SEE PAGE 73), BUT JUST AS WELL SUITED TO
ROAST CHICKEN OR PORK. SERVE WITH APPLESAUCE
OR SOUR CREAM ALONGSIDE.

5 LBS	RUSSET POTATOES	2.5 KG
2	ONIONS, FINELY CHOPPED	2
3	LARGE EGGS, BEATEN	3
1/3 CUP	ALL-PURPOSE FLOUR OR MATZO MEAL	75 ML
	SALT AND BLACK PEPPER TO TASTE	
	VEGETABLE OIL	

COARSELY GRATE POTATOES (NO NEED TO PEEL THEM)
ONTO A DOUBLE LAYER OF PAPER TOWELS. GATHER THEM
UP INTO A BUNDLE EACH TIME YOU HAVE A MANAGEABLE
PILE AND SQUEEZE OUT AS MUCH LIQUID AS POSSIBLE.
TRANSFER TO A LARGE BOWL. ONCE ALL THE POTATOES
ARE GRATED, ADD ONIONS, EGGS, FLOUR, SALT AND
PEPPER; MIX WELL.

IN A LARGE, HEAVY SKILLET, HEAT ABOUT 1/2 INCH (1 CM)
OF OIL OVER MEDIUM-HIGH HEAT. ADD HEAPING SPOONFULS
OF POTATO MIXTURE, SPREADING THEM OUT INTO SMALL,
THIN PANCAKES WITH THE BACK OF A SPOON, FRYING 4
OR 5 AT A TIME FOR ABOUT 3 MINUTES PER SIDE OR UNTIL
GOLDEN BROWN. ADD MORE OIL AS NEEDED. DRAIN ON
PAPER TOWELS AND SERVE IMMEDIATELY, OR COOK THEM
UP TO A DAY AHEAD AND REHEAT IN A HOT SKILLET OR ON
A BAKING SHEET IN A 250°F (120°C) OVEN WHEN GUESTS
ARRIVE. MAKES ABOUT 3 DOZEN LATKES.

SWEETENED-UP SWEET POTATOES

THIS CASSEROLE IS FOR PEOPLE WHO LIKE THEIR VEGGIES TO TASTE A BIT LIKE DESSERT.

2 1/2 LBS	SWEET POTATOES, PEELED AND CUBED	1.25 KG
2 LBS	CARROTS, SLICED	1 KG
2	GARLIC CLOVES, MINCED	2
2 TSP	GROUND CINNAMON	10 ML
PINCH	GROUND CLOVES	PINCH
	SALT AND BLACK PEPPER TO TASTE	
3/4 CUP	ORANGE JUICE	175 ML
2 TBSP	LIQUID HONEY	30 ML
2 TBSP	BUTTER, MELTED	30 ML

TOPPING

3/4 CUP	DRY BREAD CRUMBS	175 ML
1/3 CUP	BUTTER, MELTED	75 ML
3/4 CUP	CHOPPED PECANS	175 ML

PREHEAT OVEN TO 350°F (180°C). IN A LARGE POT OF BOILING SALTED WATER, COOK SWEET POTATOES AND CARROTS FOR ABOUT 20 MINUTES OR UNTIL TENDER. TRANSFER TO A 13- BY 9-INCH (33 BY 23 CM) BAKING DISH. IN A SMALL BOWL, COMBINE GARLIC, CINNAMON, CLOVES, SALT, PEPPER, ORANGE JUICE, HONEY AND BUTTER. POUR OVER VEGETABLES AND TOSS TO COMBINE.

TOPPING: PLACE BREAD CRUMBS IN A SMALL BOWL AND DRIZZLE WITH BUTTER. STIR WITH A FORK TO BLEND WELL. STIR IN PECANS, THEN EVENLY SPRINKLE TOPPING OVER VEGETABLES. BAKE FOR 30 TO 40 MINUTES OR UNTIL TOP IS CRISP AND JUICES ARE BUBBLING. SERVES 8 TO 10.

CHILI-SPICED ROASTED SQUASH

ROASTING DELICATA SQUASH BRINGS OUT ITS SWEETNESS AND SOFTENS THE PEEL — SO MUCH SO THAT IT BLENDS RIGHT INTO THE TENDER SQUASH. THESE RINGS ARE AS GOOD COLD AS THEY ARE HOT OUT OF THE OVEN. TRY LEFTOVERS ON A SALAD OR SANDWICH.

I	GARLIC CLOVE, MINCED	I
1 1/2 TSP	CHILI POWDER	7 ML
	SALT AND BLACK PEPPER TO TASTE	
3 TBSP	VEGETABLE OR OLIVE OIL	45 ML
I TSP	LIME JUICE	5 ML
2	DELICATA SQUASH (EACH ABOUT I LB/500 G)	2

PREHEAT OVEN TO 425°F (220°C) AND PLACE ONE RACK IN THE UPPER THIRD AND ONE IN THE LOWER THIRD. IN A LARGE BOWL, STIR TOGETHER GARLIC, CHILI POWDER, SALT, PEPPER, OIL AND LIME JUICE. CUT SQUASH IN HALF (AROUND THE WAIST, SO TO SPEAK) AND SCOOP OUT SEEDS. CUT SQUASH INTO RINGS ABOUT 1/2 INCH (I CM) THICK. ADD TO BOWL AND TOSS WITH OIL MIXTURE. SPREAD SQUASH RINGS ON TWO BAKING SHEETS LINED WITH PARCHMENT PAPER, SCRAPING LEFTOVER OIL FROM THE BOWL OVER TOP. BAKE, TOSSING ONCE OR TWICE AND SWITCHING TRAYS AROUND, UNTIL DARK GOLDEN AND TENDER WHEN PIERCED WITH A FORK, ABOUT 25 MINUTES.

SERVES 4 TO 6.

SPRING GREENS RISOTTO

A POT OF RISOTTO IS SIMPLER TO MAKE THAN MOST
PEOPLE THINK. ONCE YOU HAVE THE RIGHT RICE
(A SHORT-GRAIN RICE LIKE ARBORIO WILL RELEASE
ITS STARCH INTO THE DISH), YOU'RE HALFWAY THERE.
THERE'S NO NEED TO STAND AT THE STOVE AND STIR
CONSTANTLY, BUT STIRRING YOUR RISOTTO OFTEN, AS
YOU ADD STOCK, WILL HELP CREATE A CREAMY TEXTURE.
A HANDFUL OF GREENS ADDED AT THE END WILL WILT
INTO THE WARM RICE JUST BEFORE YOU SERVE IT. IF
YOU LIKE, TOP WITH A HANDFUL OF FRESH, PEPPERY
ARUGULA FOR CONTRAST.

2 TBSP	OLIVE OIL	30 ML
2 TBSP	BUTTER, DIVIDED	30 ML
1	SMALL ONION, FINELY CHOPPED	1
1	GARLIC CLOVE, MINCED	1
2 CUPS	ARBORIO OR OTHER SHORT-GRAIN WHITE RICE	500 ML
½ CUP	WHITE WINE (OPTIONAL)	125 ML
5 to 6 CUPS	BASIC CHICKEN STOCK (PAGE 28) OR READY-TO-USE CHICKEN OR VEGETABLE BROTH, WARMED	1.25 to 1.5 L
2 CUPS	SPINACH, SWISS CHARD OR ARUGULA LEAVES, TORN	500 ML
½ CUP	GRATED PARMESAN CHEESE	125 ML
	JUICE OF 1 LEMON (ABOUT 3 TBSP/ 45 ML)	

IN A LARGE SAUCEPAN, HEAT OIL AND HALF THE BUTTER
OVER MEDIUM-HIGH HEAT. SAUTÉ ONION FOR 3 TO
4 MINUTES OR UNTIL SOFT AND TRANSLUCENT. ADD
GARLIC AND SAUTÉ FOR 1 MINUTE. ADD RICE AND COOK,

STIRRING, FOR ANOTHER MINUTE OR TWO, TO COAT THE GRAINS WITH OIL. IF DESIRED, ADD WINE AND COOK, STIRRING, FOR 1 TO 2 MINUTES OR UNTIL THE MOISTURE COOKS OFF.

REDUCE HEAT TO MEDIUM-LOW. ADD ABOUT $\frac{1}{2}$ CUP (125 ML) STOCK AT A TIME AND COOK, STIRRING OFTEN, UNTIL EACH ADDITION IS ABSORBED. WHEN YOUR SPOON LEAVES A TRAIL THROUGH THE RICE WITHOUT FILLING UP BEHIND IT, IT'S TIME TO ADD MORE STOCK. WHEN YOU'VE INCORPORATED ABOUT 5 CUPS (1.25 L) STOCK (IT SHOULD TAKE ABOUT 25 MINUTES), THE MIXTURE SHOULD BE CREAMY AND THE RICE SOFT BUT STILL SLIGHTLY FIRM TO THE BITE. IF IT STILL HAS A CRUNCHY CORE, ADD A LITTLE MORE STOCK OR WATER AND KEEP COOKING. ADD GREENS, CHEESE, THE REMAINING BUTTER AND LEMON JUICE, STIRRING UNTIL GREENS ARE WILTED AND CHEESE IS MELTED. TASTE AND ADJUST SEASONING. SERVE IMMEDIATELY. SERVES 6 TO 8.

TIP: FOR SOME ADDED LEMONY FLAVOR, GRATE 1 TSP (5 ML) LEMON ZEST BEFORE YOU JUICE THE LEMON AND ADD IT TO THE RISOTTO WITH THE LEMON JUICE.

BEET AND BEET GREENS RISOTTO

THIS BRILLIANT RED RISOTTO USES THE BEET GREENS AS WELL AS THE ROOT VEGGIES THEMSELVES, WILTING THE GREENS INTO THE FINISHED DISH ALONG WITH CHUNKS OF SOFT GOAT CHEESE, WHICH PARTIALLY MELTS INTO THE MIX.

2 TBSP	BUTTER	30 ML
I TBSP	VEGETABLE OIL	I5 ML
I	SMALL ONION, FINELY CHOPPED	I
I CUP	ARBORIO OR OTHER SHORT-GRAIN WHITE RICE	250 ML
3 to 4 CUPS	BASIC CHICKEN STOCK (PAGE 28) OR READY-TO-USE CHICKEN BROTH, WARMED, DIVIDED	750 ML to I L
I	LARGE BEET, ROASTED OR BOILED AND PEELED, THEN COARSELY GRATED OR FINELY CHOPPED	I
I CUP	CHOPPED OR TORN BEET GREENS	250 ML
$1/2$ CUP	GRATED PARMESAN CHEESE	125 ML
$1/2$ CUP	CRUMBLED SOFT GOAT CHEESE	125 ML
	SALT AND BLACK PEPPER TO TASTE	

IN A LARGE SAUCEPAN OR DUTCH OVEN, HEAT BUTTER AND OIL OVER MEDIUM-HIGH HEAT. SAUTÉ ONION FOR 4 TO 5 MINUTES OR UNTIL SOFT. ADD RICE AND COOK, STIRRING, FOR I MINUTE, UNTIL COATED WITH OIL. REDUCE HEAT TO MEDIUM-LOW. ADD ABOUT $1/2$ CUP (I25 ML) STOCK AND COOK, STIRRING, UNTIL LIQUID IS ABSORBED. ADD BEET AND ANOTHER $1/2$ CUP STOCK; COOK, STIRRING OFTEN, UNTIL LIQUID IS ABSORBED. CONTINUE ADDING STOCK $1/2$ CUP AT A TIME, STIRRING OFTEN (NO NEED TO STIR CONSTANTLY)

UNTIL LIQUID IS ABSORBED. WHEN YOU'VE INCORPORATED ABOUT 3 CUPS (750 ML) STOCK, THE MIXTURE SHOULD BE CREAMY AND THE RICE SOFT BUT STILL SLIGHTLY FIRM TO THE BITE. IF IT STILL HAS A CRUNCHY CORE, ADD A LITTLE MORE STOCK AND KEEP COOKING. ADD BEET GREENS AND PARMESAN WITH THE LAST ADDITION OF STOCK. WHEN THE MIXTURE IS CREAMY-LOOKING AND THE RICE IS TENDER BUT NOT MUSHY, ADD GOAT CHEESE, SALT AND PEPPER, STIRRING JUST TO SWIRL THE CHEESE INTO THE RISOTTO WITHOUT ALLOWING IT TO MELT COMPLETELY. SERVE IMMEDIATELY. SERVES 4, OR 8 AS AN APPETIZER.

I MISS THE DAYS WHEN YOU COULD JUST
PUSH SOMEONE IN THE SWIMMING POOL WITHOUT
WORRYING ABOUT THEIR CELL PHONE.

BROWN AND WILD RICE STUFFING WITH APPLES, CRANBERRIES AND PECANS

THIS FALL-INSPIRED PILAF DOES WELL AS A GLUTEN-FREE STUFFING OPTION FOR YOUR TURKEY OR AS A SIDE DISH BAKED ALONGSIDE THE REST OF THE MEAL.

4 CUPS	BASIC CHICKEN STOCK (PAGE 28), READY-TO-USE CHICKEN OR VEGETABLE BROTH, OR WATER	1 L
1 CUP	WILD RICE	250 ML
1 CUP	LONG-GRAIN BROWN RICE	250 ML
1/2 TSP	SALT	2 ML
1 CUP	DRIED CRANBERRIES	250 ML
1/3 CUP	BUTTER, MELTED	75 ML
2	SHALLOTS, FINELY CHOPPED	2
2	CELERY STALKS, FINELY CHOPPED (INCLUDE LEAVES, IF THERE ARE ANY)	2
1	TART APPLE, CHOPPED	1
1 TBSP	FINELY CHOPPED FRESH SAGE	15 ML
2 TSP	FINELY CHOPPED FRESH THYME	10 ML
1/2 TSP	BLACK PEPPER	2 ML
1/2 CUP	CHOPPED PECANS, TOASTED	125 ML

IN A LARGE SAUCEPAN, BRING STOCK TO A BOIL OVER MEDIUM-HIGH HEAT. ADD WILD RICE, BROWN RICE AND SALT; REDUCE HEAT TO LOW, COVER AND COOK UNTIL RICE IS TENDER, ABOUT 45 MINUTES. REMOVE FROM HEAT AND FLUFF WITH A FORK, STIRRING IN CRANBERRIES. SET ASIDE. IN A LARGE SKILLET, MELT BUTTER OVER MEDIUM-HIGH HEAT. SAUTÉ SHALLOTS AND CELERY UNTIL SOFTENED, ABOUT 5 MINUTES. ADD APPLE AND SAUTÉ

FOR 3 TO 4 MINUTES OR UNTIL STARTING TO SOFTEN. STIR IN SAGE, THYME AND PEPPER; SAUTÉ FOR 2 MINUTES. TRANSFER TO A BOWL AND TOSS WITH RICE MIXTURE AND PECANS.

USE THE MIXTURE TO STUFF A TURKEY, OR TRANSFER IT TO A BUTTERED BAKING DISH THAT WILL ACCOMMODATE IT, COVER AND BAKE (ALONGSIDE YOUR TURKEY, IF YOU LIKE) AT 350°F (180°C) FOR ABOUT 30 MINUTES OR UNTIL WELL HEATED THROUGH. SERVES 6 TO 8.

TIP: TO TOAST PECANS, SPREAD THEM IN A SINGLE LAYER IN A SMALL SKILLET SET OVER MEDIUM HEAT. COOK, STIRRING OR SHAKING THE PAN OFTEN, FOR 5 TO 6 MINUTES OR UNTIL GOLDEN AND FRAGRANT.

ROGER'S FAVORITE RICE

GENERALLY WE'VE TRIED TO PHASE OUT A LOT OF CONVENIENCE INGREDIENTS, BUT THIS RICE WOULDN'T BE ROGER'S FAVORITE WITHOUT A PACKET OF ONION SOUP MIX.

1	CAN (10 OZ/284 ML) SLICED MUSHROOMS IN BRINE	1
1 CUP	LONG-GRAIN WHITE RICE	250 ML
1	PACKET ONION SOUP MIX (ABOUT 2 TBSP/30 ML)	1
1 TBSP	VEGETABLE OIL	15 ML
2 TSP	SOY SAUCE	10 ML
	WATER	

PREHEAT OVEN TO 350°F (180°C). BUTTER A 6-CUP (1.5 L) BAKING DISH. DRAIN MUSHROOMS, RESERVING BRINE. IN THE PREPARED BAKING DISH, COMBINE MUSHROOMS, RICE AND ONION SOUP MIX. POUR RESERVED BRINE, OIL AND SOY SAUCE INTO A LARGE MEASURING CUP AND TOP UP WITH WATER SO THAT THE LIQUID MEASURES 2$\frac{1}{2}$ CUPS (625 ML). POUR OVER RICE AND GENTLY STIR. BAKE, UNCOVERED, FOR 45 TO 60 MINUTES OR UNTIL RICE IS TENDER AND LIQUID IS FULLY ABSORBED. SERVES 4 TO 6.

IF YOU WANT BREAKFAST IN BED,
SLEEP IN THE KITCHEN.

HOMEMADE BREADS

NO-KNEAD BREAD

MADE FAMOUS IN THE NEW YORK TIMES, THIS BREAD
BY JIM LAHEY IS PERFECT AT MEALTIMES.

3 CUPS	ALL-PURPOSE OR BREAD FLOUR, PLUS MORE FOR DUSTING	750 ML
1/4 TSP	INSTANT OR ACTIVE DRY YEAST	1 ML
1 TSP	SALT	5 ML
1 1/2 CUPS + 2 TBSP	WATER	405 ML

IN A LARGE BOWL, STIR TOGETHER FLOUR, YEAST AND
SALT. STIR IN WATER UNTIL BLENDED; THE DOUGH WILL
BE SHAGGY AND STICKY. COVER WITH PLASTIC WRAP OR A
PLATE AND LET IT REST ON THE COUNTERTOP FOR 18 TO
24 HOURS. WHEN IT'S READY, THE SURFACE OF THE DOUGH
WILL APPEAR WET AND DOTTED WITH BUBBLES.

GENEROUSLY FLOUR A SMOOTH TEA TOWEL (ANYTHING
WITH TEXTURE, LIKE TERRY CLOTH, COULD STICK) AND
PLACE DOUGH ON IT. SPRINKLE DOUGH WITH A LITTLE
MORE FLOUR AND FOLD IT OVER ON ITSELF ONCE OR
TWICE, THEN ROUGHLY SHAPE INTO A BALL. DUST WITH
MORE FLOUR, FOLD THE TOWEL OVER THE BREAD OR
COVER WITH ANOTHER TOWEL AND LET STAND FOR
ANOTHER HOUR OR TWO.

MEANWHILE, PREHEAT OVEN TO 450°F (230°C) WITH A
6- TO 8-QUART (6 TO 8 L) COVERED CAST-IRON POT INSIDE.
CAREFULLY REMOVE POT FROM OVEN, LIFT OFF LID AND
FLIP DOUGH FROM THE TOWEL INTO THE POT. COVER AND
BAKE FOR 30 MINUTES, THEN REMOVE LID AND BAKE FOR
10 TO 15 MINUTES OR UNTIL DEEP GOLDEN. MAKES 1 LOAF,
SERVING 8.

CHEESY PULL-APART BREAD

THIS IS AN EXTREMELY WELL-RECEIVED SIDE FOR SOUPS OR CHILIS, OR EVEN ON ITS OWN WHEN EVERYONE IS SITTING DOWN TO WATCH A MOVIE.

1	LARGE CRUSTY LOAF, EITHER ROUND OR OBLONG (ABOUT 1 LB/500 G)	1
2	GARLIC CLOVES, MINCED	2
1 CUP	SHREDDED MOZZARELLA CHEESE	250 ML
1 CUP	SHREDDED CHEDDAR CHEESE	250 ML
1/4 CUP	BUTTER, MELTED	60 ML

PREHEAT OVEN TO 350°F (180°C). CUT DOWN THROUGH THE TOP OF THE LOAF TOWARD THE BOTTOM CRUST IN A CRISSCROSS PATTERN, WITH THE CUTS ABOUT 3/4 INCH (2 CM) APART, TAKING CARE NOT TO CUT RIGHT THROUGH THE BOTTOM OF THE LOAF (YOUR LOAF WILL LOOK A BIT LIKE A SEA URCHIN WHEN YOU'RE DONE; IF ANY PIECES OF BREAD DETACH THEMSELVES, JUST POP THEM BACK INTO THEIR SPOTS). PLACE LOAF ON A PIECE OF FOIL LARGE ENOUGH TO WRAP IT COMPLETELY.

IN A MEDIUM BOWL, TOSS TOGETHER GARLIC, MOZZARELLA AND CHEDDAR. USING YOUR HANDS, STUFF CHEESE MIXTURE IN BETWEEN CUTS. WORK IN ONE DIRECTION, THEN GO BACK AND FILL IN A LITTLE IN THE OTHER DIRECTION, ESPECIALLY AROUND THE EDGE OF LOAF. DRIZZLE BUTTER EVENLY OVER TOP. WRAP TIGHTLY AND PLACE ON A BAKING SHEET. BAKE FOR 15 MINUTES. OPEN FOIL AT THE TOP OF LOAF AND PUSH IT DOWN THE SIDES A LITTLE. BAKE FOR 5 MINUTES OR UNTIL CHEESE IS MELTED. SERVE IMMEDIATELY, LETTING PEOPLE TEAR OFF SECTIONS FOR THEMSELVES. SERVES 4 TO 6.

IRISH SODA BREAD

LIKE A BIG, CRUSTY SCONE, SODA BREAD IS A QUICK LOAF THAT COMES TOGETHER IN NO TIME — NO NEED TO WAIT FOR IT TO RISE. MAKE A PLAIN LOAF, OR ADD GRATED CHEESE OR HERBS, AND SERVE IT IN WEDGES ALONG WITH SOUPS, STEWS OR ANYTHING ELSE THAT MIGHT LEAVE SAUCE, BROTH OR GRAVY BEHIND TO MOP UP.

2 CUPS	ALL-PURPOSE FLOUR	500 ML
1 CUP	WHOLE WHEAT FLOUR	250 ML
3 TBSP	PACKED BROWN SUGAR	45 ML
1 TBSP	BAKING POWDER	15 ML
1/2 TSP	BAKING SODA	2 ML
1/2 TSP	SALT	2 ML
1/2 CUP	COLD BUTTER, CUT INTO PIECES	125 ML
2 CUPS	SHREDDED SHARP (OLD) CHEDDAR CHEESE (OPTIONAL)	500 ML
1	LARGE EGG	1
1 CUP	BUTTERMILK	250 ML

PREHEAT OVEN TO 375°F (190°C). IN A LARGE BOWL, COMBINE ALL-PURPOSE FLOUR, WHOLE WHEAT FLOUR, SUGAR, BAKING POWDER, BAKING SODA AND SALT. CUT IN BUTTER WITH A PASTRY BLENDER, A FORK OR YOUR FINGERS UNTIL WELL BLENDED. IF YOU LIKE, ADD CHEESE AND TOSS TO COMBINE. IN A SMALL BOWL, USE A FORK TO STIR TOGETHER EGG AND BUTTERMILK; ADD TO THE DRY INGREDIENTS AND STIR UNTIL A SHAGGY, STICKY DOUGH COMES TOGETHER. GATHER DOUGH UP AND KNEAD IT A FEW TIMES ON THE COUNTERTOP. SHAPE INTO A BALL, PLACE ON A BAKING SHEET LINED WITH PARCHMENT PAPER AND CUT A DEEP X IN THE SURFACE. BAKE FOR

50 TO 60 MINUTES OR UNTIL DARK GOLDEN AND SLIGHTLY HOLLOW-SOUNDING WHEN TAPPED ON THE BOTTOM. LET COOL SLIGHTLY ON A WIRE RACK, THEN CUT INTO WEDGES TO SERVE. MAKES 1 LOAF, SERVING 8.

CHEDDAR BEER BATTER BREAD

THIS QUICK BATTER BREAD IS EASY TO STIR TOGETHER WHEN YOU NEED A LITTLE SOMETHING TO BALANCE ON THE EDGE OF YOUR BOWL OF CHILI OR STEW.

3 CUPS	ALL-PURPOSE FLOUR	750 ML
1 TBSP	BAKING POWDER	15 ML
2 TBSP	SUGAR	30 ML
1/2 TSP	SALT	2 ML
1 CUP	SHREDDED SHARP (OLD) CHEDDAR CHEESE	250 ML
1	BOTTLE (12 OZ/341 ML) BEER, AT ROOM TEMPERATURE	1
1/4 CUP	BUTTER, MELTED	60 ML

PREHEAT OVEN TO 375°F (190°C). IN A LARGE BOWL, COMBINE FLOUR, BAKING POWDER, SUGAR AND SALT. ADD CHEESE AND TOSS TO COMBINE. STIR IN BEER AND BUTTER JUST UNTIL COMBINED; DON'T WORRY ABOUT GETTING ALL THE LUMPS OUT. POUR INTO A BUTTERED OR PARCHMENT-LINED 9- BY 5-INCH (23 BY 12.5 CM) LOAF PAN AND BAKE FOR 35 TO 40 MINUTES OR UNTIL GOLDEN AND SPRINGY TO THE TOUCH. LET COOL IN PAN ON A WIRE RACK. MAKES 1 LOAF, SERVING 8.

FINNISH PULLA

ELIZABETH'S HUSBAND'S FAMILY IS FINNISH, AND WHILE HIS MUM DOESN'T MAKE A LOT OF FINNISH FOOD, THIS SWEET BUTTERY BREAD IS A FAMILY FAVORITE. SERVE IT WITH SOFT BUTTER AS A SIDE WITH DINNER (THE SUBTLE SWEETNESS WOULD GO NICELY WITH LAMB) OR WITH COFFEE AFTER DINNER IN LIEU OF A SWEETER DESSERT.

I CUP	MILK	250 ML
I TBSP	ACTIVE DRY YEAST	15 ML
1/4 CUP	WARM WATER	60 ML
1/2 CUP	SUGAR	125 ML
1 1/2 TSP	GROUND CARDAMOM	7 ML
I TSP	SALT	5 ML
3	LARGE EGGS, LIGHTLY BEATEN	3
4 1/2 CUPS	ALL-PURPOSE FLOUR, DIVIDED	1.125 L
1/2 CUP	COLD BUTTER, CUT INTO PIECES	125 ML
	ADDITIONAL SUGAR	
	SLICED ALMONDS	

SCALD THE MILK BY PUTTING IT IN A SMALL SAUCEPAN OVER MEDIUM-HIGH HEAT AND BRINGING IT JUST TO THE VERGE OF BOILING. ONCE IT STARTS TO BUBBLE, TAKE IT OFF THE HEAT AND LET IT COOL TO LUKEWARM.

WHILE THE MILK IS COOLING, STIR YEAST INTO THE WARM WATER; LET STAND FOR 3 TO 5 MINUTES OR UNTIL FOAMY. TRANSFER YEAST MIXTURE TO A LARGE BOWL AND WHISK IN SUGAR, CARDAMOM, SALT, WARM MILK AND TWO-THIRDS OF THE EGGS. STIR IN 2 CUPS (500 ML) FLOUR AND THE BUTTER. WORK IN THE REMAINING FLOUR

WITH YOUR HANDS, BREAKING UP THE BUTTER AS YOU GO. ONCE THE FLOUR IS INCORPORATED AND THE DOUGH NO LONGER STICKS TO YOUR HANDS, COVER THE BOWL WITH A TEA TOWEL AND LET REST FOR 15 MINUTES.

KNEAD DOUGH FOR ABOUT 5 MINUTES OR UNTIL SMOOTH AND ELASTIC; FORM INTO A BALL. GREASE THE INSIDE OF A CLEAN BOWL AND PUT THE DOUGH INSIDE, COVERING IT WITH A TEA TOWEL. LET RISE IN A WARM PLACE UNTIL DOUBLED IN BULK, ABOUT AN HOUR AND A HALF.

DIVIDE DOUGH INTO 3 EQUAL PIECES AND ROLL EACH PIECE INTO A 36-INCH (90 CM) ROPE. LINE A BAKING SHEET WITH A PIECE OF PARCHMENT PAPER. BRAID THE 3 ROPES TOGETHER ON THE PREPARED SHEET, THEN COVER WITH A TEA TOWEL. LET RISE FOR 45 MINUTES.

MEANWHILE, PREHEAT OVEN TO 375°F (190°C). BRUSH LOAF WITH THE REMAINING EGG AND SPRINKLE WITH SUGAR AND ALMONDS. BAKE FOR 30 TO 35 MINUTES OR UNTIL DARK GOLDEN AND BAKED THROUGH. MAKES 1 LOAF, SERVING 8.

TIP: AS YOU BRAID THE ROPES, THE LOAF WILL BECOME MORE COMPACT, BUT IF IT'S TOO LONG FOR YOUR BAKING SHEET, POSITION IT DIAGONALLY ON THE SHEET.

TIP: FOR SMALLER PULLA LOAVES, SPLIT THE DOUGH IN HALF, ROLL THE DOUGH INTO 24-INCH (60 CM) ROPES AND MAKE 2 LOAVES. BAKE THEM AT THE SAME TIME, SPACED APART ON THE BAKING SHEET — THEY SHOULD BE READY IN 20 TO 25 MINUTES.

ROSEMARY FOCACCIA

FOCACCIA IS GREAT BEGINNER BREAD. IT TASTES
WONDERFUL, BUT IS USUALLY A LITTLE IRREGULAR
IN SHAPE AND RISE — WHICH MEANS THAT, HOWEVER
IT LOOKS, IT'S STILL PERFECT.

2 TSP	ACTIVE DRY YEAST	10 ML
2 CUPS	WARM WATER (SLIGHTLY WARM TO THE TOUCH)	500 ML
4 1/4 CUPS	ALL-PURPOSE FLOUR (APPROX.)	1.05 L
1 1/2 TSP	SALT	7 ML
6 TBSP	OLIVE OIL, DIVIDED	90 ML
2 TSP	CHOPPED FRESH ROSEMARY	10 ML
	FLAKY OR COARSELY GROUND SALT TO TASTE	

IN A MEDIUM BOWL, STIR YEAST INTO THE WARM WATER;
LET STAND FOR 3 TO 5 MINUTES OR UNTIL FOAMY. IN
A LARGE BOWL, STIR TOGETHER FLOUR AND SALT. ADD
YEAST MIXTURE AND 2 TBSP (30 ML) OIL, STIRRING WELL
WITH A WOODEN SPOON. KNEAD FOR ABOUT 10 MINUTES,
ADDING MORE FLOUR AS NEEDED TO FORM A QUITE SOFT
BUT SMOOTH DOUGH. LIGHTLY OIL THE LARGE BOWL (NO
NEED TO WASH IT) AND PLACE DOUGH INSIDE. COVER WITH
PLASTIC WRAP AND LET RISE IN A WARM PLACE UNTIL
DOUBLED IN BULK, ABOUT AN HOUR.

SPREAD 2 TBSP (30 ML) OIL OVER A 15- BY 10-INCH
(37.5 BY 25 CM) RIMMED BAKING SHEET. DEFLATE DOUGH,
THEN SPREAD OUT ON THE SHEET WITH YOUR HANDS
UNTIL IT FORMS A RECTANGLE ABOUT 1/2 INCH (1 CM) FROM
THE EDGES OF THE SHEET. USING YOUR FINGERS, PROD

DOUGH ALMOST THROUGH TO THE BAKING SHEET TO FORM DIVOTS. DRIZZLE WITH THE REMAINING OIL, THEN SPRINKLE WITH ROSEMARY AND SALT. COVER LOOSELY (WE INVERT A SECOND BAKING SHEET OVER THE FIRST, RIM TO RIM) AND LET RISE UNTIL PILLOWY, ABOUT 30 TO 40 MINUTES.

MEANWHILE, PREHEAT OVEN TO 450°F (230°C). UNCOVER AND BAKE UNTIL BREAD IS BROWNED AND PRODUCES A HOLLOW SOUND WHEN TAPPED, ABOUT 20 MINUTES. MAKES 1 LOAF, ABOUT 14 BY 9 INCHES (35 BY 23 CM).

VARIATION: YOU CAN REPLACE HALF OF THE ALL-PURPOSE FLOUR WITH WHOLE WHEAT FLOUR IN THIS LOAF, IF YOU WISH.

I DECIDED TO SELL MY VACUUM CLEANER.
IT WAS JUST COLLECTING DUST.

NAAN

YOU DON'T NEED A TANDOOR TO MAKE YOUR OWN NAAN — A CAST-IRON SKILLET WILL DO THE TRICK, RIGHT ON THE STOVETOP.

2¼ TSP	ACTIVE DRY YEAST (1 PACKAGE)	11 ML
1 TSP	SUGAR	5 ML
½ CUP	WARM WATER	125 ML
2½ CUPS	ALL-PURPOSE FLOUR	625 ML
½ TSP	SALT	2 ML
1	LARGE EGG, LIGHTLY BEATEN	1
¼ CUP	VEGETABLE OIL	60 ML
⅓ CUP	PLAIN YOGURT	75 ML
	VEGETABLE OIL AND/OR BUTTER	

IN A LARGE BOWL, STIR YEAST AND SUGAR INTO THE WARM WATER; LET STAND FOR 3 TO 5 MINUTES OR UNTIL FOAMY. STIR IN FLOUR, SALT, EGG, OIL AND YOGURT. KNEAD FOR 5 TO 7 MINUTES OR UNTIL DOUGH IS SOFT AND ELASTIC. COVER WITH A TEA TOWEL AND LET RISE UNTIL DOUBLED IN SIZE, ABOUT AN HOUR.

DIVIDE DOUGH INTO 6 TO 8 PIECES. ROLL OUT EACH PIECE INTO A THIN CIRCLE OR OVAL. IN A CAST-IRON SKILLET, HEAT A DRIZZLE OF OIL AND/OR A DAB OF BUTTER OVER MEDIUM-HIGH HEAT. COOK NAAN, ONE AT A TIME, FLIPPING AS NECESSARY UNTIL DEEP GOLDEN AND BLISTERED ON BOTH SIDES. ADD MORE OIL AND/OR BUTTER AND ADJUST HEAT AS NEEDED BETWEEN NAAN. MAKES 6 TO 8 NAAN.

QUICK (REALLY!) BAGUETTES

YOU CAN HAVE FRESHLY BAKED, MADE-FROM-SCRATCH BAGUETTES ON THE TABLE IN ABOUT AN HOUR. REALLY!

2¼ TSP	ACTIVE DRY YEAST (1 PACKAGE)	11 ML
2 TBSP	SUGAR	30 ML
1½ CUPS	WARM WATER	375 ML
3 to 4 CUPS	ALL-PURPOSE FLOUR	750 ML to 1 L
1 TSP	SALT	5 ML

PREHEAT OVEN TO 425°F (220°C). FILL A SHALLOW CAKE PAN WITH WATER OR ICE AND PUT IT ON THE BOTTOM RACK; MAKE SURE ANOTHER RACK IS SET IN THE MIDDLE OF THE OVEN. IN A LARGE BOWL, STIR YEAST AND SUGAR INTO THE WARM WATER. SET ON TOP OF THE PREHEATING OVEN FOR 10 MINUTES TO WARM UP.

ADD HALF THE FLOUR AND THE SALT TO THE YEAST MIXTURE, THEN ADD MORE FLOUR, ½ CUP (125 ML) AT A TIME, UNTIL YOU HAVE A SOFT DOUGH. KNEAD FOR A FEW MINUTES, UNTIL SMOOTH AND ELASTIC. (YOU CAN DO THIS WITH THE DOUGH HOOK ON YOUR STAND MIXER, IF YOU HAVE ONE.) CUT DOUGH INTO 4 PIECES AND ROLL EACH PIECE INTO A LONG, THIN ROPE. FOR EACH BAGUETTE, TWIST 2 ROPES TOGETHER. SET LOAVES ON A BAKING SHEET LINED WITH PARCHMENT PAPER, SPACING AT LEAST 2 INCHES APART. LET STAND FOR 15 TO 30 MINUTES ON TOP OF THE OVEN.

BAKE ON THE MIDDLE RACK FOR 15 TO 20 MINUTES, UNTIL GOLDEN AND CRUSTY. MAKES 2 LOAVES.

PARKER HOUSE ROLLS

THIS IS IT — THE QUINTESSENTIAL SUNDAY FAMILY DINNER ROLL. THE ROLLS BAKE CLOSE TOGETHER, RETAINING THEIR SOFT EDGES, AND THERE'S SOMETHING COMMUNAL ABOUT A PAN OF ROLLS YOU PULL APART AT THE TABLE.

2 TSP	ACTIVE DRY YEAST	10 ML
1/4 CUP	WARM WATER	60 ML
1 CUP	MILK	250 ML
1/4 CUP	LARD OR BUTTER, CUT INTO PIECES	60 ML
3 TBSP	SUGAR	45 ML
3 1/2 CUPS	ALL-PURPOSE FLOUR	875 ML
1 1/2 TSP	SALT	7 ML
1	LARGE EGG, LIGHTLY BEATEN	1
	MELTED BUTTER	
	COARSE SALT (OPTIONAL)	

IN A LARGE BOWL, STIR YEAST INTO THE WARM WATER; LET STAND FOR 3 TO 5 MINUTES OR UNTIL FOAMY.

MEANWHILE, IN A SMALL SAUCEPAN, HEAT MILK, LARD AND SUGAR UNTIL WARM BUT NOT HOT; THE LARD WILL START TO MELT, BUT DOESN'T NEED TO MELT COMPLETELY. (IF THE MIXTURE GETS TOO HOT, LET IT COOL TO A BIT WARMER THAN BODY TEMPERATURE.)

ADD THE MILK MIXTURE TO THE YEAST MIXTURE, ALONG WITH FLOUR, SALT AND EGG; STIR UNTIL DOUGH COMES TOGETHER. KNEAD FOR 5 TO 6 MINUTES OR UNTIL DOUGH IS SMOOTH AND ELASTIC. RETURN DOUGH TO THE BOWL, COVER WITH A TEA TOWEL AND LET RISE FOR AN HOUR OR SO, UNTIL DOUBLED IN BULK.

PUNCH THE DOUGH DOWN AND DIVIDE IT INTO 3 PIECES. ROLL EACH PIECE INTO A LONG RECTANGLE, ABOUT 12 BY 6 INCHES (30 BY 15 CM). CUT EACH RECTANGLE BOTH LENGTHWISE AND CROSSWISE INTO THIRDS, SO THAT YOU HAVE A TOTAL OF 27 RECTANGLES. BRUSH BUTTER OVER EACH PIECE, AND BUTTER THE BOTTOM AND SIDES OF A 13- BY 9-INCH (33 BY 23 CM) BAKING DISH. FOLD EACH RECTANGLE ALMOST IN HALF LENGTHWISE, LEAVING ABOUT $\frac{1}{2}$ INCH (1 CM) EXTENDING AT ONE END. ARRANGE ROLLS IN BAKING DISH, OVERLAPPING THEM SLIGHTLY, LIKE SHINGLES. BRUSH TOPS WITH BUTTER, COVER WITH A TEA TOWEL AND SET ASIDE WHILE YOU PREHEAT OVEN TO 350°F (180°F).

BAKE FOR 25 TO 30 MINUTES OR UNTIL GOLDEN. BRUSH TOPS OF BUNS WITH BUTTER WHILE STILL WARM AND, IF YOU LIKE, SPRINKLE WITH COARSE SALT. MAKES 27 ROLLS.

I BASE MOST OF MY FASHION TASTE ON
WHAT DOESN'T ITCH.
— GILDA RADNER

JASON'S GRANDMA'S 2-HOUR BUNS

JASON WAS ONCE JULIE'S NEIGHBOR ACROSS THE STREET, AND HIS GRANDMA'S BUNS WERE LEGENDARY. WE CONVINCED HIM TO SHARE HER RECIPE.

3½ to 4 CUPS	ALL-PURPOSE FLOUR, DIVIDED	875 ML to 1 L
¼ CUP	SUGAR	60 ML
1 TBSP	INSTANT DRY YEAST	15 ML
1	LARGE EGG	1
1½ CUPS	WARM WATER	375 ML
¼ CUP	VEGETABLE OIL	60 ML
1 TSP	SALT	5 ML

IN A LARGE BOWL, COMBINE 2 CUPS (500 ML) FLOUR, SUGAR AND YEAST. IN ANOTHER LARGE BOWL, WHISK TOGETHER EGG, WATER AND OIL. ADD FLOUR MIXTURE, STIRRING UNTIL WELL BLENDED. ADD THE REMAINING FLOUR AND SALT, STIRRING UNTIL THE DOUGH COMES TOGETHER. KNEAD FOR 5 TO 7 MINUTES OR UNTIL SMOOTH AND ELASTIC. LET RISE FOR 15 MINUTES, THEN PUNCH DOUGH DOWN AND LET RISE FOR ANOTHER 15 MINUTES.

PUNCH DOUGH DOWN AGAIN AND SHAPE INTO BUNS (MAKE THEM ABOUT HALF THE SIZE YOU WANT THEM TO BE ONCE BAKED). PLACE BUNS CLOSE TOGETHER IN A BUTTERED OR PARCHMENT-LINED 13- BY 9-INCH (33 BY 23 CM) BAKING DISH, COVER WITH A TEA TOWEL AND LET RISE FOR ABOUT 1 HOUR, UNTIL DOUBLED IN BULK.

MEANWHILE, PREHEAT OVEN TO 350°F (180°C). BAKE BUNS FOR 15 TO 18 MINUTES OR UNTIL DEEP GOLDEN. MAKES 1½ TO 2 DOZEN BUNS.

PLAIN OR CHEESE BISCUITS

A BASKET OF WARM BISCUITS IS ALWAYS A GOOD IDEA.
THESE ULTRA-TENDER BISCUITS ARE AS SIMPLE AS
THEY GET — THEY'RE DIVINE AS-IS, OR ADD A HANDFUL
OF GRATED CHEESE FOR CHEESE BISCUITS.

2 CUPS	ALL-PURPOSE FLOUR	500 ML
2 TBSP	SUGAR	30 ML
1 TBSP	BAKING POWDER	15 ML
1/4 TSP	SALT	1 ML
1/2 CUP	COLD BUTTER, CUT INTO PIECES	125 ML
1 CUP	SHREDDED SHARP (OLD) CHEDDAR CHEESE (OPTIONAL)	250 ML
1 CUP	MILK	250 ML
	ADDITIONAL MILK OR CREAM (OPTIONAL)	

PREHEAT OVEN TO 400°F (200°C). IN A MEDIUM BOWL,
STIR TOGETHER FLOUR, SUGAR, BAKING POWDER AND
SALT. ADD BUTTER AND BLEND WITH A FORK, PASTRY
BLENDER OR YOUR FINGERS UNTIL WELL COMBINED
AND CRUMBLY. IF YOU LIKE, ADD CHEESE AND TOSS TO
COMBINE. STIR IN MILK JUST UNTIL THE DOUGH COMES
TOGETHER. TURN DOUGH OUT ONTO THE COUNTERTOP
AND KNEAD A FEW TIMES, THEN PAT INTO A CIRCLE
ABOUT 1 INCH (2.5 CM) THICK. CUT INTO WEDGES, OR USE
A BISCUIT CUTTER TO CUT ROUNDS, AND TRANSFER TO A
BAKING SHEET LINED WITH PARCHMENT PAPER, LEAVING
SOME SPACE BETWEEN THEM. IF YOU LIKE, BRUSH
TOPS WITH MILK. BAKE FOR 15 TO 20 MINUTES OR UNTIL
GOLDEN. MAKES 8 TO 12 BISCUITS.

FOOLPROOF
YORKSHIRE PUDDING

OH, YORKSHIRE PUDDING, YOU HAVE A WAY OF MAKING AN OTHERWISE HO-HUM ROAST DINNER ABSOLUTELY MAGICAL. YORKIES ARE ESSENTIALLY JUST VEHICLES FOR EXTRA GRAVY, BUT WHEN YOU MAKE THEM PERFECTLY SO THAT THEY'RE CRISPY ON THE OUTSIDE AND PILLOWY SOFT INSIDE, YOU'LL BE THE HERO OF ANY MEAL. THE TRICK IS TO LET THE BATTER REST AND THEN GET IT INTO A PIPING HOT MUFFIN PAN DRIZZLED WITH OIL. YOU'LL NEED TO WORK QUICKLY, BUT ONCE YOU'VE MASTERED THE METHOD, YOU'LL BE TRYING TO FIGURE OUT WHAT TO MAKE FOR DINNER TO JUSTIFY ANOTHER ROUND OF YORKSHIRE PUD.

3	LARGE EGGS	3
1 CUP	ALL-PURPOSE FLOUR	250 ML
1/4 TSP	SALT	1 ML
1 1/4 CUPS	MILK	300 ML
3/4 CUP	VEGETABLE OIL	175 ML

IN A LARGE BOWL, WHISK EGGS, THEN WHISK IN FLOUR, SALT AND MILK. YOU WANT THE BATTER TO BE NICE AND SMOOTH AND EVEN A LITTLE FROTHY FROM WHISKING. LET REST FOR AT LEAST 30 MINUTES. EVEN BETTER, LET IT REST, COVERED, IN THE FRIDGE OVERNIGHT AND BRING IT BACK TO ROOM TEMPERATURE AS YOUR OVEN PREHEATS.

PREHEAT OVEN TO 450°F (230°C) AND PLACE A 12-CUP MUFFIN PAN INSIDE (PUT IT ON TOP OF A BAKING SHEET SO YOU CAN EASILY SLIDE THE MUFFIN PAN IN AND OUT WITHOUT TIPPING IT). ONCE THE OVEN IS PREHEATED,

CAREFULLY SLIDE THE HOT MUFFIN PAN OUT OF THE OVEN AND POUR 1 TBSP (15 ML) OIL INTO EACH CUP. SLIDE THE PAN BACK INTO THE OVEN AND HEAT FOR 5 TO 10 MINUTES OR UNTIL OIL IS SMOKING HOT.

HERE'S WHERE YOU NEED TO BE QUICK (AND CAREFUL): OPEN THE OVEN DOOR AND SLIDE THE RACK OUT SO THAT YOU CAN FILL THE MUFFIN CUPS WITHOUT REMOVING THE PAN FROM THE OVEN. GIVE THE BATTER A STIR, THEN USE A LADLE TO EVENLY DISTRIBUTE THE BATTER AMONG THE CUPS. SLIDE THE RACK BACK IN AND CLOSE THE DOOR. BAKE FOR 15 MINUTES, WITHOUT OPENING THE DOOR TO PEEK AT YOUR PUDS. WHEN THE 15 MINUTES ARE UP, TAKE A PEEK AND WHEN THEY'RE GOLDEN, PUFFED AND CRISPY-LOOKING, TAKE THEM OUT AND SERVE THEM IMMEDIATELY WITH ROAST MEAT AND LOADS OF GRAVY. MAKES 12.

TIP: SINGLE-SERVING YORKSHIRE PUDS ARE OUR GO-TO, BUT YOU CAN ALSO MAKE ONE GREAT BIG ONE TO SERVE AT THE TABLE. SIMPLY USE AN OVENPROOF SKILLET IN PLACE OF THE MUFFIN PAN, REDUCE THE AMOUNT OF VEGETABLE OIL TO 1/3 CUP (75 ML) AND POUR IN ALL THE BATTER IN ONE GO. IT MAY TAKE A BIT LONGER TO BAKE (20 TO 25 MINUTES) — JUST KEEP AN EYE ON IT AND TAKE IT OUT OF THE OVEN ONCE THE SIDES ARE CRISP AND GOLDEN.

BUTTERMILK CORNBREAD

CORNBREAD IS SO EASY TO MAKE. SERVE IT WITH STEWS, MEXICAN FARE OR A HEARTY SOUP OR STEW.

I CUP	ALL-PURPOSE FLOUR	250 ML
I CUP	YELLOW CORNMEAL	250 ML
1/4 CUP	SUGAR	60 ML
2 TSP	BAKING POWDER	10 ML
I TSP	BAKING SODA	5 ML
I TSP	SALT	5 ML
2	LARGE EGGS, LIGHTLY BEATEN	2
I CUP	BUTTERMILK	250 ML
1/4 CUP	BUTTER, MELTED	60 ML
	LIQUID HONEY	

PREHEAT OVEN TO 400°F (200°C). IN A LARGE BOWL, WHISK TOGETHER FLOUR, CORNMEAL, SUGAR, BAKING POWDER, BAKING SODA AND SALT. IN A SMALL BOWL, WHISK TOGETHER EGGS, BUTTERMILK AND BUTTER. POUR THE BUTTERMILK MIXTURE OVER THE FLOUR MIXTURE AND STIR UNTIL JUST COMBINED. SCRAPE BATTER INTO A GREASED 8-INCH (20 CM) SQUARE BAKING DISH OR A 9-INCH (23 CM) DEEP-DISH PIE PLATE. BAKE FOR 20 TO 25 MINUTES OR UNTIL A TESTER INSERTED IN THE CENTER COMES OUT CLEAN. LET COOL SLIGHTLY, THEN CUT INTO SQUARES OR WEDGES. SERVE DRIZZLED WITH HONEY, IF YOU LIKE. SERVES 8 TO 10.

VARIATION: FOR CHEDDAR ROSEMARY CORNBREAD, STIR IN I TBSP (15 ML) CHOPPED FRESH ROSEMARY AND I CUP (250 ML) SHREDDED CHEDDAR CHEESE WITH THE DRY INGREDIENTS.

Jacki's Latkes (page 225)

Beet and Beet Greens Risotto (page 230)

Finnish Pulla (page 240)

Buttermilk Cornbread (page 252)

SAUCES & CONDIMENTS

BASIC SALAD DRESSINGS

HOMEMADE SALAD DRESSINGS ARE VERY EASY TO MAKE AND CAN SAVE YOU A BUNDLE — AND JUST LIKE HOMEMADE STOCK, THEY'RE GENERALLY FAR BETTER THAN THE READY-MADE VERSION. WE HAVE THREE DRESSINGS HERE TO GET YOU STARTED.

HONEY MUSTARD VINAIGRETTE

1	GARLIC CLOVE, FINELY MINCED	1
1/2 CUP	VEGETABLE OIL	125 ML
3 TBSP	WHITE WINE VINEGAR	45 ML
1 to 2 TSP	GRAINY MUSTARD (SEE TIP)	5 to 10 ML
1 to 2 TSP	LIQUID HONEY	5 to 10 ML
	SALT AND BLACK PEPPER TO TASTE	

MAPLE BALSAMIC VINAIGRETTE

1	GARLIC CLOVE, FINELY MINCED	1
1/2 CUP	VEGETABLE OIL	125 ML
1/4 CUP	BALSAMIC VINEGAR	60 ML
1 TBSP	RED WINE VINEGAR	15 ML
1 TBSP	PURE MAPLE SYRUP	15 ML
1 TSP	DIJON MUSTARD	5 ML
	SALT AND BLACK PEPPER TO TASTE	

SESAME SOY DRESSING

2 TBSP	SLICED GREEN ONION (DARK GREEN PART ONLY)	30 ML
1 1/2 TSP	SUGAR	7 ML
1/2 CUP	VEGETABLE OIL	125 ML
3 TBSP	LEMON JUICE	45 ML
2 TBSP	SOY SAUCE	30 ML
1 TSP	TOASTED SESAME OIL	5 ML

PLACE ALL DRESSING INGREDIENTS IN A SMALL BOWL (OR A JAR WITH A LID). WHISK (OR SHAKE) UNTIL EMULSIFIED. LET STAND FOR A FEW MINUTES, THEN TASTE AND ADJUST FLAVORS TO SUIT YOUR PREFERENCE AND INTENDED USE. KEEP IN FRIDGE AND USE WITHIN 3 DAYS. MAKES ABOUT $3/4$ CUP (175 ML).

TIP: WHEN MAKING THE HONEY MUSTARD VINAIGRETTE, START WITH THE LOWER QUANTITY OF MUSTARD AND HONEY FOR A SUBTLE FLAVOR PROFILE. AFTER TASTING, YOU CAN DECIDE IF YOU'D LIKE THE MUSTARD AND HONEY TO BE BOLDER.

LEMONY HOLLANDAISE

WE LOVE OUR HOLLANDAISE WELL AND TRULY LEMONY,
TO BALANCE THE RICHNESS OF THE BUTTER AND EGGS.
SERVE WITH EGGS, ASPARAGUS, SEAFOOD OR POTATOES.

2	LARGE EGG YOLKS	2
1½ TBSP	LEMON JUICE	22 ML
	WHITE OR BLACK PEPPER TO TASTE	
6 TBSP	BUTTER, MELTED AND COOLED SLIGHTLY	90 ML
	ICE CUBE OR WARM WATER (IF NEEDED)	

IN A MEDIUM BOWL, WHISK EGG YOLKS, LEMON JUICE AND
PEPPER FOR 1 MINUTE. SET BOWL OVER A POT OF BARELY
SIMMERING WATER AND SLOWLY WHISK IN BUTTER.
CONTINUE WHISKING FOR 3 TO 5 MINUTES OR UNTIL
HOLLANDAISE THICKENS A LITTLE. IF THE SAUCE STARTS
TO LOOK GRAINY AROUND THE EDGES, TAKE THE BOWL
OFF THE HEAT AND WHISK IN AN ICE CUBE; IF IT THICKENS
MORE THAN YOU WANT (BUT DOESN'T CURDLE), WHISK
IN ½ TO 1 TSP (2 TO 5 ML) WARM WATER. USE WITHIN
AN HOUR (SEE TIP), OR 2 AT THE MOST (DISCARD AFTER
2 HOURS). MAKES ABOUT ½ CUP (125 ML).

TIP: IF YOU WON'T BE USING THE HOLLANDAISE
IMMEDIATELY, FILL A SMALL LUNCH THERMOS WITH HOT
(NOT BOILING) WATER AND SCREW ON THE LID. AFTER
10 MINUTES, POUR WATER OUT AND DRY THERMOS
WITH A CLEAN TEA TOWEL. POUR IN SAUCE TO HOLD AT
TEMPERATURE FOR UP TO 2 HOURS.

TIP: WE GENERALLY USE SALTED BUTTER. IF YOU USE
UNSALTED BUTTER, ADD SALT TO TASTE.

FLAVORED BUTTER

BUTTER IS DELICIOUS ON ITS OWN (OF COURSE!), BUT A LITTLE EXTRA FLAVOR CAN FEEL PARTICULARLY FANCY WHEN YOU'RE PUTTING TOGETHER A NICE DINNER. THE BUTTER CAN CHILL IN THE FRIDGE UNTIL YOU NEED TO CUT OFF A PAT OR TWO TO MELT ONTO A STEAK OR AN EAR OF FRESH CORN, OR TO SMEAR ONTO A CHICKEN BEFORE ROASTING.

1/2 CUP	BUTTER, SOFTENED	125 ML

LEMON HERB BUTTER

1/4 CUP	FINELY CHOPPED FRESH PARSLEY	60 ML
1 TBSP	FINELY CHOPPED FRESH THYME	15 ML
1 1/2 TSP	FINELY CHOPPED FRESH ROSEMARY	7 ML
	GRATED ZEST OF 1 LEMON	

CHILI LIME BUTTER

2 TBSP	FINELY CHOPPED FRESH CILANTRO	30 ML
1 1/2 TSP	CHILI POWDER	7 ML
	GRATED ZEST OF 1 LIME	

CURRIED BUTTER

2 TBSP	FINELY CHOPPED FRESH CILANTRO	30 ML
2 TSP	CURRY PASTE	10 ML
1 TSP	LEMON JUICE	5 ML

PLACE BUTTER IN A MEDIUM BOWL WITH THE FLAVORING INGREDIENTS. MASH EVERYTHING TOGETHER WITH A FORK SO THAT THE OTHER INGREDIENTS ARE EVENLY DISTRIBUTED THROUGHOUT THE BUTTER. PACK INTO A RAMEKIN, OR ROLL INTO A LOG, AND WRAP IN PLASTIC WRAP. STORE IN THE FRIDGE FOR UP TO 3 DAYS, OR IN THE FREEZER FOR UP TO 1 MONTH. *MAKES ABOUT 1/2 CUP (125 ML).*

PARSLEY BEURRE BLANC

A CLASSIC FRENCH SAUCE, BEURRE BLANC MEANS "WHITE BUTTER." WE USE IT ON VEGETABLES AND FISH OF ALL KINDS. WHILE THE RECIPE CAN BE DOUBLED EASILY, BEURRE BLANC WON'T RETAIN ITS TEXTURE WHEN REHEATED. WE USE LEFTOVERS TO FLAVOR RICE, POTATOES AND OTHER VEGETABLES.

2 TSP	MINCED SHALLOTS	10 ML
2 TBSP	WHITE WINE	30 ML
2 TBSP	WHITE WINE VINEGAR	30 ML
PINCH	WHITE OR BLACK PEPPER	PINCH
1/2 CUP	BUTTER, CUT INTO 1-INCH (2.5 CM) PIECES (SEE TIP)	125 ML
2 TSP	FINELY CHOPPED FRESH PARSLEY	10 ML
1/2 TSP	LEMON JUICE	2 ML

IN A MEDIUM SAUCEPAN, COMBINE SHALLOTS, WINE, VINEGAR AND PEPPER. BRING TO A BOIL OVER MEDIUM HEAT. BOIL UNTIL ONLY ABOUT 1 TBSP (15 ML) LIQUID REMAINS. REMOVE FROM HEAT AND LET COOL FOR ABOUT A MINUTE, THEN WHISK IN 1 PIECE OF BUTTER UNTIL MELTED (THE BUTTER SHOULD MELT, BUT NOT SIZZLE VIOLENTLY). WHISK IN ANOTHER PIECE UNTIL MELTED. RETURN PAN TO LOW HEAT FROM TIME TO TIME AS NEEDED TO KEEP THE TEMPERATURE OF SAUCE WARM ENOUGH TO MELT BUTTER (SLOWLY) BUT WELL SHORT OF BOILING. WHISK IN BUTTER, ONE PIECE AT A TIME, UNTIL ALL BUTTER IS INCORPORATED AND SAUCE IS THICK AND SMOOTH. STIR IN PARSLEY AND LEMON JUICE. USE WITHIN AN HOUR, OR 2 AT THE MOST (SEE TIP, PAGE 256), AFTER WHICH TIME SAUCE CAN BE TRANSFERRED TO AN AIRTIGHT

CONTAINER AND STORED IN THE FRIDGE FOR OTHER USES (USE WITHIN 3 DAYS). MAKES ABOUT $\frac{1}{2}$ CUP (125 ML).

TIP: WE GENERALLY USE SALTED BUTTER (AS THAT'S WHAT WE HAVE ON HAND). IF YOU USE UNSALTED BUTTER FOR THE BEURRE BLANC, ADD SALT TO TASTE.

VARIATION: TO MAKE A PLAIN BEURRE BLANC, OMIT THE PARSLEY. IF YOU WANT THE SAUCE TO BE COMPLETELY SMOOTH, POUR IT THROUGH A FINE-MESH SIEVE BEFORE USING.

I DON'T KNOW HOW TO ACT MY AGE.
I'VE NEVER BEEN THIS AGE BEFORE.

QUICK HOMEMADE MAYO

MAYO THAT CAN LITERALLY BE MADE IN MOMENTS, AND THAT TASTES INCREDIBLE IN AN EGG SALAD SANDWICH, IN POTATO SALAD OR ON HOMEMADE OVEN FRIES.

IMPORTANT: ENSURE ALL INGREDIENTS ARE AT ROOM TEMPERATURE BEFORE STARTING (WE PLACE THE EGG IN A HOT TAP WATER BATH TO WARM IT UP QUICKLY).

I	LARGE EGG, AT ROOM TEMPERATURE (SEE SAFETY TIP, OPPOSITE)	I
I TSP	DIJON MUSTARD	5 ML
I TBSP	LEMON JUICE OR WHITE WINE VINEGAR	15 ML
	SALT AND BLACK PEPPER TO TASTE	
$3/_4$ CUP	CANOLA OR SUNFLOWER OIL (SEE TIP)	175 ML

CRACK EGG INTO A I- TO 2-CUP (250 TO 500 ML) GLASS MEASURING CUP OR A 16-OZ (500 ML) WIDE-MOUTH CANNING JAR. GENTLY ADD ALL OTHER INGREDIENTS, IN ORDER. PLACE THE HEAD OF AN IMMERSION BLENDER ON THE BOTTOM OF THE CUP SO THAT IT COVERS THE EGG. PULSE A FEW TIMES, UNTIL YOU SEE OPAQUE SWIRLS COMING FROM THE BLENDER VENTS. CONTINUE TO PULSE, SLOWLY TIPPING THE BLENDER TO ONE SIDE AND THEN GRADUALLY LIFTING IT UP THROUGH THE OIL UNTIL THE MAYO IS UNIFORM AND THICK. COVER AND REFRIGERATE, AND USE WITHIN 5 DAYS. MAKES ABOUT I CUP (250 ML).

TIP: DON'T BE TEMPTED TO USE OLIVE OIL WHEN MAKING MAYO WITH THIS METHOD — THE RESULT WILL BE BITTER.

TIP: ENSURE THAT ITEMS MADE WITH MAYO ARE ALSO KEPT REFRIGERATED.

TZATZIKI

SERVE THIS CLASSIC GREEK DIP ALONGSIDE GREEK-INSPIRED PORK SKEWERS (PAGE 121) OR SALMON BURGERS (PAGE 82). IT'S ALSO EQUALLY GOOD AS A STAND-ALONE DIP WITH PITA BREAD.

1/2	LARGE ENGLISH CUCUMBER (UNPEELED)	1/2
1 OR 2	GARLIC CLOVES, MINCED	1 OR 2
2 TBSP	FINELY CHOPPED FRESH MINT OR DILL	30 ML
	SALT AND BLACK PEPPER TO TASTE	
1 CUP	FULL-FAT PLAIN GREEK YOGURT	250 ML
1 TSP	LEMON JUICE	5 ML

COARSELY GRATE CUCUMBER INTO A COLANDER LINED WITH PAPER TOWEL. WRAP UP AND SQUEEZE OUT AS MUCH MOISTURE AS POSSIBLE, THEN TRANSFER TO A BOWL. STIR IN GARLIC TO TASTE, MINT, SALT, PEPPER AND YOGURT, THEN STIR IN LEMON JUICE. KEEPS IN THE FRIDGE FOR UP TO 5 DAYS. MAKES ABOUT 1 1/2 CUPS (375 ML).

PICO DE GALLO

ESSENTIALLY JUST A REALLY FRESH SALSA, PICO DE GALLO HAS BOLD FLAVORS. USE IT IN BEAN SOUPS, IN WRAPS OR ALONGSIDE QUESADILLAS — OR SCOOP IT STRAIGHT UP WITH CORN CHIPS.

14 OZ	PLUM (ROMA) TOMATOES (ABOUT 5 OR 6)	420 G
1	JALAPEÑO PEPPER, SEEDS AND RIBS REMOVED, FINELY CHOPPED	1
1/2 CUP	PACKED FRESH CILANTRO LEAVES AND SMALL STEMS, CHOPPED	125 ML
1/3 CUP	FINELY CHOPPED WHITE ONION	75 ML
	JUICE OF 1 LIME	
	SALT TO TASTE	

CUT TOMATOES IN HALF AND REMOVE CORE AND SEEDS. SPREAD OVER A DOUBLE THICKNESS OF PAPER TOWELS TO ABSORB EXCESS JUICE FOR A FEW MINUTES, THEN TRANSFER TO A CUTTING BOARD AND CHOP. PLACE IN A MEDIUM BOWL WITH THE REMAINING INGREDIENTS AND TOSS TOGETHER. LET STAND FOR 10 MINUTES, THEN TOSS AGAIN. KEEP IN THE FRIDGE UNTIL READY TO USE (IT'S BEST ON THE DAY IT'S MADE). *MAKES ABOUT 2 CUPS (500 ML).*

SALSA VERDE

THE NAME JUST MEANS "GREEN SAUCE." THIS RECIPE — NOT TO BE CONFUSED WITH THE MEXICAN SAUCE OF THE SAME NAME, MADE WITH TOMATILLOS — IS SO EASY TO MAKE, AND IS A PERFECT ACCOMPANIMENT TO RICH MEATS. WE PARTICULARLY LIKE IT WITH PORK SHOULDER STEAKS.

2	GARLIC CLOVES, CHOPPED	2
1/2 CUP	PACKED FRESH FLAT-LEAF (ITALIAN) PARSLEY LEAVES (ABOUT 1 SMALL BUNCH)	125 ML
	GRATED ZEST OF 1/2 LEMON	
1 1/2 TBSP	LEMON JUICE	22 ML
1 TBSP	RED WINE VINEGAR	15 ML
1/3 CUP	OLIVE OIL	75 ML

IN A FOOD PROCESSOR, COMBINE GARLIC, PARSLEY, LEMON ZEST, LEMON JUICE AND VINEGAR; PULSE, SCRAPING DOWN THE BOWL A FEW TIMES, UNTIL VERY FINELY CHOPPED. WITH THE MOTOR RUNNING, THROUGH THE FEED TUBE, ADD OIL IN A THIN STREAM AND PROCESS UNTIL NEARLY SMOOTH (IT WILL BE VERY GREEN, WITH SOME FLECKS REMAINING). KEEPS IN THE FRIDGE FOR UP TO 3 DAYS. MAKES ABOUT 1/2 CUP (125 ML).

CHIMICHURRI

THIS IS A TRADITIONAL ARGENTINIAN CHIMICHURRI. OTHER VERSIONS USE CILANTRO OR MINT. CHIMICHURRI IS MOST OFTEN USED AS A CONDIMENT FOR COOKED MEATS, SUCH AS STEAK, BUT WE ALSO LIKE TO USE IT AS A MARINADE FOR CHICKEN (SEE CHIMICHURRI CHICKEN LEGS, PAGE 92) AND PORK.

2	GARLIC CLOVES, MINCED	2
1/2 CUP	PACKED FINELY CHOPPED FRESH PARSLEY LEAVES AND SMALL STEMS	125 ML
1 TSP	DRIED OREGANO	5 ML
1/4 TSP	SALT	1 ML
1/4 TSP	BLACK PEPPER	1 ML
1/8 TSP	HOT PEPPER FLAKES	0.5 ML
3 TBSP	OLIVE OIL	45 ML
2 TBSP	RED WINE VINEGAR OR LEMON JUICE (SEE TIP)	30 ML

IN A SMALL BOWL, COMBINE ALL INGREDIENTS. LET FLAVORS COMBINE FOR AT LEAST 30 MINUTES. KEEPS IN THE FRIDGE FOR UP TO 5 DAYS. MAKES ABOUT 1/2 CUP (125 ML).

TIP: RED WINE VINEGAR IS TRADITIONALLY USED IN CHIMICHURRI, BUT LEMON JUICE WORKS WELL TOO, AND IS ESPECIALLY COMPATIBLE WHEN YOU'RE PAIRING THE CHIMICHURRI WITH CHICKEN.

SPINACH AND WALNUT PESTO

WE LOVE THIS VERSION OF PESTO. SPINACH CAN BE
FOUND YEAR-ROUND, AND WALNUTS ADD A MILD FLAVOR
SIMILAR TO PINE NUTS — WITH NO SECOND MORTGAGE
NEEDED. WE USE THIS PESTO ON GRILLED TROUT
(SEE RECIPE, PAGE 113), ON BURGERS AND IN PLACE OF
TOMATO SAUCE AS A BASE ON PIZZA.

1	PACKAGE (5 OZ/142 G) BABY SPINACH	1
1	GARLIC CLOVE, MINCED	1
1/4 CUP	CHOPPED WALNUTS	60 ML
1/4 CUP	GRATED PARMESAN CHEESE	60 ML
	SALT AND BLACK PEPPER TO TASTE	
2 TBSP	OLIVE OIL (APPROX.)	30 ML

IN A FOOD PROCESSOR, COMBINE SPINACH, GARLIC,
WALNUTS, CHEESE, SALT AND PEPPER; PULSE, SCRAPING
DOWN THE BOWL A FEW TIMES, UNTIL SPINACH IS IN VERY
SMALL PIECES. WITH THE MOTOR RUNNING, THROUGH THE
FEED TUBE, ADD OIL IN A THIN STREAM AND PROCESS
UNTIL PESTO IS NEARLY SMOOTH, SCRAPING DOWN THE
BOWL AND ADDING A LITTLE MORE OIL AS NEEDED. KEEPS
IN THE FRIDGE FOR UP TO 4 DAYS. MAKES ABOUT 3/4 CUP
(175 ML).

BASIC GRAVY

GRAVY CAN BE THE BEST PART OF A ROAST DINNER WHEN IT'S DONE WELL! THIS IS A TUTORIAL, RATHER THAN A SPECIFIC RECIPE FOR A PARTICULAR ROAST. GREAT GRAVY SHOULD RELY MORE ON THE PAN JUICES THAN STOCK FOR ITS FLAVOR (THOUGH IT'S FINE TO USE SOME STOCK). HOW MUCH GRAVY YOU MAKE WILL DEPEND ON HOW BIG YOUR ROAST IS AND HOW MUCH IN THE WAY OF DRIPPINGS IT PRODUCES. YOU'LL NEED:

ROASTING PAN WITH CONCENTRATED PAN JUICES

THICKENER, SUCH AS ALL-PURPOSE FLOUR, CORNSTARCH OR POTATO STARCH

WATER AND/OR STOCK OR READY-TO-USE BROTH (CHICKEN OR BEEF, DEPENDING ON WHAT YOU'VE ROASTED)

SAUTÉED SHALLOTS (VERY OPTIONAL)

DRY WINE OR LEMON JUICE

SALT AND BLACK PEPPER TO TASTE

PLACE THE ROASTING PAN ON THE STOVETOP AND SPOON OUT ANY EXCESS FAT BEFORE YOU START (A LITTLE IS FINE). ADD A SPOONFUL OR TWO OF FLOUR (SEE TIP, AND IF USING CORNSTARCH OR POTATO FLOUR, DON'T ADD IT HERE; SEE METHOD OPPOSITE). BROWN OVER MEDIUM-HIGH HEAT, STIRRING, FOR A FEW MINUTES. REDUCE HEAT TO MEDIUM AND ADD 1 TO 2 CUPS OF WATER (250 TO 500 ML). SCRAPE UP ALL THE BROWNED BITS UNTIL DISSOLVED. ADD SHALLOTS AND A LITTLE STOCK (IF USING). IF THE LIQUID THICKENS BEFORE THE CONCENTRATED PAN JUICES DISSOLVE, ADD MORE WATER — YOU CAN ALWAYS SIMMER IT LONGER TO REDUCE IT.

TO THICKEN WITH CORNSTARCH OR POTATO STARCH, STIR THE STARCH INTO ABOUT THE SAME QUANTITY OF COOL WATER OR STOCK, WHISK INTO THE GRAVY AND BRING IT BACK TO A LOW BOIL FOR A COUPLE OF MINUTES, WHISKING CONSTANTLY UNTIL THE GRAVY HAS THICKENED.

TASTE, AND IF THE GRAVY IS A LITTLE FLAT, ADD A SPLASH OF WINE OR LEMON JUICE. SEASON WITH SALT AND PEPPER AND PUSH IT THROUGH A SIEVE IF YOU WANT IT PERFECTLY SMOOTH. SERVE HOT, AND REFRIGERATE LEFTOVERS PROMPTLY.

TIP: THE AMOUNT OF FLOUR TO ADD TO A ROASTING PAN IS DIFFICULT TO QUANTIFY. AS A GENERAL GUIDE, WE USE ABOUT 1 TBSP (15 ML) FOR POULTRY UP TO 3 LBS (1.5 KG), AND 2 TBSP FOR A 5-LB (2.5 KG) BIRD. BEEF TENDS TO PRODUCE A LOT LESS IN THE WAY OF DRIPPINGS, SO START WITH 1 TBSP (15 ML). ONCE WE'VE ADDED LIQUID AND LET THE GRAVY THICKEN, WE'LL USE CORNSTARCH OR POTATO STARCH TO THICKEN IT FURTHER, IF REQUIRED. THIS HAS THE ADDED BONUS OF ENSURING THAT YOUR GRAVY IS NEITHER GELATINOUS (TOO MUCH CORNSTARCH) OR PASTY (TOO MUCH FLOUR).

TIP: WHEN MAKING GRAVY FOR TURKEY (SUCH AS EASY UNSTUFFED TURKEY, PAGE 62), WE LEAVE THE NECK AND GIBLETS IN THE PAN UNTIL WE STRAIN THE GRAVY TO SERVE. THINK OF IT AS MAKING A MINI-STOCK — THEY'LL ADD A TON OF FLAVOR TO YOUR GRAVY.

BLUE CHEESE STEAK SAUCE

THIS RICH SAUCE WILL ELEVATE A STEAK TO SOMETHING TRULY SPECIAL. FOR SOMETHING A LITTLE DIFFERENT, WE LIKE TO SEAR BITE-SIZE CHUNKS OF STEAKS IN A CAST-IRON SKILLET AND SERVE WITH THIS SAUCE FOR DRIZZLING.

1/2 CUP	HEAVY OR WHIPPING (35%) CREAM	125 ML
1/2 CUP	CRUMBLED STILTON CHEESE	125 ML
1/2 TSP	DRY MUSTARD	2 ML
1 TSP	LEMON JUICE	5 ML

IN A MEDIUM SAUCEPAN, BRING CREAM TO A BOIL OVER MEDIUM HEAT. REDUCE HEAT AND SIMMER, SCRAPING SIDES AND BOTTOM OF PAN WITH A HEATPROOF SPATULA, FOR 3 TO 5 MINUTES OR UNTIL CREAM IS VERY THICK AND REDUCED BY ABOUT HALF (TAKE CARE: CREAM WILL BUBBLE UP HIGH IN THE PAN). REDUCE HEAT TO LOW AND STIR IN CHEESE. ONCE MOST OF THE CHEESE HAS MELTED, WHISK IN MUSTARD UNTIL SAUCE IS NEARLY SMOOTH. STIR IN LEMON JUICE. LET COOL SLIGHTLY, THEN STIR AGAIN BEFORE SERVING. MAKES ABOUT 1/2 CUP (125 ML), ENOUGH FOR 4 TO 6 SERVINGS.

TIP: LEFTOVERS KEEP IN A JAR IN THE FRIDGE FOR UP TO A WEEK; REHEAT SLOWLY AND WHISK SMOOTH AGAIN.

WHAT DOES "VARICOSE" MEAN?
ANSWER: NEARBY.

MUST-TRY MUSTARD SAUCE

FORGET THE YELLOW STUFF FROM THE SQUEEZE BOTTLE — THIS HOMEMADE MUSTARD SAUCE IS PERFECT WITH A CLASSIC HAM DINNER, PORK TENDERLOIN OR SAUSAGES.

2	LARGE EGG YOLKS	2
3/4 CUP	MILK	175 ML
3 TBSP	LIQUID HONEY	45 ML
2 TBSP	DRY MUSTARD	30 ML
1 TBSP	ALL-PURPOSE FLOUR	15 ML
1/4 CUP	APPLE CIDER VINEGAR	60 ML
PINCH	SALT	PINCH
2 TBSP	BUTTER	30 ML

IN A SMALL SAUCEPAN, WHISK TOGETHER EGG YOLKS, MILK AND HONEY. PLACE OVER MEDIUM HEAT AND WHISK IN MUSTARD AND FLOUR UNTIL COMBINED. STIR IN VINEGAR AND SALT. BRING TO A BOIL, WHISKING CONSTANTLY. REDUCE HEAT AND SIMMER (STILL WHISKING — IT'S ONLY A COUPLE OF MINUTES!) UNTIL THICKENED. REMOVE FROM HEAT, ADD BUTTER AND STIR UNTIL MELTED. MAKES ABOUT 1 CUP (250 ML).

TIP: IF YOU DON'T SERVE THE WHOLE LOT AT DINNER, THE MUSTARD SAUCE WILL KEEP COVERED IN THE FRIDGE FOR UP TO 2 WEEKS. USE IT ON SANDWICHES!

CRANBERRY SAUCE, TWO WAYS

EVERY TURKEY DINNER NEEDS CRANBERRY SAUCE!
WE'VE GOT YOU COVERED WITH TWO OPTIONS. BOTH ARE
VERY EASY TO PREPARE AND CAN BE MADE AHEAD OF
THE BIG DAY.

WITH ORANGE

2 CUPS	FRESH OR FROZEN CRANBERRIES	500 ML
$\frac{1}{4}$ to $\frac{1}{2}$ CUP	SUGAR	60 to 125 ML
1	LONG STRIP ORANGE ZEST (ABOUT 4 BY $\frac{1}{2}$ INCHES/10 BY 1 CM)	1
$\frac{1}{2}$ CUP	ORANGE JUICE	125 ML

IN A MEDIUM SAUCEPAN, COMBINE CRANBERRIES, $\frac{1}{4}$ CUP
(60 ML) SUGAR, ORANGE ZEST AND ORANGE JUICE; BRING
TO A BOIL OVER MEDIUM-HIGH HEAT. BOIL, STIRRING
OCCASIONALLY, FOR 15 TO 20 MINUTES OR UNTIL
CRANBERRIES HAVE ALL POPPED (YOU CAN HELP THEM
ALONG BY SMUSHING THEM AGAINST THE POT WITH THE
BACK OF THE SPOON). TASTE AND ADD MORE SUGAR IF
YOU WISH, THEN LET COOL. MAKES ABOUT 1 CUP (250 ML).

WITH WINE AND CURRANTS

$\frac{1}{4}$ CUP	DRIED CURRANTS	60 ML
$\frac{3}{4}$ CUP	DRY RED WINE	175 ML
1	CINNAMON STICK	1
2 CUPS	FRESH OR FROZEN CRANBERRIES	500 ML
$\frac{1}{4}$ to $\frac{1}{2}$ CUP	SUGAR	60 to 125 ML

IN A MEDIUM SAUCEPAN, COMBINE CURRANTS, WINE AND
CINNAMON STICK; BRING TO A SIMMER OVER MEDIUM

HEAT. SIMMER UNTIL REDUCED BY ABOUT ONE-THIRD, ABOUT 10 MINUTES. ADD CRANBERRIES AND 1/4 CUP (60 ML) SUGAR; BRING TO A BOIL. BOIL, STIRRING OCCASIONALLY, FOR 15 TO 20 MINUTES OR UNTIL CRANBERRIES HAVE ALL POPPED (YOU CAN HELP THEM ALONG BY SMUSHING THEM AGAINST THE POT WITH THE BACK OF THE SPOON). TASTE AND ADD MORE SUGAR IF YOU WISH, THEN LET COOL. MAKES ABOUT 1 CUP (250 ML).

TIP: BOTH VERSIONS WILL KEEP IN THE FRIDGE FOR A WEEK OR TWO (OR IN THE FREEZER FOR A FEW MONTHS).

HOMEMADE MINT SAUCE

WHEN YOU'RE GOING TO THE EFFORT TO ROAST A LEG OF LAMB, A BATCH OF FRESH MINT SAUCE IS WORTH THE EXTRA 5 MINUTES.

1/3 CUP	SUGAR	75 ML
1/3 CUP	UNSEASONED RICE VINEGAR	75 ML
1/3 CUP	WATER	75 ML
1/3 CUP	FINELY CHOPPED FRESH MINT (LEAVES ONLY)	75 ML

IN A SMALL SAUCEPAN, BRING SUGAR, VINEGAR AND WATER TO A SIMMER OVER MEDIUM HEAT, STIRRING UNTIL SUGAR IS DISSOLVED. REMOVE FROM HEAT AND STIR IN MINT. LET COOL COMPLETELY — THE MINT WILL STEEP IN THE SYRUP AS IT COOLS. STORE IN THE FRIDGE AND SERVE WARM OR COLD. MAKES ABOUT 1 CUP (250 ML).

EASY PEACH, MANGO OR APPLE CHUTNEY

THIS TANGY-SWEET CHUTNEY IS PERFECT WITH CURRIES, SAMOSAS, ROAST CHICKEN OR PORK, OR TO SERVE ALONGSIDE CHEESE PLATTERS.

2 LBS	PEACHES, NECTARINES, MANGOS OR TART APPLES (SEE TIP), DICED	1 KG
2	GARLIC CLOVES, MINCED	2
1	SMALL ONION, FINELY CHOPPED	1
1	JALAPEÑO PEPPER, SEEDED AND MINCED	1
1/2	RED BELL PEPPER, FINELY CHOPPED	1/2
1 TBSP	GRATED FRESH GINGER	15 ML
1 CUP	PACKED BROWN SUGAR	250 ML
1/4 TSP	SALT	1 ML
PINCH	HOT PEPPER FLAKES	PINCH
1/2 CUP	APPLE CIDER VINEGAR OR UNSEASONED RICE VINEGAR	125 ML

IN A LARGE SAUCEPAN, COMBINE ALL INGREDIENTS; BRING TO A BOIL OVER MEDIUM-HIGH HEAT. REDUCE HEAT AND SIMMER, STIRRING OFTEN, FOR ABOUT 20 MINUTES OR UNTIL FRUIT SOFTENS AND THE MIXTURE THICKENS. CONTINUE TO COOK IF IT SEEMS TOO RUNNY, KEEPING IN MIND THAT IT WILL THICKEN AS IT COOLS. REMOVE FROM HEAT AND LET COOL COMPLETELY. POUR INTO JARS AND REFRIGERATE FOR UP TO A MONTH, OR FREEZE FOR UP TO 6 MONTHS. MAKES ABOUT 8 CUPS (2 L).

TIP: IF USING PEACHES, NECTARINES OR APPLES FOR THIS RECIPE, YOU CAN PEEL THEM OR LEAVE THEM UNPEELED. MANGOS, OF COURSE, WILL NEED TO BE PEELED BEFORE THEY ARE DICED.

MARINATED CUCUMBERS FOR THE TABLE

FANCY CHEFS AND FOODIES ARE CALLING THESE TANGY CUCUMBERS "QUICK PICKLES," BUT FOR DECADES OUR FAMILIES HAVE SIMPLY BEEN CALLING THEM "MARINATED CUCUMBERS" AND SERVING THEM ALONGSIDE EVERYTHING FROM ROAST MEATS TO BURGERS.

1	GARLIC CLOVE, MINCED	1
2 TBSP	SUGAR	30 ML
2 TSP	DRIED DILL	10 ML
1 TSP	MUSTARD SEEDS	5 ML
1 TSP	SALT	5 ML
PINCH	HOT PEPPER FLAKES	PINCH
1/2 to 1 CUP	WHITE VINEGAR	125 to 250 ML
2	LARGE CUCUMBERS	2

IN A SMALL SAUCEPAN, COMBINE GARLIC, SUGAR, DILL, MUSTARD SEEDS, SALT, HOT PEPPER FLAKES AND 1/2 CUP (125 ML) VINEGAR. HEAT OVER MEDIUM-LOW HEAT, STIRRING, UNTIL SUGAR IS DISSOLVED. LET COOL.

MEANWHILE, SLICE CUCUMBERS INTO ROUNDS, THE THINNER THE BETTER. PLACE IN A GLASS OR STAINLESS STEEL BOWL. POUR COOLED MARINADE OVER CUCUMBERS, SUBMERGING THEM (TOP OFF WITH A LITTLE MORE VINEGAR, IF NECESSARY). COVER AND REFRIGERATE FOR AT LEAST 4 HOURS OR OVERNIGHT. THE CUCUMBERS SHOULD LAST IN THE FRIDGE FOR UP TO 5 DAYS. SERVES 8 TO 10.

NORMA'S ENGLISH-STYLE PICCALILLI

PICCALILLI IS A BRITISH VERSION OF INDIAN PICKLE RELISH AND GOES WONDERFULLY WITH ROAST MEATS, CHARCUTERIE OR ANY OTHER WAY YOU FEEL LIKE SNEAKING IT IN. NORMA'S VERSION IS PACKED WITH BROWN SUGAR AND TURMERIC FOR A PERFECT BALANCE OF SWEET AND TANGY.

3 CUPS	DICED MINI CUCUMBERS (SEE TIP)	750 ML
3 CUPS	CAULIFLOWER FLORETS (AS SMALL AS POSSIBLE)	750 ML
2 CUPS	ROUGHLY CHOPPED PEELED PEARL ONIONS	500 ML
1/4 CUP	PICKLING SALT	60 ML
6 CUPS	WATER	1.5 L
2 CUPS	PACKED BROWN SUGAR	500 ML
1/2 CUP	ALL-PURPOSE FLOUR	125 ML
1/4 CUP	DRY MUSTARD	60 ML
1 TBSP	CELERY SEEDS	15 ML
2 TSP	GROUND TURMERIC	10 ML
1 1/2 TSP	SALT	7 ML
3 CUPS	WHITE VINEGAR	750 ML
1 CUP	WARM WATER	250 ML

PLACE CUCUMBERS, CAULIFLOWER AND ONIONS IN A LARGE BOWL AND SPRINKLE WITH PICKLING SALT. FILL THE BOWL WITH 6 CUPS (1.5 L) WATER, COVER WITH PLASTIC WRAP AND REFRIGERATE OVERNIGHT.

POUR VEGETABLES AND BRINING LIQUID INTO A LARGE, HEAVY POT AND BRING TO A BOIL. DRAIN VEGETABLES IN A COLANDER AND RINSE OFF ANY EXCESS SALT.

IN THE SAME POT, COMBINE BROWN SUGAR, FLOUR, MUSTARD, CELERY SEEDS, TURMERIC AND SALT. PLACE OVER MEDIUM-LOW HEAT AND SLOWLY STIR IN VINEGAR AND WARM WATER. SLOWLY BRING TO A BOIL, STIRRING REGULARLY SO THAT NOTHING BUILDS UP ON THE BOTTOM OF THE POT. BOIL FOR 3 TO 4 MINUTES, STIRRING CONSTANTLY, THEN ADD VEGETABLES AND RETURN TO A BOIL. REMOVE FROM HEAT AND LET COOL.

AT THIS POINT, YOU CAN DIVIDE PICCALILLI INTO MANAGEABLE PORTIONS AND FREEZE ANY THAT YOU'RE NOT PLANNING TO USE IMMEDIATELY. PICCALILLI KEEPS IN THE REFRIGERATOR FOR ABOUT 2 WEEKS OR IN THE FREEZER FOR UP TO 6 MONTHS. MAKES ABOUT 6 CUPS (1.5 L).

TIP: THIN-SKINNED MINI ENGLISH CUCUMBERS ARE EASY TO FIND IN MOST GROCERY STORES AND WORK PERFECTLY FOR THIS PICCALILLI. DON'T USE THE KNOBBY PICKLING CUKES, WHICH CAN BE MORE WOODY.

IF IT WALKS OUT OF THE REFRIGERATOR, LET IT GO.

MARINATED ROASTED VEGETABLES

WE LOVE TO SERVE THESE HEAPED ON TOP OF SLICES OF FOCACCIA (SEE PAGE 242). THEY'RE WONDERFUL TO HAVE ON HAND TO LIVEN UP A SANDWICH OR SALAD, OR TO SERVE SIMPLY AS A SIDE DISH.

2	PEPPERS (RED OR ORANGE BELL OR POBLANO)	2
6 OZ	MUSHROOMS	175 G
2 CUPS	CHERRY OR GRAPE TOMATOES	500 ML
$\frac{1}{4}$ CUP	OLIVE OIL, DIVIDED	60 ML
	SALT AND BLACK PEPPER TO TASTE	
$\frac{1}{4}$ TSP	DRIED OREGANO	1 ML
$1\frac{1}{2}$ TBSP	RED WINE VINEGAR	22 ML

PREHEAT OVEN TO 425°F (220°C). CORE PEPPERS AND CUT INTO STRIPS ABOUT $\frac{1}{4}$ INCH (0.5 CM) WIDE. TRIM MUSHROOMS AND CUT LARGER ONES IN HALF (OR EVEN QUARTERS). PLACE PEPPERS, MUSHROOMS AND TOMATOES ON A LARGE RIMMED BAKING SHEET LINED WITH PARCHMENT PAPER. DRIZZLE WITH ABOUT HALF THE OIL AND TOSS WELL. SPRINKLE WITH SALT AND PEPPER. SPREAD VEGETABLES OUT IN A SINGLE LAYER. ROAST FOR 40 TO 45 MINUTES, STIRRING ONCE OR TWICE, UNTIL THE MOISTURE FROM THE VEGETABLES HAS EVAPORATED AND THINGS ARE QUITE BROWNED (THE PAN JUICES MAY BURN IN PLACES — NOT TO WORRY). LET COOL FOR 5 MINUTES.

IN A LARGE BOWL, COMBINE OREGANO, THE REMAINING OIL AND VINEGAR. TIP THE VEGETABLES INTO THE BOWL AND TOSS WELL. LET COOL COMPLETELY, THEN EITHER SERVE IMMEDIATELY OR REFRIGERATE FOR UP TO 1 WEEK. MAKES ABOUT 3 CUPS (750 ML).

DESSERTS

CHOCOLATE BOURBON PECAN PIE

EVERYTHING THAT'S DELICIOUS, ALL IN ONE PIE. ONE BITE AND YOU'LL FEEL LIKE YOU'RE SITTING ON A PORCH SOMEWHERE WARM (OR THAT MAY JUST BE THE BOURBON TALKING).

	BASIC BUTTER PIE PASTRY (PAGE 160)	
3	LARGE EGGS	3
1 CUP	SUGAR	250 ML
1 CUP	GOLDEN CORN SYRUP	250 ML
1/4 CUP	BUTTER, MELTED	60 ML
2 TBSP	BOURBON OR A SIMILAR STYLE OF WHISKEY	30 ML
1 TSP	VANILLA	5 ML
1 CUP	CHOPPED PECANS	250 ML
1/2 CUP	SEMISWEET CHOCOLATE CHIPS	125 ML
	PECAN HALVES	

PREHEAT OVEN TO 350°F (180°C). ON A LIGHTLY FLOURED SURFACE, ROLL PASTRY OUT INTO A 10-INCH (25 CM) CIRCLE. GENTLY FIT INTO A 9-INCH (23 CM) PIE PLATE AND TRIM AND CRIMP THE EDGES. IN A LARGE BOWL, LIGHTLY BEAT EGGS. WHISK IN SUGAR, CORN SYRUP, BUTTER, BOURBON AND VANILLA. SPREAD CHOPPED PECANS AND CHOCOLATE CHIPS OVER THE BOTTOM OF THE PIE CRUST AND POUR FILLING MIXTURE ON TOP. CAREFULLY ARRANGE PECAN HALVES ON TOP OF THE PIE (DO A RING AROUND THE PERIMETER OR SPIRAL THEM TO COVER THE ENTIRE SURFACE — IT'S UP TO YOU!). BAKE FOR 40 TO 50 MINUTES OR UNTIL FILLING IS SET AROUND THE EDGES BUT STILL A BIT JIGGLY IN THE MIDDLE. LET COOL ON A WIRE RACK COMPLETELY BEFORE SLICING. SERVES 8.

CLASSIC PUMPKIN PIE

EVERYONE NEEDS A GOOD PUMPKIN PIE RECIPE. SERVE IT AT ROOM TEMPERATURE WITH WHIPPED CREAM SWEETENED WITH A LITTLE SUGAR OR MAPLE SYRUP.

	BASIC BUTTER PIE PASTRY (PAGE 160)	
1/2 CUP	SUGAR	125 ML
1/2 CUP	PACKED BROWN SUGAR	125 ML
1 TSP	GROUND CINNAMON	5 ML
1/2 TSP	GROUND GINGER	2 ML
1/4 TSP	GROUND ALLSPICE	1 ML
1/4 TSP	SALT	1 ML
PINCH	GROUND NUTMEG (OPTIONAL)	PINCH
3	LARGE EGGS	3
1	CAN (14 OZ/398 ML) PUMPKIN PURÉE (NOT PIE FILLING)	1
3/4 CUP	HALF-AND-HALF (10%) CREAM OR HEAVY OR WHIPPING (35%) CREAM	175 ML
1 TBSP	DARK (COOKING) MOLASSES	15 ML
1 TSP	VANILLA	5 ML

PREHEAT OVEN TO 350°F (180°C). ON A LIGHTLY FLOURED SURFACE, ROLL PASTRY OUT INTO A 10-INCH (25 CM) CIRCLE. GENTLY FIT INTO A 9-INCH (23 CM) PIE PLATE AND TRIM AND CRIMP THE EDGES. IN A LARGE BOWL, WHISK TOGETHER THE REMAINING INGREDIENTS UNTIL WELL BLENDED AND SMOOTH. POUR INTO CRUST. BAKE FOR 50 TO 60 MINUTES OR UNTIL FILLING IS SET AROUND THE EDGES BUT STILL A BIT JIGGLY IN THE MIDDLE. LET COOL COMPLETELY ON A WIRE RACK BEFORE SLICING. SERVES 8.

TIP: IF THE CRUST IS BROWNING TOO QUICKLY, COVER THE PIE LIGHTLY WITH A SHEET OF FOIL AS IT BAKES.

SASKATOON PIE

IN THIS CLASSIC CANADIAN PRAIRIE PIE, SASKATOON BERRIES ARE MOST OFTEN PACKAGED UP IN A DOUBLE CRUST; TO FANCY IT UP, CUT STRIPS TO MAKE A LATTICE, OR CUT SHAPES IN THE TOP CRUST TO ALLOW STEAM TO ESCAPE.

	DOUBLE RECIPE BASIC BUTTER PIE PASTRY (PAGE 160)	
1/2 CUP	SUGAR	125 ML
3 TBSP	ALL-PURPOSE FLOUR	45 ML
5 CUPS	FRESH OR FROZEN SASKATOON BERRIES	1.25 L
	GRATED ZEST OF 1 LEMON (OPTIONAL)	
2 TBSP	BUTTER, CUT INTO PIECES	30 ML
1	LARGE EGG, LIGHTLY BEATEN	1
	COARSE SUGAR (OPTIONAL)	

PREHEAT OVEN TO 425°F (220°C). DIVIDE PASTRY MORE OR LESS IN HALF, WITH ONE PIECE SLIGHTLY LARGER THAN THE OTHER. ON A LIGHTLY FLOURED SURFACE, ROLL THE LARGER PIECE OUT INTO A 10-INCH (25 CM) CIRCLE. GENTLY FIT INTO A 9-INCH (23 CM) PIE PLATE, WITHOUT TRIMMING EDGES. ROLL THE OTHER PIECE OUT TO ABOUT THE SIZE OF THE TOP OF THE PIE. IN A SMALL BOWL, STIR TOGETHER SUGAR AND FLOUR. PLACE BERRIES IN A MEDIUM BOWL AND ADD SUGAR MIXTURE AND LEMON ZEST (IF USING), GENTLY TOSSING TO COMBINE. POUR BERRIES INTO THE PASTRY SHELL, SHAKING ANY EXCESS SUGAR FROM THE BOTTOM OF THE BOWL OVER TOP, AND TOP WITH PIECES OF BUTTER.

IF YOU LIKE, CUT THE SECOND PIECE OF PASTRY INTO STRIPS AND MAKE A LATTICE TOP. OTHERWISE, LAY IT OVER THE PIE, BRUSHING THE EDGE OF THE BOTTOM CRUST WITH A LITTLE BEATEN EGG FIRST TO HELP IT SEAL. PRESS THE TOP CRUST TO THE BOTTOM, TRIM THE PASTRY AND CRIMP THE EDGE. CUT A FEW SLITS IN THE TOP TO LET STEAM ESCAPE. BRUSH THE TOP WITH BEATEN EGG AND, IF DESIRED, SPRINKLE WITH COARSE SUGAR. BAKE FOR 15 MINUTES, THEN REDUCE OVEN TEMPERATURE TO 350°F (180°C) AND BAKE FOR 50 TO 60 MINUTES OR UNTIL GOLDEN AND BUBBLING. LET COOL COMPLETELY ON A WIRE RACK BEFORE SLICING. SERVES 8.

ECONOMICS IS LIKE THE DUTCH LANGUAGE —
I'M TOLD IT MAKES SENSE, BUT I HAVE MY DOUBTS.
— JOHN OLIVER

LEMON MERINGUE PIE

LEMON MERINGUE PIE IS UP THERE WITH THE BEST SPECIAL-OCCASION DESSERTS.

I CUP	GRAHAM CRACKER CRUMBS	250 ML
2 1/2 CUPS	SUGAR, DIVIDED	625 ML
1/4 CUP	BUTTER, MELTED	60 ML
1/3 CUP	CORNSTARCH	75 ML
I CUP	WATER	250 ML
	GRATED ZEST OF I LEMON	
1/2 CUP	LEMON JUICE	125 ML
5	LARGE EGGS, SEPARATED	5

PREHEAT OVEN TO 350°F (180°C). IN A MEDIUM BOWL, COMBINE GRAHAM CRUMBS, 2 TBSP (30 ML) SUGAR AND BUTTER, STIRRING WITH A FORK UNTIL WELL BLENDED. PRESS INTO THE BOTTOM AND UP THE SIDES OF A 9-INCH (23 CM) PIE PLATE. BAKE FOR 8 MINUTES OR UNTIL PALE GOLDEN AROUND THE EDGES. REMOVE FROM OVEN AND INCREASE OVEN TEMPERATURE TO 400°F (200°C).

IN A MEDIUM SAUCEPAN, WHISK TOGETHER 1 3/4 CUPS (425 ML) SUGAR AND CORNSTARCH. WHISK IN WATER, LEMON ZEST AND LEMON JUICE, THEN WHISK IN EGG YOLKS. COOK OVER MEDIUM-HIGH HEAT, WHISKING, UNTIL THE MIXTURE BOILS AND THICKENS. POUR INTO CRUST.

USING AN ELECTRIC MIXER, BEAT EGG WHITES UNTIL SOFT PEAKS FORM. GRADUALLY ADD THE REMAINING SUGAR, BEATING UNTIL GLOSSY AND STIFF. MOUND ON THE FILLING, SPREADING IT RIGHT TO THE EDGES. BAKE FOR 5 MINUTES OR UNTIL MERINGUE IS GOLDEN. LET COOL ON A WIRE RACK FOR A FEW HOURS, UNTIL SET. SERVES 8.

CARAMELIZED APPLE PIES

ALTHOUGH YOU CAN EAT THEM OUT OF HAND, THESE SIMPLE, FLAKY PASTRIES ARE BEST SERVED WARM, WITH A KNIFE AND FORK AND A SCOOP OF VANILLA ICE CREAM.

3 TBSP	BUTTER	45 ML
2	LARGE TART APPLES, PEELED AND DICED	2
1/4 CUP	PACKED BROWN SUGAR	60 ML
1/2 TSP	GROUND CINNAMON	2 ML
PINCH	SALT	PINCH
1	PACKAGE (1 LB/500 G) FROZEN PUFF PASTRY, THAWED	1
1	LARGE EGG, LIGHTLY BEATEN	1

PREHEAT OVEN TO 400°F (200°C). IN A LARGE SKILLET, MELT BUTTER OVER MEDIUM-HIGH HEAT. ADD APPLES AND COOK, STIRRING OFTEN, FOR 4 TO 6 MINUTES OR UNTIL TENDER AND CARAMELIZED. ADD BROWN SUGAR, CINNAMON AND SALT; COOK, STIRRING, UNTIL APPLES ARE WELL COATED WITH SYRUP. REMOVE FROM HEAT AND LET COOL SLIGHTLY.

ON A LIGHTLY FLOURED SURFACE, ROLL OUT EACH HALF OF THE PUFF PASTRY INTO A 12- BY 10-INCH (30 BY 25 CM) RECTANGLE. CUT EACH PIECE IN HALF BOTH LENGTHWISE AND CROSSWISE, MAKING A TOTAL OF 8 RECTANGLES. DIVIDE FILLING AMONG RECTANGLES, BRUSH THE EDGES WITH BEATEN EGG AND FOLD OVER TO CREATE A TRIANGLE, ENCLOSING THE FILLING. TRANSFER TO A BAKING SHEET LINED WITH PARCHMENT PAPER AND PRESS DOWN AROUND THE EDGES WITH THE TINES OF A FORK. BRUSH EACH PIE WITH A LITTLE MORE BEATEN EGG AND CUT A SMALL SLIT IN THE TOP OF EACH. BAKE FOR 20 MINUTES OR UNTIL DEEP GOLDEN. MAKES 8 HAND PIES.

PEACH CRUMBLE

THE CRUMBLY TOPPING IN THIS DESSERT PARTIALLY
MELTS INTO THE FRUIT, LEAVING A DELICIOUSLY CRISP
LAYER ON THE SURFACE. WE'VE KEPT THINGS QUITE
TART HERE — IF YOU LIKE A SWEETER CRUMBLE,
INCREASE THE SUGAR IN THE FRUIT AND THE TOPPING
BY 1 TBSP (15 ML) EACH.

FRUIT

3 TBSP	SUGAR	45 ML
1 TBSP	CORNSTARCH	15 ML
1/2 TSP	GROUND CINNAMON	2 ML
4 1/2 to 7 CUPS	FRESH FIRM-RIPE OR FROZEN PEACH SLICES (SEE TIP)	1.125 to 1.75 L
	GRATED ZEST OF 1/2 LEMON	
1 TBSP	LEMON JUICE	15 ML

TOPPING

1 CUP	ALL-PURPOSE FLOUR	250 ML
2/3 CUP	SUGAR	150 ML
1/2 TSP	BAKING POWDER	2 ML
PINCH	SALT (SEE TIP)	PINCH
1	LARGE EGG, LIGHTLY BEATEN	1
1/2 CUP	BUTTER, MELTED	125 ML

FRUIT: PREHEAT OVEN TO 375°F (190°C). IN A LARGE BOWL,
STIR TOGETHER SUGAR, CORNSTARCH AND CINNAMON. ADD
PEACHES, LEMON ZEST AND LEMON JUICE; TOSS WELL.
TRANSFER TO A BUTTERED 8-INCH (20 CM) SQUARE DEEP
GLASS BAKING DISH, SCRAPING THE JUICES FROM THE
BOTTOM OF THE BOWL. IF USING FROZEN PEACHES, BAKE
THE FRUIT, STIRRING ONCE OR TWICE, UNTIL IT COMES TO
ROOM TEMPERATURE, ABOUT 15 TO 20 MINUTES.

TOPPING: IN A MEDIUM BOWL, COMBINE FLOUR, SUGAR, BAKING POWDER AND SALT. DRIZZLE EGG OVER FLOUR MIXTURE AND TOSS TOGETHER, THEN USE A FORK TO SEPARATE LARGER CLUMPS AND WORK MOISTURE INTO DRIER AREAS OF THE MIXTURE. SPREAD CRUMBS OVER PEACHES, THEN DRIZZLE BUTTER EVENLY OVER TOP. BAKE FOR 35 TO 40 MINUTES OR UNTIL TOP IS GOLDEN AND EDGES ARE BUBBLING WITH JUICE (SOME JUICE WILL ENCROACH ONTO THE TOPPING). LET COOL SLIGHTLY BEFORE SERVING. SERVES 6 TO 8.

TIP: THERE'S A LARGE DIFFERENCE IN THE VOLUME OF PEACHES REQUIRED, DEPENDING ON WHETHER YOU'RE USING FRESH OR FROZEN. FRESH PEACHES SLUMP TOGETHER NICELY WHEN MEASURED (SO THE LOWER END OF THE RANGE IS PLENTY), WHEREAS A MEASURING CUP OF FIRMLY FROZEN PEACH SLICES WILL INCLUDE A LOT OF AIR. IF IT HELPS, WE USED ONE AND A HALF 20-OZ (600 G) BAGS OF FROZEN PEACHES WHEN TESTING THIS RECIPE (FOR A TOTAL OF 30 OZ/900 G).

TIP: IF USING UNSALTED BUTTER TO MAKE THE TOPPING, INCREASE THE SALT TO $1/4$ TSP (I ML).

I COULDN'T FIGURE OUT WHY THE BASEBALL KEPT GETTING LARGER. THEN IT HIT ME.

APPLE CRISP

A BUBBLING FRUIT CRISP IS THE QUINTESSENTIAL SUNDAY DINNER DESSERT. USE A VARIETY OF APPLES FOR THE BEST FLAVOR.

4	LARGE TART APPLES, PEELED (OR NOT) AND THICKLY SLICED	4
1/2 CUP	SUGAR	125 ML
2 TSP	CORNSTARCH	10 ML
1 TSP	GROUND CINNAMON	5 ML
1/2 CUP	ALL-PURPOSE FLOUR	125 ML
1/2 CUP	LARGE-FLAKE (OLD-FASHIONED) OR QUICK-COOKING ROLLED OATS	125 ML
1/2 CUP	PACKED BROWN SUGAR	125 ML
1/4 CUP	BUTTER	60 ML
2 TBSP	LIQUID HONEY OR PURE MAPLE SYRUP	30 ML
	ICE CREAM OR WHIPPED CREAM	

PREHEAT OVEN TO 375°F (190°C). ARRANGE APPLES IN A 9-INCH (23 CM) PIE PLATE OR SHALLOW BAKING DISH. IN A SMALL DISH OR MEASURING CUP, STIR TOGETHER SUGAR, CORNSTARCH AND CINNAMON. SPRINKLE OVER FRUIT AND TOSS TO COAT.

IN A BOWL (OR A FOOD PROCESSOR), COMBINE ALL TOPPING INGREDIENTS; BLEND WITH A FORK OR PULSE UNTIL WELL COMBINED AND CRUMBLY. SPRINKLE OVER FRUIT, SQUEEZING IT AS YOU GO TO CREATE SOME LARGER CLUMPS. BAKE FOR 40 TO 45 MINUTES OR UNTIL TOP IS GOLDEN AND FRUIT IS TENDER AND BUBBLY AROUND THE EDGES. SERVE WARM, WITH ICE CREAM OR WHIPPED CREAM. SERVES 6 TO 8.

CHOCOLATE PUDDING CAKE

MORE CHEWY BROWNIE THAN CAKE, THIS PRODUCES A THICK CHOCOLATE PUDDING UNDERNEATH AS IT BAKES.

1 CUP	ALL-PURPOSE FLOUR	250 ML
1 1/4 CUPS	SUGAR, DIVIDED	300 ML
1/4 CUP	UNSWEETENED COCOA POWDER	60 ML
2 TSP	BAKING POWDER	10 ML
1/4 TSP	SALT	1 ML
1/2 CUP	MILK	125 ML
1/4 CUP	VEGETABLE OIL	60 ML
1 TSP	VANILLA	5 ML
1/2 CUP	PACKED BROWN SUGAR	125 ML
1 CUP	HOT WATER OR BREWED COFFEE	250 ML
	VANILLA ICE CREAM	

PREHEAT OVEN TO 350°F (180°C). IN A MEDIUM BOWL, STIR TOGETHER FLOUR, 3/4 CUP (175 ML) SUGAR, COCOA, BAKING POWDER AND SALT. IN A SMALL BOWL OR MEASURING CUP, STIR TOGETHER MILK, OIL AND VANILLA; ADD TO THE DRY INGREDIENTS AND STIR JUST UNTIL COMBINED. SPREAD INTO A GREASED OR PARCHMENT-LINED 9-INCH (23 CM) SQUARE BAKING PAN.

IN THE SAME BOWL, STIR TOGETHER THE REMAINING SUGAR, BROWN SUGAR AND HOT WATER; POUR OVER BATTER, BUT DON'T STIR. BAKE FOR 20 MINUTES OR UNTIL CAKE IS SPRINGY TO THE TOUCH AND THERE IS A THICK CHOCOLATE SAUCE UNDERNEATH. SERVE WARM, WITH VANILLA ICE CREAM. SERVES 6.

LARGE-BATCH BROWNIES

A BIG PAN OF WARM BROWNIES, SET OUT IN THE MIDDLE
OF THE TABLE, IS AMONG THE VERY BEST DESSERTS.
ADD A PINT OF ICE CREAM AND PITCHER OF CHOCOLATE
SAUCE TO TAKE IT OVER THE TOP.

8 OZ	SEMISWEET CHOCOLATE, CHOPPED	250 G
1/2 CUP	BUTTER, CUT INTO PIECES	125 ML
1 CUP	SUGAR	250 ML
4	LARGE EGGS	4
1 TSP	VANILLA	5 ML
1 CUP	ALL-PURPOSE FLOUR	250 ML
1/4 CUP	UNSWEETENED COCOA POWDER	60 ML
1/4 TSP	SALT	1 ML
1/2 CUP	CHOCOLATE CHIPS OR CHOPPED WALNUTS OR PECANS (OPTIONAL)	125 ML

PREHEAT OVEN TO 350°F (180°C). IN A SMALL SAUCEPAN,
MELT CHOCOLATE AND BUTTER OVER LOW HEAT (OR MELT
THEM ON LOW IN A MEDIUM BOWL IN THE MICROWAVE).
STIR UNTIL SMOOTH AND, IF YOU USED A POT, POUR INTO
A MEDIUM BOWL. STIR IN SUGAR, EGGS AND VANILLA UNTIL
WELL BLENDED. STIR IN FLOUR, COCOA AND SALT UNTIL
ALMOST COMBINED. IF DESIRED, STIR IN CHOCOLATE
CHIPS UNTIL JUST BLENDED. SPREAD INTO A 13- BY 9-INCH
(33 BY 23 CM) BAKING PAN LINED WITH PARCHMENT PAPER.
BAKE FOR 25 TO 30 MINUTES OR UNTIL JUST SET, EDGES
ARE STARTING TO PULL AWAY FROM THE SIDES OF THE
PAN AND A TESTER INSERTED IN THE CENTER COMES OUT
WITH LOTS OF MOIST CRUMBS STICKING TO IT. LET COOL
SLIGHTLY IN PAN ON A WIRE RACK BEFORE CUTTING INTO
SQUARES. SERVES 12 TO 16.

Marinated Roasted Vegetables (page 276) and
Rosemary Focaccia (page 242)

Browned Butter Blondies (page 289)

Grandma Ruby's Fudge Ribbon Cake (page 290)

Brown Sugar Panna Cotta (page 313)

BROWNED BUTTER BLONDIES

A PAN OF BLONDIES CAN BE STIRRED TOGETHER IN 5 MINUTES AND SLID INTO A WARM OVEN AS EVERYONE SITS DOWN TO EAT; WHEN IT'S TIME FOR DESSERT, IT'S READY. IF YOU LIKE, BAKE THEM IN A 9-INCH (23 CM) ROUND CAKE PAN AND SERVE IN SLIGHTLY FANCIER WEDGES, WITH A SCOOP OF ICE CREAM.

1/2 CUP	BUTTER	125 ML
1 CUP	PACKED BROWN SUGAR	250 ML
1	LARGE EGG, BEATEN	1
1 TSP	VANILLA	5 ML
1 CUP	ALL-PURPOSE FLOUR	250 ML
1/2 TSP	BAKING SODA	2 ML
1/4 TSP	SALT	1 ML
1/2 CUP	CHOPPED DARK OR WHITE CHOCOLATE, CHOCOLATE CHIPS OR CHOPPED NUTS	125 ML

PREHEAT OVEN TO 350°F (180°C). IN A SMALL SAUCEPAN, MELT BUTTER OVER MEDIUM-HIGH HEAT. HEAT, SWIRLING THE PAN OCCASIONALLY, UNTIL THE FOAM STARTS TURNING GOLDEN AND THE MIXTURE SMELLS NUTTY. POUR INTO A MEDIUM BOWL AND STIR IN BROWN SUGAR, THEN EGG AND VANILLA. STIR IN FLOUR, BAKING SODA AND SALT UNTIL ALMOST COMBINED. STIR IN CHOCOLATE AND/OR NUTS (OR WHATEVER ADDITIONS YOU LIKE) UNTIL JUST BLENDED. SPREAD INTO AN 8-INCH (20 CM) SQUARE BAKING PAN LINED WITH PARCHMENT PAPER. BAKE FOR 20 TO 25 MINUTES OR UNTIL GOLDEN AND SET AROUND THE EDGES. SERVE WARM OR LET COOL IN PAN ON A WIRE RACK. SERVES 9.

GRANDMA RUBY'S FUDGE RIBBON CAKE

WHEN ELIZABETH WAS A LITTLE GIRL, HER MOM WOULD ALWAYS MAKE THIS — A BASIC CHOCOLATE CAKE WITH A RIBBON OF CREAM CHEESE RUNNING THROUGH — FOR HER BIRTHDAY. THESE DAYS, SHE MAKES IT FOR HERSELF.

CREAM CHEESE RIBBON

1/3 CUP	SUGAR	75 ML
1 TBSP	CORNSTARCH	15 ML
1	PACKAGE (8 OZ/250 G) CREAM CHEESE, SOFTENED	1
1 TBSP	BUTTER	15 ML
1	LARGE EGG	1
2 TSP	MILK	10 ML
1/2 TSP	VANILLA	2 ML

CAKE

2 CUPS	ALL-PURPOSE FLOUR	500 ML
1 TSP	BAKING SODA	5 ML
1 TSP	BAKING POWDER	5 ML
1/2 TSP	SALT	2 ML
1 1/3 CUPS	SUGAR	325 ML
1/2 CUP	BUTTER, SOFTENED	125 ML
2	LARGE EGGS	2
1 1/3 CUPS	MILK	325 ML
4 OZ	SEMISWEET CHOCOLATE, MELTED	125 G
1 1/2 TSP	VANILLA	7 ML

NONNA'S CHOCOLATE ICING

1/2 CUP	UNSWEETENED COCOA POWDER	125 ML
1/2 CUP	BUTTER, SOFTENED, DIVIDED (APPROX.)	125 ML
1/3 CUP	MILK (APPROX.)	75 ML

1½ TSP	VANILLA	7 ML
3½ CUPS	POWDERED (ICING) SUGAR (APPROX.)	875 ML

PREHEAT OVEN TO 350°F (180°C). GREASE AND FLOUR TWO 9-INCH (23 CM) ROUND CAKE PANS.

CREAM CHEESE RIBBON: IN A LARGE BOWL, USING AN ELECTRIC MIXER, BEAT SUGAR, CORNSTARCH, CREAM CHEESE AND BUTTER UNTIL SMOOTH. GRADUALLY BEAT IN EGG, MILK AND VANILLA UNTIL SMOOTH AND CREAMY. SET ASIDE.

CAKE: IN A MEDIUM BOWL, WHISK TOGETHER FLOUR, BAKING SODA, BAKING POWDER AND SALT; SET ASIDE. IN A LARGE BOWL, USING AN ELECTRIC MIXER, BEAT SUGAR AND BUTTER UNTIL FLUFFY. BEAT IN EGGS AND MILK. WITH THE MIXER ON LOW, GRADUALLY ADD THE FLOUR MIXTURE, MIXING UNTIL COMBINED. ADD CHOCOLATE AND VANILLA; MIX UNTIL THE COLOR OF THE BATTER IS NO LONGER STREAKY.

POUR ONE-QUARTER OF THE CAKE BATTER INTO EACH PREPARED PAN AND SMOOTH SO IT'S EVEN. CAREFULLY SPREAD HALF THE CREAM CHEESE MIXTURE OVER THE BATTER IN EACH PAN, THEN TOP WITH THE REMAINING CAKE BATTER. THE LAYERS DON'T HAVE TO BE PERFECT, BUT BE CAREFUL NOT TO SWIRL THE BATTER WITH THE CREAM CHEESE. BAKE THE CAKES FOR 35 TO 45 MINUTES OR UNTIL A TESTER INSERTED IN THE CENTER COMES OUT CLEAN. LET COOL COMPLETELY IN PANS ON A WIRE RACK BEFORE REMOVING FROM PANS AND ICING.

CONTINUED...

ICING: IN A LARGE BOWL, USING AN ELECTRIC MIXER, BEAT COCOA AND 1/4 CUP (60 ML) BUTTER UNTIL CREAMY. BEAT IN MILK AND VANILLA UNTIL COMBINED. ADD POWDERED SUGAR, ONE-THIRD AT A TIME, AND CONTINUE MIXING UNTIL THE MIXTURE HAS A SPREADABLE CONSISTENCY, ADDING MORE SUGAR OR MILK IF NECESSARY. NEXT IS WHERE THE MAGIC HAPPENS: WITH THE MIXER ON MEDIUM, GRADUALLY ADD THE REMAINING BUTTER, 1 TBSP (15 ML) AT A TIME, MIXING WELL BETWEEN EACH ADDITION. AFTER ALL THE BUTTER IS IN (AND YOU MAY WANT TO ADD A LITTLE BIT MORE THAN THE ALLOTTED 1/4 CUP/60 ML, TO MAKE IT EVEN FLUFFIER), KEEP MIXING FOR SEVERAL MINUTES, UNTIL THE ICING IS INCREDIBLY FLUFFY.

IF THE CAKES ARE DOMED ON TOP, SLICE OFF THE DOMED PART WITH A SERRATED KNIFE TO MAKE MORE EVEN LAYERS. SPREAD ICING OVER THE TOP OF ONE OF THE CAKE LAYERS, THEN SET THE OTHER LAYER ON TOP. ICE THE CAKE, COMPLETELY COVERING THE TOP AND SIDES. CHILL UNTIL 1 HOUR BEFORE SERVING. SERVES 12.

SOFT CHOCOLATE LOAF CAKE

A DIFFERENT KIND OF CHOCOLATE CAKE, THIS ONE IS MOIST AND REQUIRES NO FROSTING OR DECORATION. SERVE SLICES PLAIN, WITH ICE CREAM OR ALONGSIDE A SUNDAE, TOPPED WITH BERRIES AND WHIPPED CREAM.

1⅓ CUPS	ALL-PURPOSE FLOUR	325 ML
¼ CUP	UNSWEETENED COCOA POWDER	60 ML
1 TSP	BAKING SODA	5 ML
¼ TSP	SALT	1 ML
1½ CUPS	PACKED DARK BROWN SUGAR	375 ML
½ CUP	BUTTER, SOFTENED	125 ML
¼ CUP	VEGETABLE OIL	60 ML
2	LARGE EGGS	2
2 TSP	VANILLA	10 ML
4 OZ	SEMISWEET CHOCOLATE, MELTED	125 G
1 CUP	JUST-BOILING WATER	250 ML

PREHEAT OVEN TO 350°F (180°C). IN A SMALL BOWL OR MEASURING CUP, STIR TOGETHER FLOUR, COCOA, BAKING SODA AND SALT; SET ASIDE. IN A LARGE BOWL, USING AN ELECTRIC MIXER, BEAT BROWN SUGAR, BUTTER AND OIL UNTIL WELL BLENDED. BEAT IN EGGS AND VANILLA UNTIL PALE AND LIGHT. BEAT IN CHOCOLATE. ADD THE FLOUR MIXTURE TO THE CHOCOLATE MIXTURE ALTERNATELY WITH THE BOILING WATER, STARTING AND FINISHING WITH FLOUR AND BEATING ON LOW SPEED OR STIRRING BY HAND AFTER EACH ADDITION JUST UNTIL COMBINED. POUR INTO A 9- BY 5-INCH (23 BY 12.5 CM) LOAF PAN LINED WITH PARCHMENT PAPER. BAKE FOR 60 TO 75 MINUTES OR UNTIL SPRINGY TO THE TOUCH. LET COOL SLIGHTLY IN PAN ON A WIRE RACK BEFORE SLICING. SERVES 10.

SUNKEN FLOURLESS CHOCOLATE CAKE

THIS CELEBRATORY CAKE COMES WITH A LOW-MAINTENANCE DECORATION: FILL THE SUNKEN PART WITH A CLOUD OF CHOCOLATE-SWIRLED WHIPPED CREAM, AND OPT FOR SPARKLERS INSTEAD OF CANDLES.

CAKE

8 OZ	SEMISWEET OR BITTERSWEET (DARK) CHOCOLATE, COARSELY CHOPPED	250 G
1/2 CUP	BUTTER, SOFTENED OR CUT INTO CHUNKS	125 ML
6	LARGE EGGS	6
I CUP	SUGAR, DIVIDED	250 ML

TOPPING

1 1/2 CUPS	HEAVY OR WHIPPING (35%) CREAM	375 ML
I TBSP	SUGAR	15 ML
I TSP	VANILLA	5 ML
1/2 CUP	SEMISWEET OR BITTERSWEET (DARK) CHOCOLATE CHIPS OR CHOPPED CHOCOLATE	125 ML
	CHOCOLATE SHAVINGS (OPTIONAL)	

PREHEAT OVEN TO 350°F (180°C). LINE THE BOTTOM OF A 9-INCH (23 CM) SPRINGFORM PAN WITH A CIRCLE OF WAXED OR PARCHMENT PAPER (USE THE BOTTOM OF THE PAN TO TRACE A CIRCLE, THEN CUT IT OUT WITH SCISSORS). DON'T GREASE THE PAN; THE BATTER NEEDS TO BE ABLE TO CLING TO THE SIDES AS IT RISES.

CAKE: IN A BOWL SET OVER A POT OF BARELY SIMMERING WATER, GENTLY MELT CHOCOLATE AND BUTTER (OR MELT THEM ON LOW IN THE MICROWAVE). LET COOL SLIGHTLY.

SEPARATE 4 OF THE EGGS, PUTTING THE YOLKS AND WHITES IN SEPARATE MEDIUM BOWLS. TO THE YOLKS, ADD $\frac{1}{2}$ CUP (125 ML) SUGAR, THE WARM CHOCOLATE MIXTURE AND THE REMAINING EGGS. WHISK UNTIL SMOOTH. USING AN ELECTRIC MIXER, BEAT EGG WHITES UNTIL FOAMY. GRADUALLY ADD THE REMAINING SUGAR, BEATING UNTIL EGG WHITES FORM SOFT MOUNDS BUT AREN'T YET STIFF. FOLD ABOUT ONE-QUARTER OF THE EGG WHITES INTO THE CHOCOLATE MIXTURE TO LIGHTEN IT, THEN GENTLY FOLD IN THE REST, WITHOUT DEFLATING THE EGG WHITES.

POUR BATTER INTO PREPARED PAN AND SMOOTH THE TOP. BAKE FOR 35 TO 40 MINUTES OR UNTIL CAKE IS PUFFY AND CRACKED ON TOP, AND THE MIDDLE ISN'T WOBBLY. LET COOL COMPLETELY IN PAN ON A WIRE RACK, WITHOUT LOOSENING THE RING; THE BATTER NEEDS TO CLING TO THE SIDES OF THE PAN AS IT COOLS SO THAT IT CAN PROPERLY SINK IN THE MIDDLE AND KEEP ITS HIGH EDGES.

TOPPING: MEANWHILE, IN A LARGE BOWL, USING AN ELECTRIC MIXER, BEAT CREAM, SUGAR AND VANILLA UNTIL STIFF PEAKS FORM. PLACE CHOCOLATE CHIPS IN A MICROWAVE-SAFE BOWL AND MICROWAVE ON LOW IN 30-SECOND INTERVALS, STIRRING BETWEEN EACH, JUST UNTIL MELTED AND SMOOTH. LET COOL SLIGHTLY, THEN GENTLY FOLD INTO WHIPPED CREAM, LEAVING SOME STREAKS. SCRAPE INTO THE SUNKEN CHOCOLATE CAKE AND, IF YOU LIKE, TOP WITH CHOCOLATE SHAVINGS. SERVES 8.

TIP: THE THING TO REMEMBER WHEN MELTING CHOCOLATE IS TO DO IT SLOWLY; CHOCOLATE SCORCHES AND CAN SEIZE UP EASILY.

PINK SPICE CAKE

CARROT CAKE IS MORE FAMILIAR, BUT BEETS WORK JUST AS WELL WHEN IT COMES TO MOIST, SPICY, CREAM CHEESE-FROSTED CAKE. PLUS, BEETS TURN EVERYTHING PINK, WHICH WE COUNT AS A BONUS (UNLESS YOU USE GOLDEN BEETS, WHICH IS NO FUN AT ALL).

CAKE

2 CUPS	ALL-PURPOSE FLOUR	500 ML
2 TSP	GROUND CINNAMON	10 ML
2 TSP	BAKING SODA	10 ML
1 TSP	BAKING POWDER	5 ML
1 TSP	SALT	5 ML
1¾ CUPS	SUGAR	425 ML
3	LARGE EGGS, LIGHTLY BEATEN	3
1 CUP	VEGETABLE OIL	250 ML
1 TSP	VANILLA	5 ML
2 CUPS	SHREDDED OR VERY FINELY CHOPPED PEELED BEETS	500 ML
1	CAN (8 OZ/227 ML) CRUSHED PINEAPPLE, DRAINED	1

ICING

1	PACKAGE (8 OZ/250 G) CREAM CHEESE, SOFTENED	1
¼ CUP	BUTTER, SOFTENED	60 ML
2 CUPS	POWDERED (ICING) SUGAR	500 ML

CAKE: PREHEAT OVEN TO 350°F (180°C). IN A LARGE BOWL, LIGHTLY WHISK TOGETHER FLOUR, CINNAMON, BAKING SODA, BAKING POWDER AND SALT. STIR IN SUGAR, EGGS, OIL AND VANILLA UNTIL EVENLY COMBINED. STIR IN BEETS

AND PINEAPPLE. SCRAPE INTO A GREASED 13- BY 9-INCH (33 BY 23 CM) BAKING PAN. BAKE FOR 45 TO 55 MINUTES OR UNTIL A TESTER INSERTED IN THE CENTER COMES OUT CLEAN. LET COOL SLIGHTLY IN PAN, THEN TURN OUT ONTO A WIRE RACK TO COOL COMPLETELY.

ICING: IN A MEDIUM BOWL, USING AN ELECTRIC MIXER, BEAT CREAM CHEESE AND BUTTER UNTIL COMBINED. BEAT IN POWDERED SUGAR UNTIL SMOOTH AND FLUFFY.

SPREAD ICING OVER TOP AND SIDES OF COOLED CAKE. CHILL UNTIL 1 HOUR BEFORE SERVING. SERVES 10 TO 12.

TIP: IF YOU HAVE A GRATING DISK FOR YOUR FOOD PROCESSOR, USE IT TO EASILY GRATE YOUR BEETS. THIS RECIPE ALSO WORKS WITH BEETS THAT ARE VERY FINELY CHOPPED BY PULSING THEM IN SPURTS WITH A STANDARD FOOD PROCESSOR BLADE.

CUPCAKES ARE MUFFINS THAT BELIEVED IN MIRACLES.

SPICED PUMPKIN CAKE WITH CREAM CHEESE FROSTING

PERFECT FOR THE HARVEST SEASON, THIS CAKE MAKES GREAT USE OF LEFTOVER CANNED PUMPKIN, AND THE LAYERS FREEZE WELL, SO YOU CAN MAKE THEM AHEAD FOR THE HOLIDAYS. AS A BONUS, FROZEN CAKE LAYERS ARE EASY TO FROST, WITH MINIMAL CRUMBS!

CAKE

1½ CUPS	ALL-PURPOSE FLOUR	375 ML
1 TSP	BAKING POWDER	5 ML
1 TSP	BAKING SODA	5 ML
2 TSP	GROUND CINNAMON	10 ML
1 TSP	GROUND GINGER	5 ML
¼ TSP	GROUND NUTMEG OR ALLSPICE (OR ADD BOTH)	1 ML
¼ TSP	SALT	1 ML
1 CUP	PACKED BROWN SUGAR	250 ML
½ CUP	BUTTER, SOFTENED	125 ML
¼ CUP	VEGETABLE OIL	60 ML
3	LARGE EGGS	3
2 TSP	VANILLA	10 ML
1	CAN (14 OZ/398 ML) PUMPKIN PURÉE (NOT PIE FILLING)	1

FROSTING

1	PACKAGE (8 OZ/250 G) CREAM CHEESE, SOFTENED	1
½ CUP	BUTTER, SOFTENED	125 ML
3 CUPS	POWDERED (ICING) SUGAR (APPROX.)	750 ML
1 TSP	VANILLA	5 ML
	WATER OR MILK (IF NEEDED)	

CAKE: PREHEAT OVEN TO 350°F (180°C). IN A SMALL BOWL, STIR TOGETHER FLOUR, BAKING POWDER, BAKING SODA, CINNAMON, GINGER, NUTMEG AND SALT; SET ASIDE. IN A LARGE BOWL, USING AN ELECTRIC MIXER, BEAT BROWN SUGAR, BUTTER AND OIL UNTIL PALE AND LIGHT. BEAT IN EGGS AND VANILLA UNTIL WELL COMBINED. BEAT IN PUMPKIN PURÉE — IT MAY LOOK CURDLED, BUT THAT'S OKAY. ADD THE FLOUR MIXTURE AND BEAT ON LOW OR STIR BY HAND JUST UNTIL COMBINED. DIVIDE BATTER AMONG THREE GREASED 8- OR 9-INCH (20 OR 23 CM) ROUND CAKE PANS, SMOOTHING THE TOPS. BAKE FOR 25 TO 35 MINUTES OR UNTIL GOLDEN AND SPRINGY TO THE TOUCH. INVERT CAKES ONTO A WIRE RACK TO COOL COMPLETELY. (AT THIS POINT, YOU CAN WRAP AND FREEZE THEM FOR UP TO 6 MONTHS.)

FROSTING: IN A LARGE BOWL, USING AN ELECTRIC MIXER, BEAT CREAM CHEESE AND BUTTER UNTIL THERE ARE NO MORE LUMPS. BEAT IN POWDERED SUGAR AND VANILLA UNTIL FROSTING IS SPREADABLE. (ADD A SPOONFUL OF WATER OR MILK IF IT'S TOO THICK, AND A LITTLE EXTRA POWDERED SUGAR IF IT SEEMS TOO RUNNY.)

IF THE CAKES ARE DOMED ON TOP, SLICE OFF THE DOMED PART WITH A SERRATED KNIFE TO MAKE MORE EVEN LAYERS. SPREAD FROSTING OVER THE TOP OF ONE OF THE CAKE LAYERS, THEN PLACE ANOTHER LAYER ON TOP. REPEAT, FROSTING THE TOP OF THE SECOND LAYER AND PLACING THE THIRD LAYER ON TOP. FROST THE TOP OF THE CAKE, LEAVING THE SIDES EXPOSED OR COVERING THEM WITH A THIN LAYER OF FROSTING. SERVES 12.

UPSIDE-DOWN PEAR GINGERBREAD

ONE OF THE BIGGEST SELLING POINTS OF AN UPSIDE-DOWN CAKE IS THE FACT THAT IT NEEDS NO DECORATING. WHEN YOU INVERT THE CAKE, THE PEAR SLICES END UP ON TOP, MAKING IT LOOK GRATIFYINGLY COMPLETE, WITH NO NEED FOR FROSTING. IT DOES, HOWEVER, SCREAM FOR ICE CREAM OR WHIPPED CREAM.

TOPPING

1/3 CUP	PACKED BROWN SUGAR	75 ML
2 TBSP	BUTTER	30 ML
2 TBSP	LIQUID HONEY OR GOLDEN SYRUP	30 ML
2	RIPE BUT FIRM PEARS (OR TART APPLES), PEELED AND THINLY SLICED	2

GINGERBREAD

1 CUP	ALL-PURPOSE FLOUR	250 ML
1 TSP	BAKING SODA	5 ML
1 TSP	GROUND CINNAMON	5 ML
1/4 TSP	GROUND ALLSPICE (OPTIONAL)	1 ML
1/4 TSP	SALT	1 ML
1/2 CUP	PACKED BROWN SUGAR	125 ML
1/4 CUP	BUTTER, SOFTENED	60 ML
1 TBSP	GRATED FRESH GINGER	15 ML
1	LARGE EGG	1
1/4 CUP	DARK (COOKING) MOLASSES	60 ML
1 TSP	VANILLA	5 ML
3/4 CUP	BUTTERMILK (OR PLAIN YOGURT, THINNED WITH MILK)	175 ML

PREHEAT OVEN TO 350°F (180°C) AND BUTTER AN 8- OR 9-INCH (20 OR 23 CM) ROUND CAKE PAN OR DEEP-DISH PIE PLATE.

TOPPING: IN A SMALL SAUCEPAN, MELT BROWN SUGAR, BUTTER AND HONEY OVER MEDIUM HEAT, STIRRING UNTIL SMOOTH. POUR OVER THE BOTTOM OF THE PAN AND ARRANGE PEARS ON TOP, PLACING THEM TIGHT TOGETHER (THEY SHRINK A BIT AS THEY COOK, SO YOU CAN EVEN GET AWAY WITH OVERLAPPING THEM).

GINGERBREAD: IN A SMALL BOWL, STIR TOGETHER FLOUR, BAKING SODA, CINNAMON, ALLSPICE (IF USING) AND SALT; SET ASIDE. IN A MEDIUM BOWL, USING AN ELECTRIC MIXER, BEAT BROWN SUGAR AND BUTTER UNTIL WELL BLENDED. BEAT IN GINGER, EGG, MOLASSES AND VANILLA UNTIL THOROUGHLY COMBINED. (IT WILL LOOK SLIGHTLY CURDLED — THAT'S OKAY.) ADD HALF THE FLOUR MIXTURE AND STIR BY HAND OR ON LOW SPEED JUST UNTIL COMBINED. STIR IN BUTTERMILK, THEN THE REMAINING FLOUR MIXTURE IN THE SAME MANNER. POUR OVER PEARS.

BAKE FOR 35 TO 40 MINUTES OR UNTIL TOP IS SPRINGY TO THE TOUCH. LET COOL FOR 5 MINUTES, THEN RUN A KNIFE AROUND THE EDGE OF THE CAKE AND INVERT IT ONTO A PLATE WHILE IT'S STILL WARM. (IF IT COOLS TOO MUCH AND STICKS TO THE PAN, WARM IT IN THE OVEN AGAIN BEFORE YOU TRY TO INVERT IT.) DON'T WORRY IF ANY PEAR SLICES STICK TO THE BOTTOM OF THE PAN — SIMPLY PEEL THEM OUT AND PLACE THEM BACK ON TOP OF THE CAKE WHERE THEY BELONG. SERVES 8.

TRIPLE-COCONUT CAKE

COCONUT CAKE, COCONUT CUSTARD, COCONUT ICING.

CUSTARD FILLING

1/4 CUP	SUGAR	60 ML
2 TBSP	CORNSTARCH	30 ML
PINCH	SALT	PINCH
2	LARGE EGG YOLKS	2
1/2 CUP	HALF-AND-HALF (10%) CREAM	125 ML
1/2 CUP	COCONUT MILK (SEE TIP)	125 ML
1/2 CUP	SWEETENED FLAKED COCONUT	125 ML
1 1/2 TBSP	BUTTER	22 ML
1/2 TSP	VANILLA	2 ML
1/4 TSP	COCONUT EXTRACT	1 ML

CAKE

3 CUPS	ALL-PURPOSE FLOUR	750 ML
1 TBSP	BAKING POWDER	15 ML
1/2 CUP	MILK	125 ML
1/2 CUP	COCONUT MILK	125 ML
1 TSP	VANILLA	5 ML
1/4 TSP	COCONUT EXTRACT	1 ML
1 CUP	BUTTER, SOFTENED	250 ML
2 CUPS	SUGAR	500 ML
4	LARGE EGGS, SEPARATED	4
PINCH	SALT	PINCH

ICING

1 CUP	BUTTER, SOFTENED	250 ML
1/2 CUP	COCONUT MILK (APPROX.)	125 ML
4 CUPS	POWDERED (ICING) SUGAR (APPROX.)	1 L
	SWEETENED FLAKED COCONUT	

CUSTARD FILLING: IN A MEDIUM SAUCEPAN, COMBINE SUGAR, CORNSTARCH AND SALT. IN A SMALL BOWL, WHISK TOGETHER EGG YOLKS, CREAM AND COCONUT MILK. SET SAUCEPAN OVER MEDIUM HEAT AND WHISK IN EGG MIXTURE. COOK, WHISKING, FOR ABOUT 8 MINUTES OR UNTIL CONSIDERABLY THICKENED AND STARTING TO BOIL. REMOVE FROM HEAT AND IMMEDIATELY STIR IN COCONUT, BUTTER, VANILLA AND COCONUT EXTRACT, STIRRING UNTIL BUTTER IS MELTED. LET COOL, THEN COVER WITH PLASTIC WRAP, PLACING IT DIRECTLY ON THE SURFACE OF THE CUSTARD, AND CHILL FOR 2 TO 3 HOURS OR OVERNIGHT.

CAKE: PREHEAT OVEN TO 350°F (180°C). GREASE AND FLOUR TWO 9-INCH (23 CM) ROUND CAKE PANS.

IN A LARGE BOWL, WHISK TOGETHER FLOUR AND BAKING POWDER; SET ASIDE. IN A SMALL BOWL, STIR TOGETHER MILK, COCONUT MILK, VANILLA AND COCONUT EXTRACT. IN ANOTHER LARGE BOWL, USING AN ELECTRIC MIXER, BEAT BUTTER UNTIL LIGHT AND FLUFFY. GRADUALLY ADD SUGAR AND CONTINUE BEATING UNTIL COMBINED. WITH THE BEATERS RUNNING, ADD EGG YOLKS, ONE AT A TIME, AND BEAT UNTIL FULLY INCORPORATED. WITH THE MIXER ON LOW SPEED, ADD THE FLOUR MIXTURE ALTERNATELY WITH THE MILK MIXTURE, MAKING THREE ADDITIONS OF FLOUR AND TWO OF MILK, AND MIXING JUST UNTIL COMBINED. WASH BEATERS WELL.

IN A CLEAN LARGE BOWL, USING AN ELECTRIC MIXER, BEAT EGG WHITES AND SALT ON HIGH SPEED UNTIL

CONTINUED...

STIFF PEAKS FORM. STIR ONE-THIRD OF THE EGG WHITES INTO THE CAKE BATTER TO LIGHTEN, THEN GENTLY FOLD IN THE REMAINING EGG WHITES.

SCRAPE BATTER INTO PREPARED PANS, DIVIDING EVENLY. BAKE FOR ABOUT 25 TO 30 MINUTES OR UNTIL A TESTER INSERTED IN THE CENTER COMES OUT CLEAN. LET COOL COMPLETELY IN PANS ON A WIRE RACK.

ICING: IN A LARGE BOWL, USING AN ELECTRIC MIXER, BEAT BUTTER UNTIL FLUFFY, THEN GRADUALLY BEAT IN COCONUT MILK. GRADUALLY MIX IN POWDERED SUGAR AND CONTINUE MIXING FOR ABOUT 5 MINUTES OR UNTIL FLUFFY AND SPREADABLE. (IF THE ICING IS TOO THICK, ADD MORE COCONUT MILK; IF IT IS TOO THIN, ADD MORE SUGAR.)

IF THE CAKES ARE DOMED ON TOP, SLICE OFF THE DOMED PART WITH A SERRATED KNIFE TO MAKE MORE EVEN LAYERS. PLACE ONE OF THE LAYERS ON A PLATE OR CAKE STAND AND COVER THE TOP WITH CUSTARD FILLING. CAREFULLY PLACE THE OTHER LAYER ON TOP. COVER THE ENTIRE CAKE WITH ICING AND SPRINKLE WITH COCONUT. CHILL UNTIL A HALF-HOUR BEFORE SERVING. SERVES 12.

TIP: COCONUT MILK CAN SEPARATE IN THE CAN. FOR THIS RECIPE, TIP A CAN OF COCONUT MILK INTO A LARGE BOWL AND MIX VIGOROUSLY WITH A FORK TO COMBINE THE LIQUID WITH THE SOLIDS BEFORE MEASURING.

LEMON POPPY SEED POUND CAKE

HEAVY CREAM REPLACES BUTTER IN THIS CAKE, GIVING IT A RICH FLAVOR WITH A FINE CRUMB. SERVE SLICES WITH FRESH BERRIES, OR TURN THEM INTO ICE CREAM SANDWICHES WITH SOFT VANILLA ICE CREAM.

2 CUPS	ALL-PURPOSE FLOUR	500 ML
2 TSP	BAKING POWDER	10 ML
1/4 TSP	SALT	1 ML
1 CUP	HEAVY OR WHIPPING (35%) CREAM, CHILLED	250 ML
4	LARGE EGGS	4
1 CUP	SUGAR	250 ML
1 TSP	VANILLA	5 ML
	GRATED ZEST OF 1 LEMON	
1/3 CUP	POPPY SEEDS	75 ML

PREHEAT OVEN TO 350°F (180°C). IN A MEDIUM BOWL, WHISK TOGETHER FLOUR, BAKING POWDER AND SALT; SET ASIDE. IN ANOTHER MEDIUM BOWL, USING AN ELECTRIC MIXER, BEAT CREAM UNTIL STIFF; SET ASIDE. IN A LARGE BOWL, USING AN ELECTRIC MIXER, BEAT EGGS FOR 1 MINUTE. GRADUALLY ADD SUGAR, BEATING UNTIL THICK AND PALE YELLOW. BEAT IN VANILLA AND LEMON ZEST. SPRINKLE HALF THE FLOUR MIXTURE OVER THE EGG MIXTURE AND FOLD IT IN WITH A SPATULA. FOLD IN WHIPPED CREAM, THEN THE REMAINING FLOUR AND POPPY SEEDS. SPREAD INTO AN 8- BY 4-INCH (20 BY 10 CM) LOAF PAN LINED WITH PARCHMENT PAPER. BAKE FOR 45 TO 50 MINUTES OR UNTIL GOLDEN AND SPRINGY TO THE TOUCH. LET COOL SLIGHTLY IN PAN ON A WIRE RACK BEFORE SLICING. SERVES 8.

CLASSIC BAKED CHEESECAKE

A BAKED CHEESECAKE IS CLASSIC. MAKE IT AHEAD TO GIVE IT TIME TO COOL AND FIRM, THEN SERVE IT PLAIN, TOP IT WITH BERRIES OR DRIZZLE SLICES WITH CHOCOLATE OR CARAMEL SAUCE.

CRUST

I CUP	GRAHAM CRACKER CRUMBS	250 ML
2 TBSP	SUGAR	30 ML
3 TBSP	BUTTER, MELTED	45 ML

FILLING

I 1/2 LBS	CREAM CHEESE (THREE 8-OZ/250 G PACKAGES)	750 G
I CUP	SUGAR	250 ML
3 TBSP	ALL-PURPOSE FLOUR	45 ML
	GRATED ZEST OF I LEMON	
2 TBSP	LEMON JUICE	30 ML
I TSP	VANILLA	5 ML
3	LARGE EGGS	3

CRUST: PREHEAT OVEN TO 350°F (180°C). IN A BOWL, COMBINE GRAHAM CRUMBS, SUGAR AND BUTTER. PRESS INTO THE BOTTOM OF AN UNGREASED 9-INCH (23 CM) SPRINGFORM PAN. BAKE FOR 10 MINUTES, UNTIL PALE GOLDEN AROUND THE EDGES. REMOVE FROM OVEN AND INCREASE OVEN TEMPERATURE TO 425°F (220°C).

FILLING: IN A LARGE BOWL, USING AN ELECTRIC MIXER, BEAT CREAM CHEESE UNTIL NO LUMPS REMAIN. BEAT IN SUGAR, FLOUR, LEMON ZEST, LEMON JUICE AND VANILLA UNTIL SMOOTH. ADD EGGS, ONE AT A TIME, BEATING WELL AFTER EACH ADDITION.

POUR FILLING INTO CRUST. BAKE FOR 10 MINUTES, THEN REDUCE THE HEAT TO 250°F (120°C) AND BAKE FOR 30 TO 35 MINUTES OR UNTIL SET AROUND THE EDGES AND THE CENTER IS JUST SLIGHTLY JIGGLY (IT WILL FIRM UP AS IT COOLS). IMMEDIATELY RUN A THIN KNIFE AROUND THE EDGE TO LOOSEN IT FROM THE PAN SO THAT IT DOESN'T CRACK. LET COOL COMPLETELY, THEN REFRIGERATE FOR AT LEAST AN HOUR BEFORE YOU REMOVE THE SIDES OF THE SPRINGFORM PAN. SERVES 12.

WHEN EVERYTHING IS COMING YOUR WAY,
YOU'RE IN THE WRONG LANE.
— STEVEN WRIGHT

INDIVIDUAL NO-BAKE CHEESECAKES IN JARS

DESSERTS IN JARS ARE GREAT FOR BACKYARD GET-TOGETHERS — THEY CAN HANG OUT IN A BUCKET OF ICE TO KEEP COOL, AND EVERYONE CAN GRAB ONE WHEN THEY'RE READY. THESE NO-BAKE CHEESECAKES ARE PARTICULARLY SIMPLE; IF YOU DON'T HAVE JARS, YOU CAN ALWAYS MAKE THEM IN RAMEKINS OR SMALL SERVING DISHES.

TOPPING

2 CUPS	FRESH OR FROZEN BLUEBERRIES, RASPBERRIES, BLACKBERRIES OR PITTED CHERRIES	500 ML
1/3 CUP	SUGAR (OR TO TASTE)	75 ML
1/4 CUP	WATER	60 ML
I TSP	CORNSTARCH	5 ML
I TSP	COLD WATER	5 ML

CRUST

4	GRAHAM CRACKERS OR DIGESTIVE BISCUITS, CRUSHED (ABOUT 3/4 CUP/ 175 ML)	4

FILLING

I	PACKAGE (8 OZ/250 G) CREAM CHEESE, SOFTENED	I
1/4 CUP	SUGAR	60 ML
3/4 CUP	SOUR CREAM OR PLAIN GREEK YOGURT	175 ML
1/4 TSP	VANILLA	I ML

TOPPING: IN A MEDIUM SAUCEPAN, COMBINE BERRIES, SUGAR AND WATER; BRING TO A SIMMER OVER MEDIUM-HIGH HEAT. REDUCE HEAT AND SIMMER, STIRRING OCCASIONALLY, FOR 10 TO 15 MINUTES OR UNTIL

BERRIES ARE SOFT, SQUISHING SOME OF THE BERRIES AGAINST THE SIDE OF THE PAN WITH YOUR SPOON. STIR CORNSTARCH INTO COLD WATER AND ADD TO THE BERRIES; SIMMER FOR A MINUTE OR TWO, UNTIL SLIGHTLY THICKENED. LET COOL, THEN REFRIGERATE UNTIL CHILLED.

CRUST: DIVIDE COOKIE CRUMBS AMONG 6 SMALL (4 OZ/ 125 ML) CANNING JARS.

FILLING: IN A MEDIUM BOWL, USING AN ELECTRIC MIXER, BEAT CREAM CHEESE AND SUGAR UNTIL SMOOTH. BEAT IN SOUR CREAM AND VANILLA.

DIVIDE FILLING AMONG JARS, SPOONING IT OVER THE CRUMBS. SCREW ON LIDS AND REFRIGERATE UNTIL YOU'RE READY TO SERVE, FOR UP TO 4 DAYS. SPOON TOPPING OVER TOP WHEN YOU SERVE THEM. SERVES 6.

PUDDING IN A CLOUD

PUDDING AND WHIPPED CREAM — THE COMBINATION IS A CHILDHOOD FAVORITE. HERE, WE GO FOR HOMEMADE PUDDING RATHER THAN THE INSTANT STUFF AND DO A 2:1 RATIO (IN FAVOR OF THE PUDDING, OF COURSE), BUT FEEL FREE TO MAKE MORE WHIPPED CREAM IF YOU LIKE YOUR PUDDING EXTRA-CLOUDY.

PUDDING

1/4 CUP	UNSWEETENED COCOA POWDER	60 ML
2 TBSP	CORNSTARCH	30 ML
PINCH	SALT	PINCH
2 CUPS	MILK (NOT FAT-FREE), DIVIDED	500 ML
2	LARGE EGG YOLKS	2
1/2 CUP	SUGAR	125 ML
1 TSP	VANILLA	5 ML

WHIPPED CREAM

1 CUP	HEAVY OR WHIPPING (35%) CREAM	250 ML
2 TBSP	SUGAR	30 ML
	CHOCOLATE CHIPS	

PUDDING: IN A LARGE HEATPROOF BOWL, WHISK TOGETHER COCOA, CORNSTARCH, SALT AND 1/2 CUP (125 ML) MILK. WHISK IN EGG YOLKS; SET ASIDE. IN A MEDIUM SAUCEPAN, HEAT SUGAR AND THE REMAINING MILK OVER MEDIUM-HIGH HEAT UNTIL SMALL BUBBLES BEGIN TO FORM (DO NOT LET IT BOIL). GRADUALLY POUR THE MILK MIXTURE OVER THE COCOA MIXTURE, ADD VANILLA AND WHISK THOROUGHLY. POUR THE ENTIRE MIXTURE BACK INTO THE SAUCEPAN, INCREASE HEAT TO HIGH AND BRING TO A BOIL. REDUCE HEAT AND SIMMER FOR 2 MINUTES, WHISKING

CONSTANTLY AND MAKING SURE TO SCRAPE THE BOTTOM OF THE PAN. LET COOL SLIGHTLY, THEN TRANSFER TO A BOWL AND PLACE PLASTIC WRAP RIGHT ON THE SURFACE OF THE PUDDING. REFRIGERATE FOR AT LEAST AN HOUR OR UNTIL READY TO SERVE (NO MORE THAN 24 HOURS).

WHIPPED CREAM: IN A LARGE BOWL, USING AN ELECTRIC MIXER, WHIP CREAM AND SUGAR UNTIL SOFT PEAKS FORM.

LAYER PUDDING AND CREAM IN BOWLS OR PARFAIT CUPS AND SPRINKLE WITH CHOCOLATE CHIPS. SERVES 4.

CHEF CAM'S WORLD-FAMOUS CHOCOLATE MOUSSE

ELIZABETH'S HUSBAND'S NONNA MADE AN (ALMOST) WORLD-FAMOUS CHOCOLATE MOUSSE. ELIZABETH WAS HAPPY TO FIND A REASONABLE EQUIVALENT AT THE BRASSERIE KENSINGTON IN CALGARY. THE RESTAURANT'S CHEF, CAM DOBRANSKI, WAS KIND ENOUGH TO GIVE US HIS RECIPE FOR HIS MOUSSE, WHICH HAS NOW REPLACED NONNA'S IN OUR HEARTS.

8 OZ	SEMISWEET CHOCOLATE, CHOPPED	250 G
1/4 CUP	BUTTER	60 ML
4	LARGE EGGS, SEPARATED (SEE SAFETY TIP, OPPOSITE)	4
3 TBSP	SUGAR	45 ML
1/2 CUP	HEAVY OR WHIPPING (35%) CREAM	125 ML

PLACE CHOCOLATE AND BUTTER IN A HEATPROOF BOWL AND SET IT OVER A POT OF SIMMERING WATER, STIRRING TO MELT THE CHOCOLATE. WHISK IN 3 EGG YOLKS (DISCARD THE FOURTH OR SAVE IT FOR ANOTHER USE), ONE AT A TIME. COOK, WHISKING, FOR 1 TO 2 MINUTES OR UNTIL MIXTURE THICKENS.

IN A LARGE GLASS OR STAINLESS STEEL BOWL, USING AN ELECTRIC MIXER, BEAT EGG WHITES UNTIL SOFT PEAKS FORM. ADD SUGAR AND CONTINUE MIXING UNTIL WELL COMBINED BUT STILL AT THE SOFT PEAK STAGE. GENTLY FOLD THE EGG WHITES INTO THE CHOCOLATE MIXTURE.

WIPE OUT THE MIXER BOWL AND WHIP CREAM UNTIL SOFT PEAKS FORM. FOLD WHIPPED CREAM INTO THE CHOCOLATE MIXTURE, THEN COVER AND CHILL FOR AT LEAST 1 HOUR OR OVERNIGHT. SERVES 6 TO 8.

BROWN SUGAR PANNA COTTA

A PANNA COTTA IS A SIMPLE ITALIAN DESSERT MADE WITH CREAM SET WITH GELATIN. THE BROWN SUGAR GIVES IT A CARAMEL-LIKE COLOR AND FLAVOR.

4 CUPS	HALF-AND-HALF (10%) CREAM	1 L
1 TBSP	UNFLAVORED GELATIN	15 ML
$\frac{1}{3}$ CUP	PACKED DARK BROWN SUGAR	75 ML
PINCH	SALT	PINCH
	FRESH BERRIES	

POUR CREAM INTO A MEDIUM SAUCEPAN AND SPRINKLE GELATIN OVER TOP. LET STAND FOR A FEW MINUTES TO SOFTEN. PLACE OVER MEDIUM-HIGH HEAT AND BRING TO A SIMMER, WHISKING IN BROWN SUGAR AND SALT UNTIL SUGAR IS DISSOLVED. DIVIDE AMONG SIX $\frac{1}{2}$-CUP (125 ML) RAMEKINS OR CUSTARD CUPS (IF YOU WANT TO UNMOLD THEM, SPRAY THEM WITH NONSTICK COOKING SPRAY FIRST). REFRIGERATE FOR 3 HOURS OR UNTIL SET. UNMOLD ONTO SMALL PLATES OR SERVE IN THE RAMEKINS, TOPPED WITH A FEW BERRIES. SERVES 6.

VANILLA CRÈME BRÛLÉE

A BASIC CRÈME BRÛLÉE IS A GLORIOUS THING. MAKE THESE AHEAD OF TIME, AND TORCH THE TOPS WITH SUGAR WHEN IT'S TIME FOR DESSERT — THEN GET CRACKING.

5	LARGE EGG YOLKS	5
1/4 CUP	SUGAR	60 ML
2 CUPS	HEAVY OR WHIPPING (35%) CREAM	500 ML
1/2 TSP	GOOD-QUALITY VANILLA	2 ML
	HOT WATER	
	ADDITIONAL SUGAR	

PREHEAT OVEN TO 325°F (160°C). IN A MEDIUM BOWL, WHISK TOGETHER EGG YOLKS AND SUGAR. WHISK IN CREAM AND VANILLA. POUR INTO SIX 4-OZ (125 ML) RAMEKINS AND PLACE RAMEKINS IN A 13- BY 9-INCH (33 BY 23 CM) BAKING PAN OR DISH. GENTLY POUR IN ENOUGH HOT WATER TO COME ABOUT HALFWAY UP THE SIDES OF THE RAMEKINS. GENTLY TRANSFER TO THE OVEN AND BAKE FOR 35 TO 40 MINUTES OR UNTIL CUSTARDS ARE SET BUT STILL SLIGHTLY JIGGLY IN THE MIDDLE. CAREFULLY REMOVE RAMEKINS FROM WATER BATH, LET COOL, THEN REFRIGERATE FOR A FEW HOURS, UNTIL WELL CHILLED AND SET, OR OVERNIGHT.

SPRINKLE AN EVEN LAYER OF SUGAR OVER EACH DISH AND CARAMELIZE WITH A SMALL KITCHEN TORCH UNTIL DEEP GOLDEN (OR PUT RAMEKINS ON A BAKING SHEET AND BROIL FOR A MINUTE OR TWO). LET STAND FOR A FEW MINUTES TO ALLOW THE SUGAR TO COOL AND BECOME CRACKLY. SERVES 6.

VANILLA ICE CREAM

THIS SIMPLE HOMEMADE ICE CREAM DOESN'T REQUIRE COOKING (AND COOLING) A CUSTARD.

I CUP	HEAVY OR WHIPPING (35%) CREAM	250 ML
I CUP	HALF-AND-HALF (10%) CREAM	250 ML
1/2 CUP	SUGAR	125 ML
2 TSP	GOOD-QUALITY VANILLA	10 ML
PINCH	SALT	PINCH

IN A MEDIUM BOWL, WHISK TOGETHER ALL INGREDIENTS. POUR INTO AN ICE CREAM MAKER AND FREEZE UNTIL SOFTLY FROZEN, OR ACCORDING TO MANUFACTURER'S DIRECTIONS. IF YOU LIKE, TRANSFER TO A CONTAINER AND FREEZE UNTIL FIRM. (ALTERNATIVELY, POUR INTO A 13- BY 9-INCH/33 BY 23 CM METAL BAKING PAN AND FREEZE, STIRRING AND BREAKING UP THE CHUNKS OF ICE ABOUT ONCE AN HOUR, UNTIL IT LOOKS LIKE ICE CREAM. IT WON'T BE QUITE AS SMOOTH, BUT IT WILL STILL BE DELICIOUS.) MAKES ABOUT 4 CUPS (I L).

VARIATION: ADD STRAWBERRIES, RASPBERRIES, RHUBARB OR PEACHES, MASHED OR SIMMERED WITH SUGAR TO BREAK THE FRUIT DOWN AND CONDENSE IT, GETTING RID OF ANY EXCESS MOISTURE. (DON'T ADD MORE THAN HALF THE VOLUME OF CREAM, TO MAKE SURE THE ICE CREAM STAYS CREAMY.) LET COOL COMPLETELY, THEN ADD TO THE BASE MIXTURE OR STIR IT IN WHEN THE ICE CREAM IS STILL SOFT.

VARIATION: SWIRL IN CHOPPED CHOCOLATE AT THE END OF THE FREEZING PROCESS, WHILE THE ICE CREAM IS STILL SOFT.

FROZEN KEY LIME PUFF

THIS UPDATED VERSION OF OUR CLASSIC FROZEN LEMON PUFF TAKES ON THE TROPICAL FLAVOR OF LIME AND COCONUT. DON'T WORRY IF YOU CAN'T FIND KEY LIMES, WHICH ARE SMALLER AND ROUNDER — REGULAR OLD LIMES WILL DO THE TRICK.

2	CANS (EACH 14 OZ/400 ML) COCONUT MILK	2
5	LARGE EGGS (SEE SAFETY TIP)	5
1 CUP	SUGAR	250 ML
3/4 CUP	FRESH LIME JUICE (KEY LIMES, IF YOU CAN SNAG THEM)	175 ML
	VANILLA WAFERS OR SMALL DIGESTIVE COOKIES	
1/4 CUP	POWDERED (ICING) SUGAR	60 ML
PINCH	CREAM OF TARTAR	PINCH

CHILL THE CANS OF COCONUT MILK FOR A FEW HOURS, OR PREFERABLY OVERNIGHT.

SEPARATE 3 OF THE EGGS AND SET THE WHITES ASIDE. PUT THE EGG YOLKS IN A HEATPROOF BOWL, ALONG WITH THE REMAINING EGGS, AND SET OVER A POT OF BOILING WATER. WHISK IN SUGAR AND LIME JUICE; COOK, STIRRING CONSTANTLY, UNTIL THICKENED. LET COOL COMPLETELY.

REMOVE COCONUT MILK FROM THE FRIDGE AND OPEN THE CANS. THE WATER WILL HAVE SEPARATED, LEAVING A THICK WHITE LAYER OF FATTY SOLIDS AT THE TOP OF THE CANS. CAREFULLY SPOON THE SOLIDS INTO A LARGE BOWL AND MASH A BIT TO SOFTEN (SAVE THE THIN LIQUID FOR ANOTHER USE). USING AN ELECTRIC MIXER ON HIGH SPEED, BEAT COCONUT CREAM TO A WHIPPED CREAM-LIKE

TEXTURE. GENTLY FOLD INTO THE LIME MIXTURE. WASH BEATERS WELL.

PREHEAT BROILER. LINE THE BOTTOM AND SIDES OF A 9-INCH (23 CM) SPRINGFORM PAN WITH VANILLA WAFERS. CAREFULLY POUR THE LIME COCONUT FILLING INTO THE PAN.

IN A CLEAN LARGE BOWL, USING AN ELECTRIC MIXER, BEAT EGG WHITES UNTIL FROTHY. ADD POWDERED SUGAR AND CREAM OF TARTAR; CONTINUE TO BEAT UNTIL STIFF PEAKS FORM. CAREFULLY SPREAD WHITES OVER THE FILLING.

BROIL FOR JUST A FEW MINUTES, UNTIL THE PEAKS OF THE MERINGUE ARE BROWNED (WATCH CAREFULLY: IT WILL GO FROM WHITE TO BURNT IN A MATTER OF MINUTES). COVER WITH FOIL, TENTING IT OVER THE MERINGUE WITHOUT TOUCHING IT. FREEZE FOR AT LEAST 8 HOURS OR OVERNIGHT. REMOVE FROM THE FREEZER AND TAKE OFF THE FOIL $1\frac{1}{2}$ HOURS BEFORE SERVING. SERVES 10 TO 12.

SAFETY TIP: THIS RECIPE CONTAINS EGG WHITES THAT ARE NOT FULLY COOKED, WHICH MAY BE A CONCERN IF YOU OR A PERSON CONSUMING IT IS VERY YOUNG, VERY OLD OR HAS A WEAKENED IMMUNE SYSTEM. IF CONCERNED, LOOK FOR IN-SHELL PASTEURIZED EGGS AT WELL-STOCKED SUPERMARKETS, OR USE 6 TBSP (90 ML) PASTEURIZED LIQUID EGG WHITES FOR THE MERINGUE. WE HIGHLY RECOMMEND USING THE FRESHEST EGGS POSSIBLE, REGARDLESS.

INDEX

Library and Archives Canada Cataloguing in Publication

Best of Bridge Sunday suppers : all-new recipes for family & friends.

"Text copyright © 2017 Elizabeth Chorney-Booth, Sue Duncan, Julie Van Rosendaal."
    —Title page verso.
Includes index.
ISBN 978-0-7788-0575-5 (spiral bound)

    1. Suppers. 2. Cookbooks. I. Chorney-Booth, Elizabeth, 1975-, author
II. Duncan, Sue, 1970-, author III. Van Rosendaal, Julie, 1970-, author
IV. Title: Sunday suppers.

TX738.B48 2017   641.5'3   C2017-903563-0